MIMI BRIEN
MAKES YOU MONEYWISE

- Make sound, intelligent investments in stocks, bonds, real estate, collectibles and money markets
- Minimize federal and local taxes, legally
- Borrow money wisely, at the lowest possible rates
- Make inflation work for you
- Shop for the insurance that's best for you
- Plan for a comfortable retirement
- And much, much more.

"Hooray for Mimi Brien! How wonderful to learn that money is not only for the rich."

> —Susan K. Merzbach,
> Vice-President Creative Affairs,
> Twentieth-Century Fox

"I strongly recommend this book to all women. *Moneywise* tells the truth about investing and managing money. It's an excellent book, fun to read and without the usual get-rich-quick fairy tales."

> —Yvonne Brathwaite Burke,
> Attorney,
> Former U.S. Congresswoman

"*Moneywise* is a practical and fun approach to a serious and often dull subject."

> —Lynda Fluent,
> President and CEO,
> First Women's Bank of California

Ask your bookseller for these Bantam books of related interest:

MONEYWISE

Mimi Brien

BANTAM BOOKS
TORONTO · NEW YORK · LONDON · SYDNEY

MONEYWISE
A Bantam Book / December 1982

ISBN 0-553-22850-1

Published simultaneously in the United States and Canada

PRINTED IN THE UNITED STATES OF AMERICA

O   0 9 8 7 6 5 4 3 2 1

Dedication

To those things that money can't buy:
Love and support from my daughters Aliza and Susanna
Love, support, humor and excellent work from Barbara Iannoli
My pink slip from Ivan McGuire, M.D.

Acknowledgments

Gail Christian who named me; Sue Terry and Charles Bloch of Charles Bloch & Associates; Victoria Pasternack for editorial help and listening; Irene Webb, William Morris Agency, my agent—loyal, tough and supportive; Toni Burbank of Bantam Books, my editor—demanding, exacting, enthusiastic and always by my side; Mel Berger, William Morris Agency, my co-agent who fed me uncommon good sense and humor along with wonderful food and provided check cashing privileges.

To Pat Reeves, whose work made my work possible; Clydell Wade, who kept us clean, fed and calm; Barbara Iannoli, my research mavin and rewrite partner; Mrs. Fannie Cohen, for her constant enthusiasm and generous hospitality. Special thanks to the clients of "Moneywise" who are my teachers and my friends.

Additional Acknowledgments

Audrey Albert, C.P.A.
Los Angeles, CA

David Bazil, Esquire
Los Angeles, CA

Frank Danzig, Vice President, Investments
Dean Witter Reynolds, Inc.
Century City, CA

Lee Devril, Assistant Manager, Operations
Wells Fargo Bank
Pacific Palisades, CA

John William Dyckman, Professor
Johns Hopkins University
Baltimore, MD

Linda Elstad, Writer
Pacific Palisades, CA

Delia Fernandez
TRW
Orange, CA

Lynda Fluent, President & Executive Officer
First Women's Bank
Los Angeles, CA

Fred Glaser Insurance Associates, Inc.
Van Nuys, CA

Ed Jones, Assistant Vice President, Manager
Wells Fargo Bank
Pacific Palisades, CA

Tony Lamb, Author
The Retirement Threat

Los Angeles Public Library
Los Angeles, CA

Tody Richman
Glencoe, IL

Sandy Robbins, Atty.
California Women's Savings and Loan
Los Angeles, CA

Lynn Rogers & Associates
Beverly Hills, CA

Siavash Saeedi, Doctoral Candidate
University of Southern California Urban and Regional
    Planning Department
Los Angeles, CA

Santa Monica Public Library
Santa Monica, CA

Mary Ann Sargent, Personal Banking Officer
Wells Fargo Bank
Pacific Palisades, CA

Elizabeth Snyder
Los Angeles, CA

Regina Steele, Account Executive
Merrill Lynch Pierce Fenner & Smith, Inc.
Beverly Hills, CA

Rosemary Tribulato, C.F.P.
Drexel Burnham Lambert, Inc.
Los Angeles, CA

Venice Public Library
Venice, CA

Rebekah Verdon, Insurance Planner
Los Angeles, CA

James Zak
Merrill Lynch Pierce Fenner & Smith, Inc.
Beverly Hills, CA

Contents

Introduction

Nobody is born moneywise. Believe me, I know. I only started to balance my checkbook at age 33. It wasn't that I couldn't do it before, I just didn't. When I was divorced and could no longer afford this attitude I started doing my checkbook regularly—very regularly! When I look back at how long I chose to live with money anxieties and a nagging sense of being bad and lazy, I am amazed. Today I stress to my clients and to my readers that not knowing where you are financially can drain you emotionally and physically. Knowing where you stand in terms of financial planning is *always* better than not knowing.

When I finally decided to investigate the field of money management, I was delighted to find out that I already had some of the tools necessary to figure what return I could get on my money. These tools were simply addition, subtraction, multiplication, division and the use of the decimal point—all grade school arithmetic skills. (And, all these functions can be done with great speed and accuracy on a simple, inexpensive calculator.) I also knew that I wanted and deserved the good things of life—and they are many—that money *can* buy.

What I didn't know were the advantages of one investment over another. I didn't understand risk and I didn't know the wide variety of investments open to me—or how they worked. When I began to explore the areas of management and investment, I found it all fascinating. It is not a difficult field, very commonsensical really, packed with facts and with its own jargon that was a bit confusing in the beginning. But I pressed on with my financial education and could soon converse with the best of them.

After spending a great deal of time running from one "expert" to another—accountants, bookkeepers, stockbrokers, bankers, lawyers, etc.—and then trying to balance and use their information, I recognized the need for some kind of one-stop financial service. I started my financial consultation firm in order to meet that need and to provide objective, conscientious advice to women.

I myself have been a single working woman, married, divorced, widowed, a single parent, a trustee for a stepson and the executor of a complicated estate. I've been a renter, a homeowner and a landlord. Most of the financial problems that face women I've faced myself. This has been a great advantage in my work because when I listen to my clients, I understand the road that they are taking and I know from firsthand experience where the potholes are. I also know ways to make that road smoother and easier.

I come to my profession with a background in economics and real estate. However, background alone is not enough to help you understand the confusing marketplace of the 1980's. The old rules have changed. *Moneywise* will teach you the new rules and the new tax laws that affect all investments. When you understand the game of investing, you'll feel confident to play for fun and profit.

I have counseled hundreds of clients with diverse histories, varied goals, and from different financial situations. My clients range from widows on pensions to women who work in the home and want to participate in financial decisions, to bright young professionals just starting out, and even a few women earning six-figure incomes. I have single mothers, married mothers, and women who wonder if they should have ever been mothers at all. I even had one basket case who couldn't get by on $96,000 a year.

My clients usually come to me with certain specific problems—from budget messes to questions about what to do with a large inheritance. Women come to me who want to get divorced and need advice about what to negotiate for. They come when they are marrying again and want to keep their own money separate from their husband's. After dealing with the problem in consultation, my client leaves to get on with her life. I'm left, like the Ancient Mariner, with the tale only partially told. I've helped with the problem at hand but what I really would like to do is tie each and every one of my clients to the chair and say, "I'll only release you when you've heard it all." That is why I'm writing this book.

Moneywise is for women with household incomes of $15,000 and up a year, who want to make the most of investments but who, like me, turn pale—and off—when reading about risk arbitrage and commodity straddles. This is *not* a get rich quick book for the 1980s, nor is it a book about how to snap your fingers and click your heels in the Boardroom while your male secretary picks up your cleaning. I will not discuss high-flying, maddeningly sophisticated schemes that promise you giant tax write-offs. I will not offer advice that involves being on top of your investment eight hours each day and reading in the field four hours each night. I will leave this to other authors who write books such as "How To Make A Fortune In Real Estate With No Money Down And No Monthly Payments," "How To Borrow Money Below Market Interest Without Mortgaging Anything You Own," or "How To Make A Million In The Stock Market In One Year By Investing Only $1.39 A Week." The only way I've found to become rich overnight is to inherit a fortune.

Unlike most other money books written for women I will not tell you how to be a thrifty consumer. Women know a lot about shopping wisely; it's the wherewithal to shop with we need to know more about. A contest for penny-pinching would be won hands down by women, but we might not score so high in a contest of making money grow! *Moneywise* is written for the woman who wants the knowledge to make money with money for a secure and enriched life.

In *Moneywise* I will discuss investments that are sensible and feasible. In each chapter I cover financial strategies, investments and the principles behind them. Knowing *why* an investment works the way it does is as important as knowing why people behave the way they do—only it's much easier to learn. I cover all the major fields of investment, their risks and rewards and how they are affected by the economy of the 80's, as well as the Economic Recovery Tax Act of 1981. I address the common financial problems that come up in women's lives repeatedly. Many of my clients' stories are included as illustration. As Anna in the *King of Siam* put it, "By my pupils, I've been taught."

Moneywise will tell you how to make your way in the world of money; how to provide security for yourself—and your children, if you have them—whatever your age and marital status; how to finance a home in today's difficult real-estate market; how to make more money than you ever thought you could from your income or available capital; *and* how to be a full financial partner in your marriage (or divorce).

I stress flexibility, growth and change in all my financial

consultations because women go through more changes than men—from little girls to single working women to married working women to mothers to divorcee and single parents to widowhood, so many possible roles and combination of roles. The life of a woman is not a novel, but rather, a series of short stories or vignettes. As they deal with changes, women grow and become more flexible and more interesting. Clearly, change is part and parcel of a woman's life, and I'd like to tell you about some of my own experiences with it.

I met my first husband one year after moving from New York City to Los Angeles. After our marriage we worked together in the building business, and I learned every aspect of that business from land analysis right straight through to renting. I became interested in real estate and got my license in that field.

After a year or so I wanted a baby and a house. Both items were reasonable in those days. While I never discuss how old I am, except to explain to people that both my daughters lie about my age, I *will* tell you that the interest rates when we borrowed for our first home were around four percent, and we both thought that unbearably high!

Now I felt on track. I had a husband, a house, a child on the way: everything a woman could want in the fifties! These changes weren't too scary because I was doing everything that I'd been brought up to do. Each move—marriage, buying a house, and getting pregnant—brought some emotional rocking and rolling, but all the changes I was going through I had been expecting and fantasizing about from childhood.

After the birth of my first daughter, Aliza, I really became frightened. Frightened—no, I was terrified! I had left my parents and I knew if my marriage didn't work for me, I could leave that, too. But here was a relationship, a beloved and longed-for child that I could never walk away from as long as I lived. This small baby was the one to whom I was bound, in sickness and in health, for richer for poorer, as long as we both shall live. I couldn't walk out anymore. I was a hostage to fortune for the first time in my life and I was now earthbound because of her. I continued working in a limited way with my husband in the building business that he and I had started, but my main work and most wonderful job was Aliza.

I soon learned to live with another change, a cash-flow problem. A cash-flow problem is when the cash doesn't flow into your life as fast as it flows out. Builders like my husband David always need money. It takes a long time to find a deal, buy the land and construct and rent the building. During that time no money comes in—none—and money is always going out. In this situation, I started to worry about money a whole lot. I didn't know or understand enough and, therefore, had no control over the money problems that we had. But then I was a wife/woman and David a man/husband, and he was supposed to provide. Ah, the funny, wonderful fifties!

Susanna came twenty-two months later, another miraculous daughter. By the time she was two and one-half, my father had started his slow, quiet slide into death and my life turned upside down. There was grief, impending loss and change, not only for me, but the whole family. When the grieving was over, I faced what I had really known for a year or so. My marriage had died, too. We separated when Aliza was seven and Sue was five.

Twelve years had taken me from New York City to Los Angeles, from student to worker, from single working woman to marriage and the building business, to motherhood, to death of a parent, and to divorce with two small children.

The next five years were devoted to the children and part-time work for the Office of Economic Opportunity. Then I met Jacques, a French-Canadian psychoanalyst. Within three months we were married. I became part-time stepmother to Jacques's son, moved into a lovely home, and started once again to live happily ever after.

Less than three years later, Jacques was diagnosed as having brain cancer and was given three to six months to live. And live we did, the girls, Jacques, and I. Because of some new experimental drugs, Jacques lived another two and one-half years, and when he could no longer work or talk, or dress himself, he killed himself with the knowledge and blessings of all those who loved him so much. A most extraordinary man!

The next year I don't remember too well.

I sold my house, and Aliza, Sue, and I moved to an apartment. At the end of the year, Aliza left for an eastern university three thousand miles away. Sue followed two years later, and I moved to a small apartment and began selling real estate. Six months later I left work to study to become a real estate broker. After passing the examination I started making plans to go into business for myself. I decided to use my knowledge of money, investing, and real estate and my life experience to become a financial adviser to women.

My daughter Aliza now practices law in Washington, D.C., and Susanna is working as a speech and language pathologist in San Francisco. Both are newly married and I am a mother-in-law to a doctor and lawyer. I went from marriage to being a single working parent, from a happy second marriage to being alone again, from being a full-time mother to seeing my children only during their university holidays, from a brief third marriage, into a full-time career, into my own business, and now I am a writer, to boot.

Change, creeping slowly as the girls grow up, go away, marry, and come home only as visitors. Change, coming rapidly as the doctor tells me, "Jacques will live three to six months." Change, whipsawing from life to death, from being comfortable and loved to being cash-short and alone, from part-time work to a business of my own. I am not that unusual.

Each change brought anxiety, depression, and fear and then resolution and solutions. There were periods of apathy, of failure, of regression, of tears, and, ultimately, of growth. Change and risk are the threads that connect me to my childhood and the constants in my life. Change is no longer the faceless enemy; I know her well. I know that change will always bring with it fear, anxiety, and depression. Thank God, it will also bring resolution, productivity, and growth.

During the course of all these changes I was busy educating myself about money. When Jacques died, in 1971, I put the money I received from his life insurance into the hands of my stockbroker and abdicated all responsibility to him as I tried to put my life back together.

Six months later, when I finally took a look at my financial situation, I found I had lost forty percent of my money as the stock market had zoomed downward during the recession of 1971. I took over my own investing, sold my stock, and chalked my losses up to experience. With increasing savvy and renewed confidence in my own judgment, I was able to triple my remaining money in eighteen months. I know the mechanics of investing *and* rely heavily on my gut level feelings and intuition to manipulate my investments. In this book I expect to give you the tools to do the same—to understand how money works and how to use your own feelings to work with it, *and* to have fun doing so!

BLOCKS TO MANAGING MONEY

Let's face it, it's human to want to be taken care of. It feels delicious to be taken care of. It is also absolutely necessary to trust people enough to allow yourself to be taken care of. But being cared for in a childlike way can be a trap leaving you ignorant and vulnerable. In an adult relationship, being cared for means sharing knowledge and preparing one another to go forward, even if your partner isn't with you. We teach children to take more and more responsibility for themselves as they grow, knowing they will need knowledge to become functioning adults. We teach children because we love them, and we must learn as adults because we love ourselves.

The most debilitating problem I have found in my consulting work is what I call the "Baby Doll Syndrome." The baby doll thinks that being taken care of is being loved. She wears many faces. Some baby dolls are highly competent women in the work world but have abdicated all power over financial matters at home. Whether the syndrome is caused by a lack of time, or fear, or is a way to keep their husbands happy, or arises from a genuine feeling that they want and need to be taken care of, makes no difference in the end. A baby doll has handed over the financial reins and has lost control of a large measure of her own life. There is one face of the baby doll that concerns me most of all. It is the face of the woman who thinks it is cute to be dumb about money. She will say things such as "Oh, Bill doesn't want me to worry about 'that' [money, bills, investments, insurance, checkbooks, etc.]. He takes care of it all."

Oh, Bill, Billy boy, my Bill. What will happen to the infant wife at divorce or death? Darling Bill will be cursed by the very woman who was so "cute" about being taken care of. In my office I hear the cries, "That son of a bitch and I are split and he's hidden the money. I can't get credit! I never had a checkbook!" Or, "How could he have died and left me like this? My God, I don't know anything! Why did I allow myself to be treated like an idiot?"

My client Jean was a successful owner of a high-style boutique. For six years her shop had made excellent money and she socked it away. Her husband paid her taxes for her, so everything she made was pure profit.

Jean had her fingers on the pulse of the retail business. In that business if you don't know what's "in," you're "out" very quickly. Not only did Jean need to anticipate tastes, she had to buy enough—but not too much—in order to make a profit. She had to keep track of the inventory, the bookkeeping, state and federal taxes, window display, and sales help.

Jean came to see me about her finances because she wanted a divorce. In order to find out how much money she and her two children needed to live on each month, I started to ask the usual questions. How much is the mortgage? How much are the monthly payments? How much does insurance cost? —telephone, car maintenance and gas, food, entertainment, medical? and on and on. Jean couldn't answer one question. She couldn't even give me a ball-park figure, and I couldn't track it down for her because she didn't know the bank or savings institution that had the mortgage on her home. She also had no idea if her husband had stock, a pension plan, what his salary was, or where their money was—if there was any money.

At the end of the consultation I told Jean that she wasn't ready for a divorce. She wasn't even ready to see a lawyer. My advice was to ask for a separation for a year or so while she learned what was what and where was what, and what what cost.

After she left, I daydreamed about this chic, successful businesswoman. I pictured her leaving her home each morning to go to work. In my fantasy she was five years old and so small her foot had great trouble touching the gas pedal of her car. As she drove to her business I saw her growing bigger and bigger, and older and older. By the time she reached the store she was fully grown, thirty-six years old, and ready for anything that might happen in her highly competitive business. At the end of the day, in my fantasy, I saw her get into the car and as she drove home she grew smaller and smaller, and younger and younger, until she was five and a little girl again. She was "Alice in Wonderland," a baby doll at home and a success at work!

Jean has learned a lot since then. She's still separated, but if she does divorce and remarry, I know she will remain full size.

Another client, Terry, is 33, single and doing very well in a large corporation. Not only is her work exciting but her salary is excellent. When she first came to me she was broke and swore she couldn't manage money. She wanted to give me her salary to manage. I was to give her only some "walking around money." Since I don't manage money for clients I sent her to someone who did. Two years later she came back to see me in a very angry mood. Her money manager had conserved her money so well that she now had a down payment for a house. Terry wanted to know how in the devil he did it. What magic had he used and why couldn't she do it. . . . "I'm not stupid," she said. No, she is not; she's highly professional and competitive and she was actually furious that her money manager had succeeded so well where she had failed. By God, if her manager could do it she would learn to do it.

Terry had been a baby doll without a husband as backup. While adult and self-sufficient in most important areas of her life, she had remined childlike in regard to money. It was almost as if she was saying, "Look, Ma, I'm just playing grown up. I'm really still a kid." Her good competitive instincts were aroused when she found she could have a house. The reward for being an adult suddenly outweighed the gratifications of being taken care of. She is now reading *The Wall Street Journal* every day and managing her investments very well. Terry is even thinking of writing a book in her spare time on how to manage money. I've convinced her, I think, that she'd be happier learning to hang glide.

Never, never take it for granted that a man knows more about money than you do. Men are not *born* knowing everything about money any more than women are *born* with a mop in their hand. Men just talk a better game! Many women are temporarily less knowledgeable about money than men, true. This is changing now. However, some men are total financial ignoramuses, only kept from bankruptcy by clever mothers, wives, or lovers. Knowledge of how to handle money is *not* in the genes.

What happened to a client of mine, Rene, happens over and over again. Her story, however, is particularly dramatic.

Rene was never concerned about money because her husband, John, an internist, made a very good living. Rene's three children were under sixteen when John left her. She was hurt and confused but never dreamed that she would have serious money problems. John had always talked with such confidence and pride about their investments that Rene felt financially secure. Shortly after John's departure, Rene discovered that she had only $500 in a joint checking account—and that was all. In going through desk drawers, she came across unopened bills from as far back as six years before that had been casually tossed, unpaid, into corners. She hired a lawyer and discovered, through John's deposition, that there were no investments and that John was now working only half time. Rene had made the common assumption that because John talked a good line he knew what he was doing.

In order to make ends meet, Rene decided to try writing sitcoms for TV. She grossed $5,000 during her first year—which in her financial situation was nothing to sniff at. Today, four years later, she is story editor on one of the most successful TV series in the country. She earns over $250,000 a year and knows *everything* about where her money is and what it's doing.

In order to gain financially—or just stay even—you have to risk loss. There is nothing morally wrong with failure or loss. They are two of our best teachers and anyone who dares to try has met them both. Don't let fear of risk keep you from making money decisions.

The endless choices in investing must always end in a decision or the money goes under the mattress and though that's a decision, too, it's a highly unsatisfactory one. The paradox is that *not* making a decision is simply making another type of decision. However, if we don't actively decide, we tend to think we will not be held responsible for the outcome, and that feels very good—temporarily. Of course, you can see the next paradox coming. If you don't decide, and therefore don't risk, you are simply taking another sort of risk.

You can *learn* to take intelligent risks—it's simply a matter of weighing one factor against another. The more knowledge you have about a situation, the easier it becomes to take risks. We all differ in our ability to tolerate risk due to factors in our current life, as well as our early environment.

My client Anya felt she was unable to tolerate any risk at all. She had all of her savings in a passbook account at 5¼%. I pointed out to her that with inflation at 10%, she was *losing* 4¾% on her money (10 − 5¼ = 4¾). She thought she was safe and she was. She wasn't a risk taker but she was a surefire loser! When she was able to clearly see all the factors and weigh them, she took my suggestion and moved her savings into a money instrument with a much higher yield.

Risk taking is a part of life—we do it every day. From my own observation, getting out of bed in the morning is the greatest risk a person can take—and most of us do it without thinking, and under the great disadvantage of being only barely awake.

Some women feel, not without reason, that all they can do is survive from week to week, so why bother about investments. One of my favorite clients is Nikki, a single mother of two who earns $1,400 a month as a legal secretary. She came to me because she could barely make ends meet every month. She never dreamed she could invest. I gave her a brochure on investment clubs (see Chapter 1) and convinced her to take her kids out of private ice skating lessons and put them into group lessons. This freed up $50 per month for investing.

She called friends and colleagues and got together a group of twelve people who were willing to invest $50 a month in an investment club. Three years later Nikki and her club have realized a substantial profit—much more than if they had not pooled their money. They've also talked with a great number of financial experts, increased their knowledge of investing AND they had a good time, to boot.

Women today are really doing a miraculous job! They assume the major responsibility for the kids as well as doing their jobs and keeping their homes running smoothly. I'm not talking about the superwoman in her executive suite, who really represents only a minuscule portion of all working women. I'm talking about the average working woman on the nine-to-five shift at work and the twenty-four hour shift at home. Her husband may be a great father, but she is still the one who stays home when the child is sick, dispenses the vitamins, knows when the next dental checkup is due, worries about new school clothes, hunts for the Halloween costume, and on and on and on.

Given the responsibilities, it is more important today than ever to know where the money is coming from and how to manage it. This is true for all women, whether they are married to a gem of a man or are single parents.

The difficulties of a woman's financial life are exacerbated by the fact that women still earn only fifty-nine cents for every dollar a man earns. (This figure has remained relatively constant since the Industrial Revolution.) If you wonder why it's harder for you to get ahead than the guy next door, it's because he has forty-one more cents on every dollar than you do. Media coverage tends to focus on the women on the "fast track" who are perfectly coiffed, expensively dressed, and reside in beautiful offices with two windows and a secretary. Reality for the majority of women is very different. When you go to your high school or college reunion, you'll probably find everybody in the same boat as yourself—each one secretly wondering why she is not a vice-president by age thirty-five. It's not your fault! Women's struggle for economic equality in our society continues.

Your decision to buy this book or to go for a financial consultation is a big step toward acquiring a positive attitude about money. You *are* entitled to money and to the rewards that it brings.

Few women, when asked their goals, will reply, "I want to make pots of money." Yet every rich person is comfortable with this goal, comfortable with the idea of making money, understands how to do it and most important, feels entitled to do so! You are entitled too.

I see women at their *most* attractive. No matter how their life-styles or opinions may differ, they are all trying to get control over their financial lives. Some feel silly because they think they can't balance their checkbook, and some want to know how to invest surplus money. Any woman trying to learn new skills to become moneywise looks terrific to me.

Questions for New Clients

I ask every new client the following questions. When you finish *Moneywise*, you'll be able to answer these for yourself—and many more.

1. How much is your mortgage or rental payment? Be sure to include homeowners' dues, if any.

2. What's your income and what tax bracket are you in?

3. How much do you owe, to whom and at what rate?

4. What investments do you have and how are they doing?

5. Do you have credit? Is it in your own name?

6. What is contained in your insurance portfolio?

7. If you became unable to work or were fired from your job, could you support yourself? How?

8. Do you contribute to the support of any relative? Will you have to help support anyone in the future?

9. Do you expect to inherit money or property at some time in your life?

10. If you have a child, have you started to plan how you are going to provide for his/her education?

11. Have you made out your Will?

12. What are your financial plans for retirement?

I

Money Management

1

Becoming a Financially Responsible Woman

Understanding how money moves around in the system and how to make that system work for you can provide you with a sense of security and independence. The process of developing financial awareness is fun, can be profitable, and will increase your self-esteem. Taking charge of your finances, as well as those of the family, is vital to your survival. Provide yourself with the necessary tools to make informed decisions and to function well in the financial world no matter what your marital status.

Know-How and Know-Where

Keeping records is crucial to financial know-how and know-where. Every woman, wage earner or not, must have two items, a desk of her own and a filing cabinet. I know it's easy for me to tell you to start here, and difficult for some of you in a busy and crowded household to insist on this for yourself, but it is necessary. A one-drawer filing cabinet can be stuck in a closet if you have no other place. I recommend the letter size hanging file type. You'll also need letter size folders and plastic tabs for labeling them. Next, gather up all those odds and ends of things you don't have a place for, put them in folders, label the folders, and file them away.

If you're the type who files alphabetically, do so. If you're not, file any old way that makes sense to you. My first folder is for receipts, the next is unpaid bills, and then insurance. Behind that I have income tax returns for the last five years and bank statements starting with January of this year. Then comes a fight folder for the fights I'm in with Mastercharge—I didn't go to Chicago last April—the fight I'm in with the Public Utilities Commission, the County Assessor's Office, and a few other select groups. I also have a file marked, "Important Papers," which contains important papers as well as information I don't know where else to file. I also have a file of unanswered correspondence, a dues file for subscriptions, a file for membership cards, and for my children's birth certificates, my divorce papers, Jacques' death certificate, and Janet's recipe for cold cucumber soup.

Don't ask me why this arrangement works for me. It does, and I'd bite the first hand that tried to change it. Remember, nobody will grade you on filing—it's for your use only.

My two most important files are marked "Where It's At" and "Investment File."

Here is my "Where It's At" list:

"Where It's At"

NAME: DATE:

1. Life insurance   Policy location

2. Attorney and Will   Location of copies

3. Bank accounts   Address and number

4. Savings and loan accounts address and number

5. Brokerage account   Location and number

6. Company benefits
   a. Pension plan
   b. Life insurance
   c. Medical/dental
   d. Other

7. Family Social Security numbers

8. Safe deposit box
      Number   Location

9. Items in safe deposit box

10. Certified public accountant address and telephone

11. General information
    (Location of health insurance policies, passports, tax returns, etc.)

12. Debts   Describe

13. Emergency addresses and telephones
    Sister:
    Brother:
    Child:
    Best friend:
    Clergy:
    Other:

14. Special considerations
    (Burial wishes, etc.)

Things on my "Where It's At" list, with the exception of my Will, are in my safe deposit box with a photocopy in my file. My Will is at my attorney's. This list can be amended to cover anything else you think of.

I sent this list to my mother who could not discuss money with her children. She filled it out and put a copy in her safe deposit box and one in her files. Thus, she could keep her reserve about money and still provide me with necessary information when she died.

Many parents can't bring themselves, for a variety of reasons, to discuss money with their grown children. The "Where It's At" list is the most delicate way I've found for them to let you know where things are so that when they die, you and the probate attorney can easily find their assets.

Hundreds of millions of dollars are sitting in banks today unclaimed by heirs who are unaware that their parents ever opened a bank account in the First National Bank of Cripple Creek, Colorado. Unless claimed within a certain number of years (each state has a different time period), the money goes forever to the state in which the bank is located.

Investment File

Your investment file should contain all papers pertaining to your financial matters. For example, it might hold your mortgage or trust deed, your bank passbooks, and a list of any of your stocks, bonds, or Treasury Bills. It should also contain a list of the prices at which you bought your stocks and bonds, any notes of money owed to you or that you owe, partnership agreements, car leasing agreements, leases, etc.

Now that you have your files set up, you're going to need a desk. It will serve as a room, or at least a space, of your own. A desk is a serious place for serious work. Children must be taught not to touch it, not even to breathe on it. Your desk should hold all the tools you'll need. My desk has:

Paper clips
Stapler, extra staples
Scotch tape
Stamps
Writing paper
Envelopes, small and business size
Brown envelopes—small and business size
A pocket calculator
Pens
Pencils
Pencil sharpener
Blotter
Liquid paper
Letter opener
Reading glasses

I also keep today's mail, as well as notes to myself about whom to call and why. I have a calender showing a month at a glance on which I note any upcoming events, appointments, birthdays, invitations, and dates when payments are due.

None of these items need cost a fortune. The desk doesn't have to be Chippendale or Hepplewhite. It can be a good old unfinished bargain from a garage sale. The stationery items can be bought at Saks or at *my* favorite, a discount office supply store. The only thing I still *can't* get at a discount is MONEY.

Record-keeping, record-keeping!—a bore, but it gets to be a habit like brushing your teeth, so that after a while, if you don't keep records you begin to feel grubby and uncomfortable.

Separate but Equal

You may think that you can escape the chore of setting up records because you are married and your husband already has a file system. Wrong! Sorry. As a financial consultant I've seen too many divorced women left holding an empty file cabinet. I've also met too many widows who discover that their husbands never really had a decent record-keeping system at all! He may have had good intentions but a short attention span.

Many women believe that because they pay the bills they also have their finger on the pulse of the family finances. This is true, but only to a limited extent. There's more to managing money than writing checks.

Every woman *must* have copies of every bit of financial information concerning her and her family. Where are those insurance policies? Where is the passbook? What company carries the pension plan? Where and how is your money invested? This information should be filed in your very own separate-but-equal file.

A Good Money Relationship

You may ask yourself, "How am I ever going to get all this information for my files?" Good question. If you already pay the bills in your household, you are in a stronger position than those women who do not. But in either case, there are several approaches you can take to obtain this information.

The first thing to do is discuss your needs with your husband and explain what you're trying to do. Many men will be delighted to sit down and share the burden of record-keeping with you. If your husband has kept poor or scanty records he'll probably be relieved to have you take over the organization.

Some husbands, however, see money management as strictly a male role, part of their job as breadwinners and protectors of the family. A husband who feels this way can be a bit of a problem but he's not impossible to budge. Let him know how crucial it is for you to be able to handle money and give him several reasons why.

Statistics can be very convincing. You should point out that the average age of a widow in the United States is fifty-six and that the average woman may be alone, handling her own affairs, for as many as twenty years. Tell him that husbands die before their wives four times out of five. No husbands really want to leave their wives uninformed widows—and yet so many do.

This subject could threaten an already tense marriage or cause temporary cracks in a strong one. Your husband may not budge one inch, and the price of going to the mat may be high. But the cost of *not* knowing, in case of divorce, sickness, or death can be much higher!

If your husband still won't cooperate, there *is* a last resort that some of my clients have used with great success. Get Form 4506 from the Internal Revenue Service, fill it out, and send it in. It is a request for last year (or years) income tax forms filed by you and your husband. When you receive your back tax returns take them to an accountant of your own. He or she will be able to reconstruct what the family assets are. Every cent of wages, interest, bonuses, rents, mortgage payments, payments of debt, etc. that was reported to the IRS will be there. This might sound like a rotten way to proceed, but not knowing in case of divorce or death is a lot more rotten. You can then either confront your husband with your new knowledge or not.

My client, Jan, did just this and her husband reevaluated Jan and her determination. They were then able to start a good money relationship, and they both feel better for it.

The Business of Money

Money isn't nice or not nice; neither is it clean or dirty. It's only money. The things we learned as young girls—be kind, be sweet, yielding, don't make a fuss—have nothing to do with money and have no place in financial management. Unfortunately, we often carry these attitudes over into our business relationships.

These postures are not bred in the bones, they are learned. Unlearn them! The business of money is *not* unfeminine, unladylike, or vulgar. It is just the business of money and learning to manage it is essential to your well-being.

Determining Your Nut

A basic component of money management is determining your monthly nut (your basic cost of living). Step one is to start with your fixed (you-can't-get-out-of-them) expenses. List

Form **4506**
(Rev. February 1978)

Department of the Treasury – Internal Revenue Service
Request for Copy of Tax Form
(Please read the instructions on the back of this form before you complete it.)

Name and address of taxpayers as shown on tax form

Requester's telephone number

Document locator number (if known)

Taxpayer's social security number

Kind of tax (income, estate, excise, gift, etc.)

Current address if different from above:

Spouse's social security number

Tax form number

Mail copies to:

Employer identification number

Tax period ended

Internal Revenue Service office where tax form was filed

Do you want copies of all pages and attachments?
☐ Yes ☐ No

How many copies of each page requested do you want?

If no, do you want copies of ☐ Page 1 only? ☐ Schedules only? ☐ Other?

If you check "Other," please specify what copies you want.

If you are requesting certification, please check here, ☐ (See instructions on back.)

Signature of taxpayer (or requester)

Signature of person attesting, if corporate return (See instructions on back.)

Date

Form 4506 (Rev. 2-78)

them. Then list what money comes in each month and what you'll owe the government on April 15th. This isn't fun and is highly charged emotionally, but it must be done.

Monthly expenses:
    Rent or mortgage payment(s)
    Food
    Utilities
    Telephone
    Insurance (life, health, home or renter's, car)
    Car or transportation (train, bus, subway, taxi, carpool)
    Childcare
    Wardrobe
    Support of relatives
    Credit card payments
    Loan payments
    Contributions
    Entertainment
    Magazine subscriptions
    Additional education (you and/or children)
    Vacations
    Personal requirements (beautician, cosmetics, wine, liquor)

Monthly income:
    Take-home pay or household allowance
    Rents due you
    Alimony
    Child support
    Loan payments due you
    Bank interest
    Stock dividends
    Trust fund payments
    Monthly money from relatives
    Other sources

If what's coming in is more than what's going out, that's wonderful and you should invest the difference. If what's going out is more than what's coming in, you must change your budget.

Dealing with Cash-Flow Problems

If you're living above your head you can change things around to cut back on your lifestyle. Nothing is permanent and retrenching isn't the end of the world. Phone bills can be cut, food bills can be cut, utilities can be cut, entertaining can be fun and still not cost much. Clothes, if you have flair and style, need not come from the best stores or carry a chic label. If you can't afford where you live, consider moving or taking a roommate or renting out one room. Cut out all credit buying but hang on to the cards. You may want to increase your insurance deductible amounts which will bring down the cost of your insurance. Be careful however, and don't be caught underinsured. You may also be able to increase the number of dependents that you declare on your employee witholding form. If you are expecting a tax refund, you may claim more dependents and thereby increase the size of your paycheck. If you are unsure of how many you can legally claim (believe it or not, 14 can be listed before an employer must report you to IRS), check with your local Internal Revenue Service Office.

During a drastic retrenchment period, find one luxury that makes you feel good and keep it. My friend Gabby had to do all of the above and more during a financial reversal. But she was addicted to eating breakfast out. She should have cut it out of her budget, but leaving it in was important psychologically. This is a money book, but I believe there's a lot more to life than money. So keep doing whatever makes you feel good, if at all possible.

Remember, during a financial crisis or in a time of terrible reversals, you're not poor, you're broke. There's a big difference. Poor is when you have no education, no skills, no health, no strength. Broke is when you have no money. Broke is something you can change.

Plugging Up Leaks

Keeping one luxury in times of financial difficulty is fine and even necessary. Two or three luxuries can be a disaster. Money can be leaking out of your pocket in ways you could never imagine.

A client of mine, Sharon, though earning a good living, found herself short at the end of every month. We went through her last year's check stubs looking for the le~~ there it was. Fresh flowers. When we added fresh flowers during the year, it was ⌐

is now a jungle of grape ivy plants, and fresh flowers are reserved only for her birthday and leap years.

I've found serious leaks in my clients' budgets in the area of transportation. It's so easy to hail a taxi in New York rather than to grab a bus. In Los Angeles, it's simpler to pull into the $3-an-hour lot than to hunt for a twenty-five-cent meter. These small indulgences can add up to big leaks in the long run.

And big leaks can become torrents, as proved by my client Ruth. Her one luxury was a classic Mercedes. Custody of this beautiful machine was divided equally between Ruth and her mechanic. However, total support for the car was provided by Ruth. She spent $6,500 in one year on this luxury.

Ruth's salary as a journeyman plumber was sufficient to afford a new Buick. However, she could not afford this Mercedes. With a heavy heart, Ruth sold her car, thereby plugging her leak. She bought a reliable new car and invested her excess savings in a stock portfolio, a long-time goal of hers.

Determining Your Net Worth

Once you've determined your monthly nut and rearranged your budget as necessary, then you must figure your net worth. You may think you're only worth about $4.33; but I can assure you, you're wrong!

What is net worth? It's the value of everything you have in the world—every bit of your real and personal property. Real property means real estate. Personal property means all your cash, investments, and personal articles such as art, furs, furniture, silver, jewelry, etc. Add the value of all you own, subtract what you owe on any debts, and the result is your net worth.

My friend Aleisha, a widow for ten years, recently died and left an estate worth more than a million dollars. During her lifetime, accumulating money had been the least of her interests. However, she and her husband had owned a lovely little home since 1940. She also owned a small nursery school and the land and building housing it. With inflation and appreciation, Aleisha's original net worth of $30,000 had grown to over a million dollars in a period of forty years.

When Aleisha became terminally ill, she figured out her
for the first time. She was concerned about how to

divide her property among her children and grandchildren. She was amazed to discover what she had amassed. Had Aleisha calculated her net worth earlier, she would have made very different decisions about estate planning. Unfortunately, her heirs will pay a very heavy inheritance tax. With proper planning, this could have been avoided.

It's crucial for you to know your net worth. It's necessary when applying for credit, negotiating a divorce settlement, and in case of bankruptcy or death. It's a good idea to reevaluate your net worth at regular intervals as you move through different stages of your life.

Net worth is basic to planning your investments. Any excess money from your monthly expenses should be invested so that net worth can grow. Your investment portfolio should be diversified for maximum safety and growth. For instance, you might put some money in real estate, some in stocks, and some in bank instruments.

Keeping a Diversified Portfolio

Your portfolio is an itemized account of your investments. Diversification is a must; it cuts down your risk factor. In other words, never put all your eggs in one basket!

A client of mine, Marsha, is divorced with two children. She owns her home. However all the money she received from the divorce is tied up in an industrial building occupied by one tenant. The tenant has given notice that he will move at the end of his lease. When that happens, a good deal of money will have to be spent preparing the building for a new tenant, and there will be the loss of rent until a new tenant is found. As the major part of Marsha's income is from this building, she is in serious trouble. This is a classic example of what can happen to people who keep all their eggs in one basket and do not diversify their assets.

I'll give you three examples of possible ways to diversify your assets. Thorough explanations of each of the investment instruments mentioned are in the appropriate chapters.

1. Anna is single and earns approximately $20,000 a year. Over the past eight years she's managed to save and invest $10,000 and has a plan to increase this every year. She has $2,000 in the stock market. She has $5,000 in a money market fund and $3,000 in a time-sharing condominium at Stowe, Vermont. (This means that as part-owner she gets to

spend three weeks a year in her own comfortable place and ski to her heart's desire.)

2. Sybil is married, has two children, and owns her home. She inherited $20,000 from her mother; and this is how she invested it: $10,000 went for a three-month Treasury Bill and $5,000 went into a money market fund. She has a $5,000 stock portfolio that is also diversified—one-half is in income stocks, one-half in growth stocks.

3. Joanne is fifty-eight years old and has been widowed for two years. Joanne works as a receptionist in a doctor's office and earns $13,000. She received $75,000 from her husband's life insurance policy. She loaned $10,000 to her daughter to set up her law practice. She loaned her son $10,000 to help with the down payment on his house. Both loans are being paid back with 10 percent interest. She has two Treasury Bills at $10,000 each and she's begun to contribute $2,000 every year to an IRA. She has $13,000 in a money market fund, and the rest of her money is in certificates of deposit.

Determining Your Financial Goals

Perpetual Savings is the name of a savings and loan in my city. Can you imagine saving perpetually, for all eternity? What a dreadful thought—absolutely dreadful! When I save, I save for something I want or need. I save for a goal.

Determining financial goals is a very important aspect of money management. As a child, my earliest financial goal was to save enough from my Sunday allowance to get to next Saturday's movie. If I failed, there was always my thrifty little brother to take me. Through the stages and ages of my life my goals have changed, but if I want something I still must plan and save for it. I don't want to save perpetually. I just want to save long enough to get what I want.

A primary financial goal for anyone is to make money, of course. You also want to hang on to as much of the money you make as the IRS will permit. You also want to use your money for pleasure for yourself and your family, with enough left over to invest to make even more money.

For many single young women, this goal may be a vacation, additional education, or a down payment on a car. More and more young women are saving for big ticket items like a house.

Couples must decide in concert what their goals are. Anything from a baby to a house must be planned for. Goals must also be given priorities. Is it more important to be able to eat out and see first-run movies twice a month or to save that money and have two weeks a year on a vacation? Sometimes, by cutting back to more modest recreation, you can reach both goals.

Some of the most common goals are listed here by stages of life. Pick the ones that are important to you or add your own and give them an order of priority. When you're saving for them you won't feel so deprived because you'll be saving for something you want at the top of your list. It's much like dieting; you may want a dessert very much but you want to keep your figure even more—so that's your goal.

1. **Young and single.** This is the time to look for growth (capital appreciation) from your investments. This is also the time when you can best tolerate risk.

> Education
> Clothes
> Car
> Vacation
> Furniture
> Entertainment
> A home
> Investments
> A pension plan
> Insurance

2. **Young and married.** This is also a time when you should be securing your future with growth investments, provided, of course, that your income is sufficient.

> A home
> Car
> Furniture/appliances
> Vacation
> Investments
> Children (yes, it costs a fortune to have them though
>   they're still inexpensive to make)
> Further education
> A pension plan
> Insurance

3. **Thirty-plus.** Growth is usually still the appropriate goal at this age. Some money, however, should be in low-risk instruments such as Treasury Bills or money market funds, with the interest from them being constantly reinvested.

Education for you
A larger home
Saving for college for the kids
Orthodonture for the kids
Vacation (with or without the kids)
Camp for the kids
Investments
A pension plan
Insurance
Fee for health or sport clubs
Part-time help in the home

4. **Forty-plus.** The same as for Thirty-plus. However, this is usually a time of heavy expenses for college tuitions, appliance replacements, etc. You will probably need to be spending your interest and even some of the principal from your low-risk income investments.

Continuing education
College and gratuate school for the kids
Camp or trip for the kids
Vacation for you
Contributing to elderly parents
Investments
A pension plan
Insurance
Part-time help in the home
Replacing furniture/replacing appliances

5. **Over fifty.** Now is also a time of heavy expenses and, statistically, a peak time for earned income. Growth investments should be reevaluated and, depending on your own situation, gradually changed to income-producing investments.

Continuing education
Children's wedding
Helping the newlyweds get started
Vacation and travel
Investments
Pension plans

Insurance
Retirement planning
Contributing to elderly parents
Money to spoil grandchildren

Each one of us must personally decide how we can best balance the need for security with a desire for capital appreciation. There are those who live only for today and others who live only for tomorrow. My mother always said, "Live every day as though it's your last and as though you will live forever."

STEPPING OUT INTO THE WORLD OF MONEY

Finding Your Team of Pros

Every woman who's interested in becoming moneywise will need professional advice at some point. An accountant, a lawyer, and an insurance agent are the basic three. As you go further with your investment plan, a stockbroker will be added to this list. Criteria for each professional will be discussed in every appropriate chapter as the need arises.

How do you find a good professional? First, ask your friends whom they recommend and why. Keep asking until you have several names and numbers.

Call those that have been highly recommended and ask for a brief interview, it is usually given free of charge. Check on this to be sure. Remember, the purpose of the interview is for you to see if you like the professional and if she or he is someone you feel comfortable with. You are the client. The person you hire works for you and he or she must fill *your* needs.

In the interview, ask what the fee schedule is. Also, ask for a general picture of how this particular firm operates. Give a quick run-down about yourself and your situation. Do not commit yourself until you've found someone you like. Tell anyone you interview that you will get back to them and then do so.

At first it may be hard to call a lawyer and say you've decided to go elsewhere. The reasons you might give are:

1. It's closer.

2. I really would prefer a woman.

3. I really would prefer a man.

4. I feel I could work better with someone else. The first time I had to do this audacious thing I spent at least three hours in turmoil. How could I tell a man, a *professional* man, who had been nice enough to let me through the door, that I did NOT WANT HIS SERVICE! Would I be struck down? God, how I suffered! However, after a little practice I could do it either with no emotion or with a glint of pure joy, depending on how I had been treated.

I stay away from, or get rid of:

1. Professionals who don't return a phone call within 48 hours. (A call from their secretary that they are out of town, in trial, sick, or dead is, of course, the same as having the professional call.)

2. Anyone who is in any way condescending or patronizing or who treats me like "a little woman." *Why?* I'm fully grown, can take care of myself, and I'm tired of listening to jokes about women.

3. Anyone I find I don't like. Why? Because I don't *like* them!

4. Anyone who doesn't give service. Why? Because they don't give service.

With the dramatic increase in women professionals, I can now work a lot with women. Naturally, I apply the same judgment to women as to men. Since it is still more difficult for women to get into most professions, when they *do* they're likely to be excellent.

A special word about lawyers is needed. In smaller cities and towns or in the country, you will probably still find a family lawyer, just like the family doctor. These rare birds can be wonderful. But in big cities, where the law has become highly specialized, you'll need a lawyer who specializes in the areas in which you have a problem. Don't see a real estate lawyer for wills and probate. Don't see a personal injury man for a divorce, even if your marriage has been nothing but personal injury for twenty-two years!

You're the Boss

Remember with any professional that you hire, you are the client. As the client you call the shots and are the boss because you pay the bill!

To assert yourself is difficult and often goes against your upbringing. Women are raised to be "nice," which is a code word for compliant. You can't be compliant in your business dealings but you *can* still be nice.

I told my stockbroker to sell a stock if it went down. I gave him my bailout figure (my bottom line). The stock did go down, and he didn't sell because *he* felt it was the wrong time for me to sell. I was ready to kill him until I cooled down and looked at my options. They were: 1. I could forget it. 2. I could fire him and tell him why. 3. I could go to his boss and insist he make good on the money I lost. I chose the second option because I hadn't lost enough money to make it worthwhile to go through the hassle of option three.

I called him and told him I was furious that he hadn't followed my orders and that I no longer trusted him to handle my business. I also reminded him that he had no right to substitute his judgment for mine without calling me. Even if I had *made* money on the deal I would still have fired him.

I didn't yell at him. I was firm, businesslike, and brief. I didn't attack him personally. I attacked the way he handled the issue.

Being businesslike is a two-way street. You know how you want to be treated and you should treat people who work for you the same way. Tell them what you want up front, and if they can't do the same, find someone who can. Your goal is not to be thought of as a "darling lady" but rather as a clever, businesslike woman.

Negotiating is an art, and you've been doing it all your life. "Give a little, get a little" is negotiation at its best. In business, you must know what you want before you negotiate. Then you'll know what you can give away in order to get what you want. When I bought my first house I *needed* three bedrooms and I *wanted* two baths and a separate dining room. I had a price limit, and after a bit of negotiation I ended up with three bedrooms, one-and-a-half baths, and a small dining area. I had to give a little, but I got what I needed.

Going first-class with the best professional you can find is always cheaper in the end than trying to find a bargain. Learn to trust your gut reaction! The best for me may not be the best for you. Demand good treatment—you're paying for it and you deserve it!

Networking

From the beginning of time, women have exchanged information with one another, whether it was about the location of the warmest and driest cave or the early secrets of midwifery. Women's history has been passed down by word-of-mouth—mother to daughter and sister to sister. This kind of natural communication has recently been given the official name of networking.

For years we've been passing along the names of our pediatricians and obstetricians when they give good service. Financial networking is a simple outgrowth of this age-old custom.

One way you can involve yourself as well as get some support in the financial world is by networking, either formally or informally.

Wendy, a client of mine, is a new physical therapist. She was denied a MasterCard at her bank. I sent her to my bank (her bank but a different branch), where they were delighted to have her business and give her a credit card. They did this because I have such good relationships with the women at my bank. This is the kind of informal networking through which women can lend a hand to one another.

Another example of informal networking is to keep each other informed about job openings and advancement opportunities. Many women who have reached excellent positions in their field become mentors of younger women who in turn become mentors themselves. Women now have their own "old girl" network.

Formal networks for women have sprung up all over the country. There are groups called Women in Business, Women in Management, National Association of Women Business Owners, Women's Yellow Pages, and Women's Referral Service. Ask around to see what groups are in your area and check your phonebook too.

Read the Paper, Learn the Lingo

When you open your cookbook and prepare to tackle a new recipe, you probably deal with some very peculiar words and expressions. However, phrases like "clarify the butter, gently simmer, lightly grease, or separate the eggs" do not throw you because your cooking vocabulary is pretty well developed.

There is a financial vocabulary that you can and should learn. It's even easier to pick up than extremely precise cooking directions. Start by reading the financial news every day. You'll soon learn the jargon and begin to incorporate it in your everyday language.

Remember, jargon does two things: It forms a kind of shorthand just as in cooking directions, which is useful, and it tends to mystify a particular subject, which is not very useful at all. For example, premium in the insurance world means what you owe—it's just a bill that your insurance company decides to call a premium. In the bond market, a premium is what you are paid above your cost when you sell a bond that has increased in value. In the bond market, your premium is your profit. At the grocery store, premium ground beef is the top grade, and if you have a cents-off coupon, that too is called a premium. (See the glossary in the Appendix for a complete list of financial terms and their definitions.)

I am completely comfortable with the financial pages of my newspaper, but do *not* give me the sports section. "Sudden death overtime" and "linebackers vs. tight ends" will happily remain a mystery to me forever!

Investment Clubs

Investment clubs are formed when people get together and pool their money to invest. Club members are able to own more substantial investments than they could as individuals.

A typical investment club consists of between ten and twenty people who invest anywhere from $20 to several hundred dollars per month in the stock market. They get together and make investment decisions after doing research and consulting with experts. The ideal investment club aims to increase the investment knowledge of its members while evenly distributing investment risks and rewards.

There are over 15,000 investment clubs across the nation. Many of these that have been in operation for two or more years are showing a profit. Some of these clubs have surpassed even the Dow Jones average and many have done better than professional money managers.

You can start an investment club for fun and profit by rounding up ten or twenty of your friends and colleagues. You can then jointly decide on how much each member will invest each month. Your next decision is whether to have wine and canapés *or* coffee and cake.

It's important to have a lawyer help set up the club and draw up an agreement for the members. Also, it might be a good idea to join the National Association of Investment Clubs (NAIC), P.O. Box 220, Royal Oaks, Michigan 48068. A small fee will get you valuable literature as well as $25,000 worth of insurance against misuse of funds by one of your club members.

NAIC has a yearly convention and puts out a monthly newsletter. The letter contains stock information and recommendations. These were spectacularly successful in early 1980 when the recommended list produced a 52 percent profit while the Dow rose only 9.8 percent!

Many clubs follow the four NAIC investment guidelines:

1. Invest regularly.
2. Reinvest profits.
3. Buy growth stocks.
4. Diversify your portfolio.

After your club has defined its goals, the next step is to choose a good broker from a reputable firm who is *not* related to a club member. This broker will carry out your orders.

Your club should meet at least once a month to study investment philosophy and to exchange research on current stock opportunities. With ten or fifteen members you are bound to have people with expertise in different firms and you might do well to start your portfolio of stocks using their special knowledge. Bring in outside speakers such as real estate and stock brokers, insurance agents, etc., who will add to your knowledge. These people will be happy to speak to you because you are all potential clients. The amount of self-education that members do will be reflected in the club's success.

I've found investment clubs to be a wonderful vehicle for women, who usually are operating with limited financial resources. It provides group support as you learn about investing and begin to make decisions about your money. It makes the process of financial discovery painless and often a lot of fun. Also, when an investment club loses money, which sometimes happens, analyzing the reasons for the loss can be almost as profitable as realizing a gain. And everything is easier and less mysterious when it's done in a group of supportive people.

2

Banking: The Banking Revolution

Prospective Landlord: If you want me to hold this apartment, I'll need two bank references.

Prospective Tenant: Of course. You can check my accounts at Sears and Merrill Lynch.

Prospective Landlord: Lady, I'm not interested in where you bought your refrigerator or who your stockbroker is. What I *need* is two *bank* references.

Prospective Tenant: Mr. Rose, Sears and Merrill Lynch *are* my bankers and I'm expecting you to supply the refrigerator.

Are *you* banking at Sears or Merrill Lynch these days? If you aren't, you may be soon! This is a brand new development in banking—exciting, creative, and profitable.

Forget everything you ever knew about banks. With the passage of the Depository Institutions Deregulation and Monetary Control Act of 1980 (DIDMC), the world of banking is being completely revolutionized. The nice brick building that houses your bank will only *look* the same. In a matter of a few years, this new legislation will create a wildly competitive and vigorous banking environment.

The DIDMC Act will bring about a number of drastic changes. This act is very complex but these are some of the highlights:

1. Regulation Q, which controls how much interest a bank can pay its depositors, will be completely phased out by 1987. Banks will be free to compete with other financial institutions for your investment dollars. Small banks will be unable to compete with larger banks and many will be swallowed up like Jonah in the belly of the whale. As of 1986, banks can pay any interest they wish on consumer deposits.

2. Mortgage rates will probably remain high but there will be a larger and more imaginative selection of mortgages to choose from. (See Real Estate chapter.)

3. One-stop banking will be available as differences between commercial banks, savings and loans, and thrift institutions evaporate.

4. Services from bank to bank will become more uniform. Every bank will be forced to match competitors' services. For example, the difference among airline prices and service today is mainly the color of the stripe on the plane's body. If Pan Am offers a special, it's matched by all the others. So when Citibank gives away toaster ovens, you can bet your boots that Wells Fargo is going to offer an Espresso maker!

5. With transfers of funds being made electronically from coast to coast, complete interstate banking services are just around the corner.

6. The banking system previously weighted down by obsolete regulations, will become streamlined and more efficient.

7. Fixed rate interest will go the way of the icebox as banks and other financial institutions will immediately pass on any increase in their costs to the consumer.

However, until the financial revolution is completed and all the repercussions are understood, we still have to deal with banks as they are right now.

What Is a Bank?

All the various financial institutions have one thing in common—they are *all* middlemen. This will remain true even *after* the revolution. Whether your money is deposited in a commercial bank, a savings and loan, or a credit union, it is held by a banking institution that gives you certain services and interest in return. They take the money they are holding, your money included, and lend it out to individuals, companies, and other nations at a higher rate of interest. Or at least they try to do this. Their profit comes from this "spread"— the difference between what they pay you and what they get paid. That is the essence of the banking business.

Example:

On my passbook *I receive* 5.25% per year.

On my loan from the same bank *I pay* 17% per year.

The bank is making 17%−5.25%=11.75%. Even with their overhead, that ain't hay!

The basic list of banks now is as follows:

1. Consumer Banks. Like your basic black dress, a commercial bank serves for almost every occasion. It offers checking and savings accounts, safe deposit boxes, business, consumer and real estate loans, pension plan management, bus tokens, and blood pressure machines!

2. Savings and Loans. Savings and loans now offer the same services as commercial banks. Their emphasis, however, has been and remains on real estate loans.

Savings and loans are also called thrift associations, building and loan associations, cooperative banks, etc.

3. Credit Union. These are non-profit savings and loan cooperatives. Membership is restricted to people with common interest, such as a common work place, profession or residence. They are not able to provide the variety of services that banks and savings and loans do. Primarily, they offer low interest consumer loans and some financial counseling services.

4. Brokerage Houses. Did you say brokerage houses? Yes, brokerage houses. These are the new boys on the block in the banking industry.

Brokerage houses started offering high yield money market funds (see Lending chapter) as a service to their customers and as a way of attracting new business. It was only a small step to offering check writing privileges against these funds. Another tiny step was to issue a credit card that is paid for each month from your money market account. Sounds just like a bank, doesn't it?

In order to keep track of these transactions, your money market fund managers started issuing monthly statements—just like your bank. This statement shows you the value of your money market fund (bank balance), dividends paid (interest), a list of all the checks you wrote, your credit card charges, and cash deposits. In case of error, the fund keeps a microfilm record of all transactions—just like your bank.

Depending on your brokerage house, there are different types of accounting, different check writing limits, and different minimums to set up an account. The minimums can be cash or stocks and bonds.

A major feature of these accounts is computerized record-keeping. While handy for tax purposes, an error can be disastrous. Have you ever tried to reason with a computer? If these accounts are yours, be sure to keep your own set of records.

5. Department Stores. Sears was the first department store to offer a high yield place to store money. With banks still restricted during the phase out of Reg. Q, nonfinancial institutions such as Sears, unhampered by regulation, are looking to meet consumer financial needs. Now these stores sell money market accounts, real estate loans, and insurance. And you thought Sears was only good for refrigerators!

Brokerage houses, department stores, and possibly everybody including your local market, are probably in the banking business for the long haul. Since these alternative banks are not controlled at all by government regulation (although banks *are* trying to have these bonanzas for the small investor regulated) they might be just the ticket for you.

Each financial institution has worked in different areas historically. For instance, savings and loans were set up after the Depression to provide long-term loans for home buyers. Each type of bank is regulated and insured by a different federal agency. Banks can be state banks or federal banks. If they are state banks they are regulated by the state as well as the federal government.

HOW TO SHOP FOR A BANK

I feel like Leonard Bernstein conducting a good orchestra when I go into my bank to conduct business. I enjoy my bank because I understand what it can do for *me*. I know what its limits of service are and I know what strings to pull to make it play for me.

Consumer banks woo you with ads and interest and new gimmicks so that you will come in and put your money with them and not the bank across the street. Banks are the supplicants and you are the beloved. If a bank falls out of favor with you, you can pull your money out of the bank with the proud knowledge that just across the street or around the corner another bank will embrace you and your money with all the passion and promise of a new lover.

In the old days when most Americans lived in smaller towns, they knew their banker, his kids, his wife, his dad, and a century's worth of gossip about his family. He knew just as much about you, your family, its gossip, and just about everything about your business. He knew if you were "expecting," if your crops or lumber business were doing better or worse than last year. With this knowledge he was able to be a compassionate and wise banker, if he so chose, or an s.o.b. if that was his nature. The well-being of a bank depended on, and still depends on, the well-being of the community. So even if your banker is an s.o.b., he still wants and needs his community to be prosperous.

This still holds true in some rural areas and small towns. For most of us, however, banking has become quite impersonal.

Big Bank, Little Bank

If there are only one or two banks in your town, you may have to settle for the first suitor. But how do you choose a bank in a big city with everybody wooing you?

With Regulation Q in full force, shopping for a bank really only involved looking for the best possible service. As this regulation is phased out, you'll want good service *and* the highest possible interest on your money. Before you can make an educated decision as to which bank to use, you must familiarize yourself with what a bank offers and how a bank works.

Before I understood banks I went through them like Sherman through Georgia. If I couldn't figure out how much money I had in an account, I changed banks, leaving my old account open for three months, so any check I had written on it would be paid. After a few years of this, I met Lee. She was then a teller in a small bank I was using because it was close to my home. I called once too often to ask my balance (how much was in my account), and she invited me to lunch. She showed me how to enter each check I wrote by number, date, and amount. She also showed me how to enter my deposits and how to balance my statement. Of course I knew all this in theory, I was just poor in practice. Partly, my behavior was motivated by fear. If I didn't know how much money I had, I also didn't know how much money I *didn't* have. In those days I'd go a country mile not to face reality.

It dawned on me as I learned to keep an accurate register of checks and deposits that the register was for me, for my private knowledge. I wasn't being watched or graded, I was only keeping a money diary.

Lee could take an interest in me because she worked for a small bank with only two branches. Each customer was important and known by name. It was a small-town bank in a big city. The only drawback to a small bank with a very limited number of branches is that there are just a few offices where you can cash a check or deposit money—services only your own bank will provide.

Alas, one morning my little bank wasn't there. It had been purchased by Wells Fargo, an old California bank. The deal had been in the making for some time. Between three in the afternoon, when Beverly Hills National closed, and ten the next morning, my little bank and I had been acquired by Wells Fargo, a big bank, in a quiet, successful maneuver that would make the CIA green with envy. Now I had to deal with a large bank but, thanks to Lee, I knew what I was doing.

Meeting Your Bankers

When you start to shop for a bank, Lee had said, interview the manager. Call first to see when it's convenient, and then go and introduce yourself. I don't care if you're only putting $500 into a checking account. Get the name of the manager and tell him or her a little about you and your work or family—general chit-chat. The idea is for him or her to remember you so that when you call he or she will know who you are. Dress in a businesslike fashion. However, if you're depositing $10,000 into a checking account and $20,000 in savings, you can probably slump in wearing jeans and tennis shoes if you want—you'll be remembered!

Whether you have lots of money or just a little money, tell the manager what you're looking for in a bank. For example, I don't want my checks bounced. Nowadays I want a check guarantee card, a credit card, and preferential treatment when I want to borrow. When I first started out I didn't ask for all these services because I had very little money. So I started modestly with my manager and told him I wanted the bank to phone if I was overdrawn and not to bounce my checks. He agreed because the bank wanted my business.

Lee told me that next to the manager, the operations officer was the most important person for a bank customer to know. They oversee the tellers and "approve" many transactions. So ask your bank manager to introduce you to the operations manager. Chit-chat with the OM also so that you'll be remembered. People are always flattered when you remember their name, from the bank manager to the teller in training. So *you* remember too, and you've got the beginning of what may be a meaningful relationship.

What Services to Look For

There are two types of bankers, creative ones and "by-the-book" ones. A creative banker, when presented with a problem, looks for a solution. For instance, he or she will help you establish credit, clear out-of-town checks for you immediately, or get you that new car loan. A "by-the-book" banker is one whose favorite word is "no." No matter what you want, he or she will cite a regulation that says you can't have it. These bankers forget that they are not just working for the bank, they are also working for *you*. If your banker is a naysayer, find a new banker!

Other features to look for are convenient hours and a location either near your home or business. You might want a night deposit service and an automatic teller machine so you can get cash at odd hours. Look for a bank with pleasant tellers who stay on the job for longer than thirty days! Insist on bank employees who are willing to explain their procedures to you in plain English.

My check guarantee card permits me to cash a $300 check at *any* branch of my bank (even when the computers are down!). Some check guarantee cards are accepted by merchants as identification when you are writing a check. Others offer overdraft protection that will cover a check even if there's not enough money in your account.

Some banks offer free safe deposit boxes, free travelers checks, and free checking accounts—although these usually require you to maintain a hefty minimum balance. I even got my encyclopedia on a group discount rate from my bank!

I have also been given my own personal banker, Maryann. The personal banker idea is spreading. Maryann cuts across all departments and is there to solve any problem I may have—bank problems that is!

Shopping for Interest Rates

The impact of Regulation Q's phaseout has yet to be fully felt. When all banks and savings and loans were under this regulation, their interest rates were fixed by the federal government. Now banks will be able to attract customers with offerings of higher interest rates than their competitors. So, you'll not only be shopping for the best services but also for the highest rates of interest.

WHAT THE BANK SELLS

The basic service a retail, or consumer bank sells, is safe storage of your money. There are many different kinds of storage and retrieval systems.

1. Checking Accounts. The most widely used banking service is a checking account. These accounts have become more complex lately. The basic premise, however, remains the same. You deposit a certain amount of money and write checks transferring portions of this money to your butcher, baker, and candlestick maker (mainly the butcher!).

These days there are many ways to get money in and out of a checking account. You can have your paycheck deposited automatically. You can telephone transfer funds from one account to another. You can pay your bills by phone and have the money automatically deducted by your bank. There are checking accounts called Negotiable Orders of Withdrawal (NOW) that pay interest on your balance. You can combine your checking account with your savings account. You can get overdraft protection (sometimes called a line of credit) in case you spend more than you have. Some banks offer all of these services with their checking, others do not. You should inquire at your own bank.

You would think when you deposit a check from another bank that your new account is officially open. It isn't. First, your check has to "clear"—go for collection to the bank it is written on. After all, you might be opening a new account with a bum check!

When I opened my new account Lee asked me to fill out a form that included my mother's maiden name. It's for identification when I call for information about my account. I think it's a brilliant idea. Nobody, but nobody, knows my mother's maiden name except me, my sister, and my brother.

When the bank notifies you that your account is open, you'll get temporary checks until the checks you ordered come in. Do have your phone number printed on your checks as well as your name and address. Since bad checks are on the increase, when you write a check you are almost always asked for your phone number.

Here is what all those numbers on your check stand for:

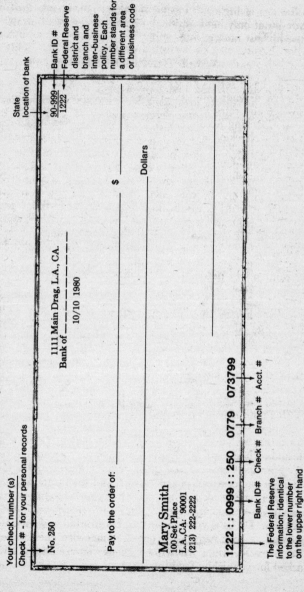

Your check number (s)
Check # - for your personal records

State
location of bank

Bank ID #
Federal Reserve
district and
branch and
inter-business
policy. Each
number stands for
a different area
or business code

90-999
1222

No. 250

1111 Main Drag, L.A., CA.
Bank of _____
10/10 1980

Pay to the order of:

$ _____
_____ Dollars

Mary Smith
100 Set Place
L.A., CA: 90001
(213) 222-2222

1222 : : 0999 : : 250   0779   073799

Bank ID#   Check #   Branch #   Acct. #

The Federal Reserve
information, identical
to the lower number
on the upper right hand
side of check

Never assume that a bank statement is correct. Balance your checkbook and reconcile your bank statement every month. This is especially important if you use an automatic teller. Errors must be corrected within certain time limits or they will stand; and if the error is in the bank's favor, you'll be out of luck!

If you are married and have a joint account with your husband, be sure to maintain a bank account of your own in addition. You need and deserve money of your own and you'll always need a bank history of your own. The law varies from state to state, but some or all of your spouse's assets are frozen immediately after his death, making the contents of a joint account inaccessible at a time of great need. In case of a divorce, you'll want to empty the holdings of your joint account into one of your own. And in case you're happily married, it really is much nicer to pay for his birthday present out of your own account. (See Love and Money chapter.)

2. Passbook Accounts. This is the most common form of savings account and one that unfortunately is guaranteed to lose you money. These accounts are paying between five percent and six percent, and in periods of high inflation they are sure losers.

For instant cash in case of an emergency, you should keep about one month's income in a passbook account. But, really, there is no other reason to store your money in these archaic instruments. Like the dinosaurs, they shall pass from this earth.

Remember, on passbook accounts interest is paid quarterly at the very *end* of the quarter (March 31, June 30, September 30 and December 31). So, if you have $1,010 in your passbook and decide to close it out June 28th, you will receive NO INTEREST for the entire quarter—nada—nothing! If, however, you decide to withdraw $1,000 in May and leave the $10 in until the end of the quarter you will receive interest on the $1,000 until the day you withdrew it and interest on the $10 for the quarter. The difference is between CLOSING and WITHDRAWING. Check with your own bank on current minimums; they could change. Remember, it's the principle I'm discussing here, not actual figures. While state banks and federally chartered banks don't always have the same regulations, the principle remains the same. Check!

3. Time Deposits. Time deposits now have as many names as the flowers in the field but a rose is a rose is a rose, and a

time deposit is a time deposit is a time deposit. They work very simply. You put your money into the bank for an agreed amount of time, and the bank pays you an agreed amount of interest.

Many of these accounts carry an early withdrawal penalty. When you invest your money in a time deposit, the bank counts on your money for a given period of time. When you withdraw your money early and upset their plans, they penalize you. The penalty usually is the loss from three to six months' interest and, in some drastic cases, interest is dropped back to passbook rates. Before investing in a time deposit, ask your banker what the penalty is for early withdrawal.

Here are the names of some time deposits in common use in this year of our Lord.

Certificates of deposit (CDs)
Long-term market yield CDs
Six-month market yield CDs
T-Bill plus accounts
Fixed time and automatic renewal CDs
Investment and planned saving CDs
Retirement passbooks
Christmas Clubs
All Savers accounts
Jumbo CDs
Six-month money market certificates
Small Savers accounts

Remember, these are *all* time deposits and they all work essentially the same way!

4. Other Instruments. Banks also sell United States Treasury Bills, bank paper, and commercial paper. These instruments differ from time deposits and will be discussed further in the Lending chapter.

5. Trust Departments. Banks sell the service of their trust departments. This department will manage your stock portfolio, serve as trustee for an estate, invest for you in mutual funds, be executor of your Will, and do just about everything but windows! However, trust departments traditionally are unimaginative, stodgy, conservative, and sexist! They are Dickensian in their outlook towards women and children. Use trust departments at your own risk as an absolute last resort.

6. Life Insurance. Some banks sell life insurance in its

various forms. Generally, this is a good place to buy reasonable insurance. Comparison shopping, however, is still necessary. (See Insurance chapter.)

LOANS

The lion's share of your bank's income comes from making loans. Banks lend to everybody from the U.S. government and large corporations to people needing car loans. Naturally, they only make loans to people who can repay, which leads to the old saw: "Banks only lend to people who have money." If you were a bank, you'd set the same criterion.

When you apply for a loan, banks ask for a financial statement. A financial statement is fascinating but hell to fill out. Most people are dumbfounded to find out how much a bank wants to know about them. Some borrowers could win the Pulitzer prize for fiction by just submitting their financial statement!

What is the bank looking for in a prospective borrower? Well, it wants three things—an ability and willingness to repay, a good credit record, and collateral. Your ability to repay depends on your income, balanced against any outstanding debts and obligations. Your credit record will show if you pay your bills regularly and promptly. Your collateral is any asset that you own and will pledge to cover the debt should you become unable to pay. (See Credit chapter.)

Banks are interested in your liquidity, because if you fail to repay they want what they hold as collateral to be easily converted to cash. (A liquid asset is one that can be quickly turned into cash.) The following things are considered liquid:

Cash—naturally!
Gold or silver
Jewels—a forced sale will bring some money
Bank instruments
Money market accounts
Stocks and bonds

Groucho Marx told a wonderful joke about liquidity. When asked by a friend for a loan he said he would be delighted to help but his money was all tied up in cash!

* * *

Those things that are *not* liquid are:
Real estate
Second trust deeds or second mortgages
Businesses
Boats
Valuable furniture and other collectibles
Insurance

Your nonliquid assets may be the most valuable things you have but they can't be cashed in quickly.

Banks do love nonliquid things that are likely to continue to pay you so that you can pay the bank. The ideal borrower is a tenured professor with a trust fund that pays a monthly income and stipulates that she cannot invade (withdraw from) the main body of the trust. This professor is the kind of borrower that would allow a banker to sleep well at night! Good luck.

However, if you *only* have money or stocks and bonds or a house, banks will still accept you because you can use all of these things as collateral. They use the equity in your home— the difference between what you owe and market value—and tie that up. You will also be able to pledge the required amount of stocks and bonds, but once pledged they can't be sold. Even cash is acceptable if you leave it on deposit with the bank. That says you don't intend to run off to your Latin American retreat.

When Should You Borrow?

There are good reasons to borrow for a healthier financial life and for a richer emotional life. I'll tell you my reasons for borrowing, and then we'll look into some other reasons that are valid.

In 1976, I borrowed $83,000 at nine percent interest for a mortgage to buy my condominium. I couldn't have bought it without borrowing. I receive a tremendous tax break in the form of an interest deduction—which I need. Practically everybody does!

So I borrowed $83,000 at nine percent. My monthly payment is $663. Most of this is interest and is tax deductible. So if I am in the fifty percent tax bracket, one-half of my interest is taken off my taxes. So, really, I am only paying about $330. (Sadly, these low interest thirty-year mortgages have passed into history.)

Just last year I borrowed against the equity in my condo—the difference between what I owe on it and what I can sell it for. Part of the money went to finance a two-and-one-half week trip to Italy with my daughters. They asked me to join them, and I felt it was both very flattering and a moment of truth. Aliza and Susanna are young women, and their future trips are unlikely to include their mother. They'll travel with husbands, kids, lovers, and friends. That's how it should be. I didn't have the cash to go (it's almost all invested), but this opportunity was worth borrowing for, and I did. It *was* worth it!

Other good reasons for borrowing might be to go into business for yourself, to buy a car, or simply because you need cash but don't want to sell something you own that's producing a good profit. So you might decide to borrow rather than sell.

However, I wouldn't have borrowed to buy my condo or take my trip if I wasn't betting on constant inflation. In periods of high inflation, each dollar I borrow today will be paid back in cheaper dollars next year or twenty years from now. Just think what a dollar bought ten years ago on the housing market and what it buys today.

Example: The average price of a house in 1972 was $30,000. In 1981 it was $64,200. Oh, if only we could buy at 1972 prices! But we can't.

In order to curb inflation, the federal government tries to make borrowing unattractive and difficult with high interest rates. This does, indeed, prevent many people from borrowing. In a recession, interest rates drop as businesses and individuals pull in their horns. With fewer people borrowing, banks, like stores, must lower their rates in the hopes of making loans more attractive. This method of controlling interest rates does not always work, which is one of the reasons economics is called the "dismal science."

Borrowing Strategies

Getting a loan is just like getting anything else that you want—only more so. It's a skill and you can learn it.

Let's take the story of Charlotte, one of my clients. She is a successful chiropractor, divorced, with a newly married daughter. Charlotte wanted a home improvement loan to turn her daughter's bedroom into a super deluxe bathroom, complete with jacuzzi and lush tropical plants.

She came to me for advice, and we developed a strategy that I felt would give her the best chance for securing her loan. Charlotte had no particular bank relationship, but her ex-sister-in-law's best friend was an operations manager at a large local bank. I also have some good banking connections that could be helpful for getting a loan. We decided to try both these connections.

My advice to Charlotte was to stay away from the platform loan officer and go directly to Mel at my bank and to her connection, Anne, at the other bank. I told her to use their names and to get and use the names of anyone else that she dealt with. If she had a memory like mine, I advised her to jot everything down, including dates of conversations.

After her initial visit she filled out a loan application. I suggested that she write a brief thank-you note to the loan officer. If this person had been especially helpful, she should also send a letter to the bank manager. You can still get a lot of things with honey.

A loan officer must submit some loans to a loan committee. This can take some time. I suggested that Charlotte bird dog her loan by calling the loan officer regularly. Loan documents can get put at the bottom of the heap, get lost, or get hurried along. Calling is a combination of a gentle reminder and a gentle irritant.

Charlotte did as I advised, but complained about feeling uncomfortable and exposed. She felt like a supplicant even though she is a successful working woman. This feeling is not at all unusual. Just bear with it. The anxiety diminishes as you become familiar with the process.

Charlotte got her loan and her bathroom. Anne, the loan officer, got two bottles of white wine as a thank-you for the extra effort she had put in. If somebody gives you special help in any way, a gift is always appreciated and you will be well remembered for doing so.

The next loan Charlotte applies for will be much easier for her. She has the tools necessary to finesse her way through a loan application. She also has a good relationship with Anne, the loan officer. She's developing a good banking reputation and can expect good treatment as a reliable customer if she applies for another loan in the future. Networking is as useful in banking as it is in assembling your professional team. The old girl network proves again that whom you know is just as important as what you know!

Charlotte's income was such that she didn't need a cosigner for her loan. I once needed a cosigner on my first loan as a single woman, and my younger brother Jeremy provided the signature. Let's face it, he had been in business longer, had a higher income, more assets, and was of the right gender! If you need a cosigner for a loan, get one. Don't stand on false dignity. (Remember, though, that cosigning works two ways. If your husband borrows money in a state where both spouses must sign for a loan, know what you are signing! You will be responsible for repaying that loan, no matter what happens to your husband.)

On the other hand, if for any reason you feel discriminated against because you are a woman, take action against the institution. Details are in the Credit chapter and in the Appendix.

There are some loans that you don't need to shop for and you don't need to buy wine for. A Simon Legree or a Sister Theresa will give you the identical loan, to the penny, because these are by-the-book loans.

Auto loans are a perfect example. Banks can give you only a certain amount based on the make, model, extras, age, and mileage of the car. In such installment loans, the bank's only area of discretion is in the repayment time period.

There is some flexibility in obtaining loans, either business or personal. A good banking relationship can bring you a lower interest rate and greater loan amounts. There is always more flexibility on short-term loans of thirty, sixty, or ninety days. In these days of roller coaster interest rates, however, bankers are inflexible about being flexible over the long haul.

Two Bottles of Wine Loans	*By-The-Book Loans*
Home improvement	Auto
Commercial	Real estate
Swing	
Line of credit	
Consumer	

BANK INSURANCE

Banks and savings and loans have been touted as the safest refuges for your money. Banks are insured by the Federal Deposit Insurance Corporation (FDIC), formed by the banks themselves after the 1929 Depression. Savings and loans are insured by the Federal Savings & Loan Insurance Corporation (FSLIC), formed by the savings and loans in the early 1930s. The main job of both agencies is to inspect and regulate banking practices in order to keep everyone honest. All deposits are now insured up to $100,000.

Remember the book and movie called *I Remember Mama*? It was about a Scandinavian family living on the edge of poverty. Every time the family had a financial crisis, Mama would tell them not to worry. She, Mama, had a bank account and if things got really desperate, she would go to the bank and give her family the money. The kids in the family grew up secure in the knowledge that nothing dreadful would ever happen because Mama's bank account stood between them and doom. At the end of this wonderful story it turns out Mama never had a bank account. She just made it up to make her family feel safe and secure—and they did.

Our bank insurance is just a bit like Mama's bank account. Oh, it's real as far as it goes, but it couldn't stand up to more than a couple of major bank failures. It has been wonderful with small banks like Franklin National, which failed a few years ago. However, if two major banks failed, so might the insurance. If you read the FDIC Insurance Act you'll see that they don't promise what we think they promise. Like most insurance policies, the small print is difficult to read.

The United States Code Annotated, Title 12, states: "Whenever an insured bank shall have been closed on account of inability to meet the demands of its depositors, payment of the insured deposits in such banks shall be made by the Corporation (FDIC) as soon as possible . . ." Now this is not exactly the kind of promise I'm looking for when I want insurance. I wouldn't buy car insurance that promised to pay "as soon as possible" or any insurance that contained such a vague promise.

However, I'm not buying FDIC or FSLIC; they are given to me. I know that they have a little more than a dollar for every $100 on deposit, so they are limited.

Many women want to invest (and even a passbook account is an investment—lousy as it is) *only* if their money is insured by a Federal insurance agency. They should rethink this position. While the FDIC and FSLIC are nice to have and perform many important functions, they can not offer total protection. When small banks run into trouble they merge with larger healthy banks in marriages arranged by the FDIC. It has been against government policy to let a bank or a savings and loan fail. Thus the FDIC and FSLIC have rarely been called upon to pay out insurance.

3

Credit: What Is It and What Do I Need It For?

The dictionary defines credit as "belief," "faith," and "trust." It is also described as trust in a person's ability and intention to pay. When you buy something or borrow and agree to pay back later, that's credit!

Even if you'd rather have spaghetti out of a can at home than charge a fine lasagna dinner out, you still need credit. Whether you are single or married to a man with a pocket full of credit cards, you need credit in your own name.

You often need a credit card as identification so you can cash a check. You need credit in an emergency. If your refrigerator dies along with your car and you have only enough cash to fix one, you can charge the other.

You need credit to take advantage of inflation—buy now and pay later in cheaper dollars.

You need credit if one of your goals is to buy your own home.

Paper money is rapidly becoming obsolete. With new technology, plastic money—credit and debit cards—is replacing your checkbook.

According to your lifestyle, you will need different kinds of credit for different things. There are many varieties of credit. Charge card credit, credit card credit, bank credit; all of these are consumer credit, including accounts at places as varied as Tiffany's or your local dry cleaner.

These kinds of cards have been lumped together and called credit cards but they're not identical. Without understanding the various types of cards, you might find you have gotten something you didn't want and can't pay for.

Charge Cards

Many people confuse a credit card with a charge card—also known as a T&E card, which stands for travel and entertainment. American Express, Diner's Club, Carte Blanche, and the airline cards are charge cards. On these charge cards, you must pay back in full within thirty days. There is a way to arrange repayment in installments on all but the airline cards, but the installments are LARGE and the interest is steep. Also, T&E cardholders are charged an annual fee for the privilege of using the card. Check for changes when you apply for these cards—T&E companies are forever switching their policies around.

I am a devoted user of American Express and Carte Blanche for all travel because they offer air travel insurance. American Express and Carte Blanche also insure you while you're traveling in a public carrier—taxi, limo, bus, subway—from the moment you leave for the airport, throughout the flight, and until you reach your destination. I fly a lot and don't expect the plane to go down. I don't even know how they get up! My only major accident was as a passenger in a taxi on the way to the airport for a trip to San Francisco. The taxi was totaled by an uninsured driver.

The insurance is limited to death or loss of a limb or sight, but the next uninsured driver might cause more destruction than the last who only managed to break my jaw and ribs.

T&E cards are also good for cash loans, travelers' checks, and some useful information on things like English-speaking doctors throughout the world.

Credit Cards

1. Bank Cards. MasterCard and Visa are the industry giants. They can be used at retail stores, restaurants, gas stations, beauty parlors, or anyplace that accepts them. They have become the everybody card. They are your passport to the financial world. In most large cities you must show one as a form of ID in order to cash a check.

MasterCard and Visa authorize various banks throughout the world to issue cards. Each bank establishes its own standard of credit worthiness. So, if you are turned down for a MasterCard, it's the bank that's turned you down and not the bank card company. Another bank may accept you because it has different standards. Both MasterCard and Visa will start you with a low credit limit. If you pay your bills on time, they will raise your credit line after one year either automatically or upon request. Credit limits and interest rates on these cards change in response to changes in federal monetary policy. The rate you pay is clearly stated on the face of your bill and should be checked.

2. Department Store Cards. These are perhaps the easiest cards for women to get today. Stores are accustomed to women buying for themselves and their families. Traditionally, it has not been the privilege but rather the duty of women to buy for the family—hers, his, and theirs. Whether it's the usual day-to-day buying, the gift buying, the holiday buying—who does it? You, me, my sister, your sister, our women cousins, and our aunts!

Each store, from J.C. Penney to Neiman-Marcus, issues its own card. Most stores offer revolving charge accounts with no interest if you pay your bill in full within a stipulated number of days. If you don't pay at that time or elect to pay only in part, naturally you will be charged interest. Since each store sets its own policy, check when opening a charge to be sure you understand the terms of payment.

3. Debit Cards. These instruct your bank to deduct the money you've spent from your account and put that money into the account of the person you've made a purchase from. It is *not* a credit or charge card. It can be useful for women who don't qualify for a credit card. It's also nice for those of you who can't bear to owe money—even for a minute.

Bank Credit

Bank credit is not the ability to *charge*, it is the ability to *borrow*. Bank credit is essential to capital accumulation. You need it to borrow to expand your business, buy a home, buy a car, and to take advantage of good investment opportunities.

A good strategy for establishing credit is to take out a small personal bank loan. Borrow a few hundred dollars, even if you don't need it, and pay it back faithfully.

However, the bank will only give larger loans under certain conditions. You may be the darling of American Express and still be unable to obtain a bank loan. So what is needed in order to borrow a substantial amount of money?

Naturally, the bank is interested in your income and credit

record and they also want *two* ways of assuring repayment. One would be your ability and willingness to repay the loan. The other source would be collateral to secure the loan. Ability and willingness can seep away, but collateral held by the bank is its ace in the hole.

For example, if you borrow to buy a car (one of the most popular forms of bank loans), the bank holds ownership of your car until the loan has been repaid. Your car is a handy form of collateral.

If you've had an auto loan or a consumer loan and have a good credit record, you do get brownie points when you apply for a big ticket item such as a home loan. Your ability and willingness to pay have been established, and your new home is collateral on the loan.

(For more about loans, see the Banking chapter.)

Credit Discrimination

Sexist attitudes die hard. Credit discrimination against women has been with us since the Phoenicians traded their first load of goods. We now have some laws on our side but it is difficult to legislate against the *attitudes* that persist in our institutions by the men who run them. Only by knowing our legal rights and by being willing to fight for them will we get a fair shake in the world of credit.

The history of women's ability to obtain credit started only in 1975. Then the ECOA (Equal Credit Opportunity Act) passed, which states that it is illegal to discriminate on the basis of sex and marital status in granting credit. It was amended in 1977 to include prohibitions on discrimination on the basis of race, color, religion, national origin, age, and receipt of public assistance benefits. Before ECOA, credit was almost automatically denied to women.

The retail credit industry has done statistical research that indicates women are *better* credit risks than men. Women tend to take a more responsible attitude toward paying their debts.

Yet the most obscene and blatant discrimination against women seeking credit was practiced by banks before ECOA became law. Since the principal source of income to any bank comes from loans, why would they refuse to deal with women who represent half the potential borrowers in this country?

What intelligent businessman would refuse to sell to half the customers who want his goods?

Banks and the men who run them label women with every known stereotype—too frail, too given to whim, too given to pregnancy, too often premenstrual, menstrual, premenopausal, menopausal, postmenopausal. Women couldn't be trusted with money. I sometimes think banks secretly believed we had too much power already. Through only a short encounter with a male, a woman could bring forth the greatest miracle in the world—a baby!

Without some way to command money, own property, and accumulate wealth, women were possessions of those who *could* command money. If women didn't need men financially, what would happen to the traditional roles of men and women? If women could do without men financially, the world, as men knew it, surely would fall apart! Nothing quite so dramatic happened, as we know.

Credit for Married Women

If credit is *only* in your husband's name, you don't exist. I don't care if you've paid every bill that has come into the house in the last twenty-eight years—you don't *exist*. And if you get divorced or your husband dies and you have no credit history, then you must start from square one.

When Jacques died, my first letter of condolence was from a credit card company. They said I should pay off our remaining balance of $582, destroy the card, and, oh yes, they were sorry to have heard of Dr. Brien's death. (A number of widows I know did not get "caught" as I did, and still charge on their dead husbands' cards. If they did not meet the standards to get credit as widows, I told them, "Keep charging and keep your mouths shut." After all, if a dead man's credit is better than a live woman's credit, so be it! If the law is a bit crazy, swing with it.) This took place before ECOA and could not happen now. Not only was I a nonperson, but almost all women in the United States were nonpersons. Now you can get credit under your own name, and go to bed secure in the knowledge that you do indeed exist.

What's His Is *Not* Necessarily Yours

Take out your credit cards and look at them. If the card reads Mr. and Mrs. J. Q. Adams, it's only in your husband's name, and you have a spouse card. Your name is not Mrs. J. Q. Adams. Your name is Judith Adams. If your card reads Judith Adams, it may or may not be in your name. It is quite possible this is also only a spouse card. A spouse card can disappear along with your spouse. It ain't yours. Call your credit card companies and ask if you're contract responsible. If you are not contract responsible you have no credit. Simply send a letter to all your card companies asking to become "contract responsible" and both you and your husband sign the letter. You'll then have credit in your own name and you will also be equally responsible for the bills. You should also do this with department stores and charge accounts.

Community Property States *vs.* Noncommunity Property States

Married women in community property states (see Appendix) can use their community assets and income when applying for credit, since half of what comes into the house as income is theirs. This gives them a great edge over women in a state not having community property laws. The only drawback is if your husband has bad credit, then half that bad credit applies to you also. I have two clients who used their maiden name when applying for credit to avoid being hung with their husbands' bad credit records.

In noncommunity property states a woman must make enough money on her own to merit credit of her own. However, even if a woman is ineligible for credit, she can still maintain a separate credit history based on her and her husband's credit repayment record.

Married women in any state should be sure that a credit history is being maintained in both names. That way, should there be a divorce or death, she will have a great advantage in applying for credit for herself.

Credit Reporting Agencies

Your credit history is maintained in places called credit reporting agencies. There are one or two of these credit bureaus in every major city in the United States. These are connected to every hamlet, village, and borough in every state. TRW, Trans Union, and Pinger are three of the largest credit reporting agencies. These may sound like the CIA or the KGB, but they are open, rather friendly organizations, and are tightly controlled by government regulations.

Banks and merchants subscribe to certain credit reporting agencies. They send credit repayment information on individuals to the bureau. This entitles them to a credit report on any person applying to them for credit.

JUDGING YOUR CREDIT WORTHINESS

Any woman who has ever applied for credit knows that there's a catch-22 at work. The first time you apply for credit at a department store, they want to know your credit history. If you have no history for whatever reason, the store is unlikely to give you credit. It's the old story: "You must have experience to get a job, and you have to have a job to get experience."

In small town and rural areas, it is easier to get credit because people know each other. But in urban areas, getting that first card can seem quite impossible.

According to the law, you must be given a credit card if you have the *ability and the willingness* to pay. You could drive a fleet of trucks through the holes in this law. What is ability? What is willingess? This law causes frustration for women applying for consumer credit for the first time.

Let's look at the word "ability." What does it really mean? It simply means that after you've paid all your normal monthly expenses you can also cover your payments to the credit card company. Who makes the judgment about your ability? The person who takes your application. This person uses the company's formula in determining your eligibility. Unfortunately, this formula is often weighted heavily in favor of middle to upper income men.

A credit grantor freely admitted to me that subjective judgment is used in extending credit. Subjective judgment is discriminatory and against the law. It is also difficult to prove. If you have not had credit before, how can a credit grantor judge your *willingness* to pay? It can't be done. So again, a subjective judgment must come into play.

The Three Cs

The formula used to determine credit worthiness is called the big Three Cs. These are character, capacity, and collateral.

Character has nothing to do with how you treat your mother, husband, children, or best friend. Vicious, miserable people of wretched character are walking the streets, their wallets and handbags bulging with credit cards. Character has to do with how long you've been at your job and how long you've had your checking account. Do you have savings? Do you have life insurance? Do you pay your bills regularly?

Capacity, the second C, questions your ability to pay your bills. Do you have enough income to repay the credit extended to you?

Collateral, the third C, consists of whatever assets you own. These would be other sources of repayment that can be used to secure a loan aside from your salary. Examples are stocks, bonds, real estate, etc. Having this C is essential to getting credit from banks.

In England, if you are an heir you can borrow on your expectations. Large estates are usually "entailed" so that it is impossible to will land and money away. Banks and merchants carry heirs for years and years until the heir's father dies and he can get his hands on the cash. Delicious to have great expectations. Don't try this in Denver or Des Moines or even Dallas. In the U.S., you're not an heir until your parent is dead and you can't borrow on expectation. Parents can change their mind on their deathbed and leave all their money to charity and the ever-waiting cat hospital.

Remember, credit is built slowly. It usually takes at least one year to develop a track record. A track record consists of how reliably you pay your bills and meet your obligations. The better your track record, the more credit you can get.

A Warning!

Having too much credit can affect your capacity to repay and therefore can affect your credit rating. Banks, one of the main credit grantors, are suspicious if you get too much credit too quickly. They're afraid you'll go off on a spree and then—Brazil.

For example, if you have:

a Visa card with a limit of	$1,400
A MasterCard with a limit of	2,000
an American Express card with a limit of	5,000
A Carte Blanche card with a limit of	3,000
you have a potential to be in debt for	$11,400

The credit card companies aren't interested in this information. Banks, however, will take into account your potential credit debit when weighing a request for a bank loan.

How to Establish a Credit Rating

A. Establish Your Financial Identity

1. Open a checking and a savings account in your legal name. Remember, your legal name is your first name and your maiden name, your husband's last name, or a combination of both last names. You are Mary Jones or Mary Smith Jones and *not* Mrs. John Jones!

2. If possible, keep your utilities in your legal name. These are not included in your credit history but are evidence of stability.

3. Keep the phone listed in your legal name, as well as your spouse's.

4. Write to the credit reporting agencies listed in your phone book and request your credit file. If you're married, be sure that separate credit histories are being maintained in your legal name as well as your husband's name.

B. Start Your Credit Rating

1. Apply for a credit card at a small local retail store or food market. Pay all bills promptly.

2. Apply for a credit card at a major department store. Make small purchases and pay your bill promptly.

3. If necessary (say the above two steps fail) apply for a small consumer loan at your bank, whether you need it or not. Have a cosigner if necessary. Put the loan money into an interest-bearing account and make your loan payments promptly.

C. Increase Your Credit Limit

1. Take advantage of special credit plans at your bank such as check guarantee cards or overdraft protection with limited lines of credit for first-time credit users.

2. Having established a few small accounts, apply for bank credit cards such as MasterCard and Visa.

3. Request extension of credit limits after one year.

4. Review your credit history file periodically to be sure it's accurate.

ADVANTAGES OF CREDIT

1. Credit and the Float. One great advantage of using credit is that you benefit from float. Float occurs because you charge an item and don't have to pay for it immediately. This is wonderful because you get to use other people's money for the period between purchase and payment. During this time you continue to earn interest on your own money, which should be in safe harbor in an interest-bearing instrument. When your bill comes in, you pay it in full and there is no interest charge.

2. Credit and Record-Keeping. You have the advantage of excellent record-keeping for business deductions if you keep your card billing. It itemizes where you spent your money and on what. Check all deductible expenses and keep the billing. When tax time comes around, there's your record.

3. Credit in Dry Spells. There are certain jobs that don't pay regularly, such as writing, acting, interior decorating, painting, real estate sales, and other jobs based on commission. These jobs can create feast or famine situations. When a check comes in it's usually big, but payment is so irregular that planning is difficult. During those dry spells when you've spent your last check and the next one isn't due for two months, it's vital to have credit. Baby still needs new shoes and your car still needs gas.

4. Credit and Inflation. During inflation, you can borrow at today's dollars and pay back with tomorrow's cheaper dollars. You can also buy at today's prices and avoid tomorrow's higher prices. For example, let's say a refrigerator is selling for $500 this year and will be selling for $600 next year. Even with high interest rates, it's probably cheaper to charge that refrigerator now. Depending on your tax bracket, you can also deduct part of the interest paid from your federal tax return.

5. Credit and the Tax Man. Interest payments are tax deductible. The formula for interest deductions is based on your tax bracket. If you are in a 25 percent tax bracket then 25 percent of your interest figures out to be deductible. Should you be in a 50 percent tax bracket then 50 percent of your interest figures out to be deductible.

Let's say you've paid $500 interest on a MasterCard this year. So 20.5 percent interest in the 50 percent bracket is really 10.25 percent interest after your tax break. All card companies send you your total interest payment at the end of the year, so you can use it at tax time.

As we see in this example, credit is more useful to rich people. The amount of interest you can deduct goes up with your tax bracket. Why can you only deduct 25 percent of interest if you're in the 25 percent income bracket, while the lucky lady in the 50 percent bracket gets to deduct 50 percent of the interest she paid? Well, unfortunately most of the tax laws in this country favor the rich.

Better Sooner Than Later?

So now you'll be able to figure out if it's better to pay in full now or charge and pay later. I'll put you in the 50 percent tax bracket for this example (how nice of me!).

Let's go back to that $500 refrigerator. Five hundred dollars at 20.5 percent interest is really $500 at 10.25 percent interest in your 50 percent bracket. So, 10.25 percent on $500 is $51.25. Okay, this year the fridge will cost you $551.25. Next year it'll be $600. Common sense tells you to use credit. Remember, this is only an example. If the cost of credit changes, use the correct current costs instead of my 20.5 percent example.

This is a simplified example since you will be making monthly payments on your $500 credit card item. The interest will only be 20.5 percent (10.25 percent to you) on $500 the first month. As you start to pay off you'll be paying on your reduced balance, so the interest will really be less than $51.25 for the year.

THE TROUBLE WITH CREDIT

Credit and Hard Times. There are times when you can't pay all that's due on your credit cards no matter how carefully you've planned. An accident, sickness, a job change, almost anything can cause a temporary cash shortage.

This can happen to anybody. When the credit card billing comes through, pay what you can and send a letter of explanation. Most creditors will be understanding and allow you some time to get back on your feet.

Credit Abuse. "Don't leave home without it" is the slogan of a card company, and it wins my Seduction Award of the Year. I feel naked if I leave home without it. I think my slip is showing or that people with x-ray eyes will know my underwear isn't coordinated—God, the guilt!

Unfortunately, credit abuse is rampant. Charging goodies on a credit card is sometimes just too easy. My godmother has the same problem with checks. She finds it amazing and wonderful that people are willing to take her little checks and give her big bundles of goodies in return.

If you are a credit card abuser you're *not* alone. There are some steps you can take to kick the habit.

1. Put all your cards away except for one to be used *only* for identification. Put them in your safe deposit box or some other difficult-to-reach spot.

2. Pay each bill down until you don't owe anything. No matter how long it takes, keep chipping away at the debt.

3. Never use your cards again except when you have a real emergency. Example: The stove, washer and dryer, and car go out on the same day.

4. See a consumer credit counselor in your area. These nonprofit agencies are all over the country, and are listed under Consumer Credit Counseling Service and also under Family Service Association. (See list in the Appendix.)

These agencies will assist you in establishing a debt management program so that you will be able to pay your bills regularly. They act as a liaison between you and your creditors. They can help to put you back on the road to financial health. Remember, some people can't drink, some can't stop at one cookie and some can't resist the lure of credit.

CREDIT LAWS

ECOA

We currently have some potent laws to protect us in seeking and using credit. We, as women, must take the responsibility to see that these laws, so hard won, are complied with. None of us *really* wants to spend years in litigation. What we do want is credit when we need it and honest dealings when we use it. Wise and judicious use of credit laws begins with knowledge of these laws and some guidelines in how to apply them to our benefit.

The Equal Credit Opportunity Act (ECOA) is a most important credit law. As I've said, this act makes it unlawful for a prospective creditor to discriminate against *any* credit applicant on the basis of race, color, religion, national origin, *sex*, marital status, or age. Furthermore, you may not be penalized and denied credit solely because any part of your income is public assistance. And you cannot be denied credit for exercising your rights. So, if you *do* make a nuisance of yourself to a prospective creditor who's denying you, he or she cannot refuse on the grounds that you are a pest.

However, ECOA doesn't guarantee that women will be granted credit. Some women will be denied, as will some men. The question you must always ask yourself if you are denied credit is, "Would a man be denied under the same circumstance?" If you think the answer is no, then you are possibly being denied credit illegally. This can lead to some funny scenarios. If you're facing a credit grantor during your seventh month of pregnancy, you may find it hard to ask yourself this question without laughing. The question is, however, still the test question! Your pregnancy is no longer a valid issue in refusing or granting credit. Some very *unfunny* scenarios unfold too. But at least we now have some ability to challenge these areas of discrimination—and win!

Credit Application Know-How

Women must be evaluated for credit worthiness on the *same* basis as men. A prospective creditor must use the *same* criteria for both sexes. When applying for credit, the following guidelines apply:

1. A prospective creditor may not treat you less favorably than another applicant because of your sex or marital status.

2. You may not be asked your sex on a credit application. There is an exception. If you apply for a loan to buy or build a home, the lender is required by the federal government to ask your sex so that the government can monitor compliance with ECOA. They must ask, but *you* don't have to answer.

This exception has always amused me. When applying for a real estate loan, you usually do so in person. Even in my jeans and Adidas with no make-up, there is no need to ask my sex. I have never met a man named Mimi either! Even if someone is in drag, loan officers should be able to make a pretty good stab at the sex of the person they're dealing with.

3. You *do not* have to choose a courtesy title (Miss, Ms., Mrs.) on a credit form.

4. A prospective creditor *may not* request your marital

status on an application for an individual unsecured account (a bank credit card, a debit card, or a checking account, for example) unless you live in a community property state or rely on assets located in a community property state to support your credit worthiness. A prospective creditor *may* request your marital status in all other cases. However, you can only be asked if you're married, unmarried, or separated (unmarried includes single, divorced, or widowed). You might well ask what other situation you could possibly be in? You could be living with someone. Southern California, being in the vanguard for just about everything, has come up with a new form for doctors. You know how they have all those little boxes to check when you're a new patient:

—married
—divorced
—separated
—widow
—single

Well, they've added a new one:

—live-in

You don't have to answer that question anyway unless you're using your husband's insurance to pay the doctor. I always check *all* the boxes and nobody has yet asked me how I manage so many relationships.

5. A prospective creditor cannot refuse to consider your income because you are married, even if it is only part time work.

6. You cannot be asked about birth control methods or your plans to have children. (Yes, they could and did ask before ECOA.)

7. A prospective creditor may not refuse to consider as income *reliable* alimony, child support, or separate maintenance. However, you don't have to disclose such information unless you think it will improve your chances of getting credit. If you do disclose this information, then a credit grantor has a right to be shown proof of reliability, e.g. court orders, etc.

8. A prospective creditor cannot consider if you have a telephone listed in your own name. That would discriminate against married women!

9. Your sex can *not* be considered as a factor in deciding whether you are a good credit risk.

10. Your marital status cannot be used to discriminate against you.

To find out if some of these things are being done despite the law, listen *very* carefully. Often in a one-on-one situation, the real reason for your denial is revealed, and it can be an illegal one. So listen carefully and write things down.

Cosignatures

Before ECOA, many credit grantors required all women to have a male cosigner. Now they can only do so if all applicants are required to do so, regardless of sex or marital status. There are two exceptions:

1. If a woman applies for *secured* credit by pledges, property, and/or other assets, the prospective creditor may ask for the signature of her husband or any other person who jointly owns the assets she is pledging. This may be done *only if* state law requires it in order for the creditor to take possession of the assets should she default.

2. If a woman applies for unsecured credit in a community property state and she does not have enough property or assets in her own name only (outside the community property) to qualify for credit or the state law denies her power to separately manage and control enough of the community property to qualify for credit.

Example: Only a few years ago in California, a husband was considered sole manager of the community property. Now, under the community property law, both husband and wife are comanagers of the community property with equal right to pledge the community assets.

Allowable Questions

When applying for credit, a prospective creditor *may* ask the following and only the following:

1. Your name.
2. Your age.
3. The source of the income upon which you are relying for credit.
4. The number of dependents you have, their ages, and the financial obligations you may have to them.
5. Any obligation to pay alimony, child support, or separate maintenance.
6. Your permanent residence and immigration status.
7. A list of all your assets and whether they are owned by you alone or with someone else.

8. Your income.

9. Where you're employed.

10. The length of time you've worked at your job.

11. Any outstanding debts you may have.

12. Whether you have a telephone at home.

13. Whether you rent or own your residence and how long you've lived there.

14. Savings and checking accounts in your name.

Remember, these are the allowable subject areas. Some of these are *not* sufficient in and of themselves to cause the granting or denial of credit. Number twelve, for example, should carry little weight on your application.

Use It or Lose It

The history of discrimination against women is long, and only very recently have we gotten some laws that can protect us. My young women clients react with horror when they learn how recently they became credit-equal under the law. Only by remembering and knowing women's fight for financial equality can we make sure we are alert enough to keep these rights. There are religious and political groups in this country that want to turn back the clock, and they are making themselves heard. They are well organized, have money to spend and political savvy. Women must care enough to work for our hard fought gains or we stand to lose them. All women are potential divorcees and widows. *Do* you want control over your financial life? *Do* you want to earn equal money for equal work? *Do* you want the same chance as a man to become rich. THAT IS THE QUESTION!

A classic and often recounted example of credit discrimination and ECOA violation is in the stories of women who have sent in identical credit applications to the same companies. One application included the first name and the other only initials. Time after time the applications have come back denying credit to the applicant with the female name and granting credit to the initialed one.

Will companies like these ever comply with the law? Only if we go after them when we have been discriminated against.

If You've Been Denied

If you are denied credit and you believe your denial to be unfair and/or illegal, there is recourse. The recourse is like a formal mating dance. Each move and countermove must be done well and in order. You must follow each step closely.

1. Request the reason for the denial in writing. Keep a copy of the letter.

2. *If* the answer is unsatisfactory to you, phone the person in authority who can make credit decisions, such as credit managers or the vice president of loans and mortgages.

3. Tell that person that you have the willingness and ability to pay and that the denial seems to be based on other factors. Firmly and calmly explain that under ECOA you can't be denied on the basis of sex or marital status. (Remember your assertiveness training!) This may seem silly because, after all, they know the laws, don't they? Not necessarily. The laws are complicated and new. Also, the prospective creditor may know the law but not like it. If a credit grantor wants to go along with old biases and you don't know how to force his or her hand, then he or she can ignore the law and get away with it. Forcing compliance with the law is up to us.

4. At this point the prospective creditor should reexamine your application to decide if a mistake has been made. The majority of women who proceed to this point will obtain credit if they're creditworthy. Credit grantors, who have based their decision on sex or marital status will continue to fly in the face of reality and the law and continue to deny you credit.

5. If you are *still* denied credit, call the company or bank that's denying you and get the name, address, and proper title of the credit manager *and* the president of the company. Write to the president and send a copy of the letter to the credit manager. Your letter should state all the facts of the case, your awareness of ECOA, and how you believe you've been discriminated against. Repeat the magic phrase concerning your ability and willingness to pay. Be polite and firm *and* give the business a way to get off the hook—by extending credit to you, of course. Send your letter to the president, certified mail, return receipt requested. The receipt is proof the letter was received and by whom, since someone must sign for it.

6. Be sure to keep copies of all your letters. You'll need them to proceed. Also keep notes on all conversations and telephone calls, including the names of whom you talked to and the date of the contract.

7. If the prospective creditor says you don't have enough of

a credit history or that you have a history that shows an unsatisfactory payment record, you have the right to know the name of the credit reporting bureau from which the information came.

8. Write or go to the credit bureau and get a copy of your credit history. If you don't understand how to read a credit report (they are written in computer code), a credit counselor will translate. The credit bureau *must* respond to your request for your credit history within thirty days of the credit denial—and for free. If it doesn't, follow the steps outlined in the Fair Credit Reporting Act section of this chapter.

9. If you have no reported credit history, call creditors with whom you have already established a relationship. Ask them what credit reporting bureau they use. Your credit history may be at another credit bureau. Contact the company that denied you credit and give it the correct bureau's name and tell it to check there.

I love fighting when I feel my rights are being violated. I wade into battle with delicious fury. Some women don't like the fires of battle, and so they retreat. Credit is an issue that is just *too* important in your financial life to let yourself back down when wronged. Be the mouse that roars, if that's your style. Be quiet, mean, pathetic, loud, abrasive, demanding, anything—but don't retreat.

10. If all else fails, send a letter of complaint to the agency that enforces ECOA compliance for that kind of business. (See list in Appendix.) This agency will investigate to determine whether the creditor is practicing discrimination.

You should also send copies of your complaint to the Consumer Credit Project, 261 Kimberley, Barrington, Illinois 60010. Request the booklet called *New Credit Rights for Women*. It contains lots of valuable information and a complaint form to fill out and return. Or simply write. This nonprofit organization will review your situation to determine whether you have a legally valid complaint. If valid, it will advise you how to proceed further. Other remedies are local government agencies or consumer organizations and knowledgeable attorneys.

If you do use the Consumer Credit Project, send a tax deductible contribution; it performs a useful service for women and COULD USE THE MONEY.

11. If, after following the above procedures, you feel you have a bona fide discrimination case, consider filing a lawsuit.

A credit grantor *may* be required to pay actual damages *and* punitive damages of up to $10,000.

12. At the very least, if you feel wronged by a company or bank, stop dealing with them and tell all your friends to do the same. Write the president of the company to tell him/her that you're boycotting the company, and say why. Creditors need to do business and until they treat women fairly, give them all the bad publicity they deserve.

There are several other laws that lend support to the ECOA and aid us in using credit wisely and to our advantage.

Fair Credit Reporting Act

One of the best things you can do is keep tabs on and maintain an accurate credit history that is independent of your spouse. We may not be in the age of Big Brother, as many pessimists believe, but we are definitely in the age of the Big Bureau. Our spending habits are being carefully monitored. Well, maybe not too carefully. Therefore, it's our responsibility to be sure that the reports on file for us in the credit bureaus are correct.

The Fair Credit Reporting Act (FCRA) is very helpful to us in keeping our records up-to-date and complete. Basically, the FCRA helps you keep tabs on your credit history by giving you the right to:

1. Review your file at any time and free of charge, if you've been denied credit within 30 days.

2. Know who has received your report in the last six months.

3. Have pertinent information adjusted that has been disputed and judged in your favor.

4. Keep a statement in the records to dispute the accuracy of any item in question.

5. Have an updated report sent to any credit information requestors within the last six months.

6. Erase adverse information pertaining to you after seven years, ten years for bankruptcies.

The FCRA also limits access to your report by spelling out the circumstances under which that report can be given out. Any Joe or Mary Blow off the street cannot just walk into a credit reporting agency and look at your file! He or she must have appropriate reason and credentials.

How to Review Your Credit File

First, look up the credit reporting agencies in your local telephone directory. If there are two or more, check each of them regarding your file. Call them to see if they'll send you a report by mail. If so, they'll send you a form to fill out first and you'll be charged a small fee (probably—and *only* if you have *not* been denied credit in the past thirty days). If you must go there in person, bring identification and some money to pay the expected fee.

If you don't understand your credit history report, the FCRA requires the credit reporting agency to provide a counselor to explain your file. Do take advantage of this as most credit reports look like gobbledygook.

That Is Simply Not True . . .

Uh, huh. So now you've read your report and discover a glaring error. The reason you didn't make that $40 payment to Feminine Fashions was because that new blouse disintegrated upon touching water! Furthermore, the store's credit department and you have already ironed the problem out. Yet, on your report, the $40 is recorded as a default, nonpayment.

Stay calm. The law requires the agency to reinvestigate these kinds of problems. If the dispute cannot be cleared up, you are allowed to put an explanation of up to one hundred words in your file. When inaccurate information is removed or explained in your file, you may request that these updated versions be sent to *any* business that requested your credit information within the last six months.

Investigative Reports—These Must Be Watched!

Some credit reporting agencies collect investigative information. Your prospective insurance companies and/or prospective employers are most likely to request the investigative type of credit report. These deal with information about your character and lifestyle, as well as your credit history. Inaccuracies can be devastating.

The FCRA requires anyone who requests one of these to notify you. You may then request of the inquirer (say, the insurance company) a complete and accurate description of the nature of the investigation. Do so, and challenge *any-thing* that demands it. Follow the steps described for correcting errors on your credit file.

Possible Solutions to Possible Problems

If you feel that your rights under FCRA have been violated, either by a creditor or a reporting agency, and your efforts to resolve the matter have proved futile, there's another step you can take. You can file a complaint with the Federal Trade Commission (address in the Appendix). You can also file a civil lawsuit against the bureau believed to be in violation. Your attorney, an invaluable member of your team of pros, should be consulted.

Other Helpful Laws

Several other pieces of legislation deserve mention. These are all part of the larger Consumer Credit Protection Act and can be *very* useful in insuring honest credit transactions. Remember, observing and acting on unfair or discriminatory credit practices is up to the individuals involved. We need to make these laws *work* for us. Where to write in case of suspected violation of any of these acts is in the Appendix.

1. Truth-in-Lending. This requires a creditor to *clearly* state the *exact* terms of any credit arrangement *before* the first transaction takes place. You have the right to know, in clear and simple terms, exactly how much a credit arrangement is going to cost and the methods used to determine these costs.

2. Fair Credit Billing Act (FCBA). Under this act, a creditor is required to notify you of your rights under the act and tell you where to direct any billing complaints or inquiries. There are certain steps in this game that must be followed. A letter must be sent within sixty days of the alleged billing error. The letter should include your name, address, account number, description or explanation of the error, and the dollar amount involved. *Keep copies of everything.*

Now the ball is in your creditor's court, so watch his/her moves. Within thirty days (count them), your creditor must acknowledge your letter *or* correct the error. If the error remains disputed, a written explanation must be sent to you within ninety days.

Meanwhile, in your home court, you are paying all undisputed charges, right? Right. Hopefully, you can resolve this in these allotted time slots.

However, the game *can* continue. For instance, you have ten days following the creditor's explanation to respond, and on and on, ad nauseam. Remember, if your creditor makes a foul move and doesn't comply with the above steps, the first $50 of the disputed bill does *not* have to be paid—whether the bill was correct or not. So, keep a sharp eye on that calendar!

3. Fair Debt Collection Practices Act (FDCPA). This act applies only to businesses whose business is to collect debts. It absolutely prohibits your money-or-your-life type practices. The act specifically forbids debt collection devices that involve misrepresentation, deception, or harassment against the debtor.

II

Investing

4

Basic Economics for Fun and Profit:
What You Need to Consider
Before Investing

The troika of taxes, inflation, and interest rates affect every person, every day. One becomes painfully aware of these factors when going to the market or when buying a new car or appliance. You are affected in less obvious ways when the price of your bus pass goes up, your phone rates increase, your shoe repair service charges higher rates, or your child's day care fees climb out of sight.

This chapter illustrates just how you are affected by the troika and how to take these factors into account when planning your investments and figuring their return. Most of the ideas and concepts will be familiar to you. I am simply taking the various pieces of this economic puzzle that we all live with and putting them together to form a picture.

In order to illustrate how these pieces fit, I have used some of the easiest and clearest charts you'll ever see. I tested them on my most chart-phobic friends, and received their stamp of approval.

The principles explained in this chapter are essential to understanding how money moves around in our economic system. Even if you have only $50 a month to put in an investment club, you need to have a working knowledge of the causes and effects of taxes, interest, and inflation to make the best decisions.

TAXES

Determining Your Tax Bracket

You may not think you have partners. You may not want partners. But you have partners and have had them from the day you earned your first penny. Your partners are Uncle Sam as well as your state and/or your local tax collectors.

Your partners want their share of whatever money you earn or get from other sources. On April 15th of every year, you must report to them and their henchmen what the partnership has earned. They will then decide what share they want. The rest is yours. These reports are in writing and are called income tax returns.

Figuring your federal tax bracket is basic to making knowledgeable investment decisions and for comparing investments. You need to know what you really have after taxes before you decide how much you can invest.

Get out last year's Federal income tax form and you'll find your taxable income on line 34 of form 1040 or line 12 of form 1040A. This is your adjusted gross income less deductions. Then look at the charts on p. 68 if you are filing a joint return and p. 67 for a single return, and find your tax bracket. (Remember, if you have had a substantial change in earnings, you'll have to work up a quick estimate of current adjusted gross income less current deductions.)

Tax Rates—Marginal and Effective

There are really two tax rates—your marginal rate and your effective rate. Your marginal rate is also called your tax bracket. So if you are in the 35 percent tax bracket, your marginal tax rate is 35 percent. This means that you pay 35 percent on your *last* dollars earned.

The effective tax rate is the rate that you *really* pay on all your taxable dollars. This is best shown by example.

The chart below demonstrates the effective tax rate for a single woman in the 35 percent tax bracket with an annual *taxable* income of $25,000.

Single return
Taxable income $25,000
Tax bracket 35%
Effective tax rate 14.88%

Taxable Income	Dollar Amount	Tax Bracket %
$ -0-–$ 2,300	$-0-	-0-
2,300– 3,400	-0-	12
3,400– 4,400	132	14
4,400– 6,500	140	16
6,500– 8,500	336	17
8,500–10,800	340	19
10,800–12,900	437	22
12,900–15,000	462	23
15,000–18,200	483	27
18,200–23,500	525	31
23,500–25,000	864	35
Total Tax	$3,719	35

In the example, this woman pays $132 on her first $4,400, $140 on her next $2,100, $336 on subsequent $2,000, and on down the line. She pays a *total* tax of $3,719 which is 14.88 percent of her total taxable income of $25,000.

The Economic Recovery Tax Act of 1981

Franklin D. Roosevelt's New Deal changed our political system, which in turn changed our tax laws. The system carried a commitment to help those "in the dawn of life, in the dusk of life, and in the shadow of life" as Hubert Humphrey so eloquently characterized it. Our tax dollars were funneled through government agencies formed to put the commitments of our political system into action. While not always effective, attempts to care for the young, the old, and the less fortunate were always being made.

Under the 1981 Economic Recovery Tax Act, the change in our tax laws has led to a change in our political system. As the new tax laws are interpreted and digested, it is clear that the changes in our tax structure transfer wealth from middle income people to the very rich. Since the government still needs money in ever increasing amounts, and since the rich will no longer pay their share, once again the middle class and the poor will be expected to pay, the middle class with money, the poor with reduction in services. To cover the deficit in revenue to the federal government, there will most certainly be more new taxes or tax increases at state and local levels—and probably in places you never even dreamed of!

What's in the new tax legislation for you? There's precious little of anything. The new laws are complicated, and the ins and outs require professional advice. I will cover some of the changes in general here and in each pertinent chapter.

1. Twenty-five percent Across-the-Board Income Tax Cut. The most widely touted break under the new tax law is the across-the-board tax cut for everybody. The absolute fairness of it all is being stressed over and over again. The chart below shows a very different picture indeed. (Chart uses figures from a married couple filing a joint return.)

Tax Bracket Changes
Economic Recovery Tax Act of 1981

Taxable Income	1981 Bracket	1982 Bracket	1983* Bracket	1984* Bracket
20,200–24,600	28%	25%	23%	22%
24,600–29,900	32%	29%	26%	25%
29,900–35,200	37%	33%	30%	28%
35,200–45,800	43%	39%	35%	33%
45,800–60,000	49%	44%	40%	38%
60,000–85,600	54%	49%	44%	42%
85,600–109,400	59%	50%	48%	45%
109,400–162,400	64%	50%	50%	49%
162,400–215,400	68%	50%	50%	50%
215,000–	70%	50%	50%	50%

*Due to unstable economic conditions in the United States, the 1983 and/or 1984 tax cuts may be rolled back, delayed or repealed.

For those earning between $20,200 and $24,600 you'll notice the bracket drops from 28 percent in 1981, to 25 percent in 1982, to 23 percent in 1983, and finally to 22 percent in 1984. At the other extreme, for those lucky folks earning over $215,000 a year, in 1981 they were in the 70 percent bracket and in 1982 miraculously dropped twenty long percentage points (or 28.5 percent) to the 50 percent bracket!

For those in the middle of the chart, earning between $45,800 and $60,000, the brackets move from 49 percent in 1981, to 44 percent in 1982, 40 percent in 1983, and 38 percent in 1984.

Two things should be noted here. The first is that an across-the-board cut of 25 percent on $20,200 is considerably less than on $45,800 and up. The second notable item is that the incredible drop for those earning big bucks is due to the change in the way unearned income (i.e., income from any source other than wages, salaries, and tips) is taxed. Prior to the new tax law, unearned income could be taxed up to 70 percent while earned income had a maximum taxation rate of 50 percent. Starting in 1982, unearned income is taxed at a maximum of 50 percent, exactly like earned income. This creates an immense tax advantage for the wealthy and makes mockery of the touted across-the-board cuts!

2. Reduction of the Maximum Capital Gains Rate. Another feature of the Economic Recovery Tax Act is the reduction of the maximum taxable rates on long-term capital gains, which is retroactive to June 10, 1981. The maximum gain to be paid has been reduced from 28 percent to 20 percent because of the bracket changes. Sixty percent of the gain is still excluded from taxation. However, in the olden days 40 percent of a taxable gain times the 70 percent maximum bracket meant a 28 percent maximum taxation on the total gain. Today, 40 percent of a gain times the new maximum bracket of 50 percent means only a 20 percent taxation on total profit. This dramatically illustrates the tremendous advantage given to the wealthy under the new tax program. As you can see, the 1980s are a great time to be rich!

3. Sweeping Estate and Gift Tax Changes. Vast changes in the estate and gift tax laws have taken place. These include giving away larger portions of an estate through gifts, lower inheritance tax rates, and other quirks that demand a review of the entire field of estate planning. In a nutshell, because of the tremendous tax breaks to the wealthy they can now accumulate even *more* money to pass on tax free! (See chapter on Wills and Estate Planning.)

4. Larger Limits and Fewer Restrictions on IRA and Keogh Plans. New pension laws now permit anyone, even people already enrolled in employee pension accounts, to open an

Individual Retirement Account (IRA) with earned income. This is the only real break—and it's very good—in the 1981 Economic Recovery Tax Act for middle income people. The maximum yearly deposits have been raised from $1,500 to $2,000 for an individual. The Keogh plan limit for self-employed people has been raised from $7,500 to $15,000. Remember there is no tax until withdrawal on money put into a pension plan. (See the Retirement chapter.)

5. One-Time All Savers Certificates with Limited Tax-Free Interest. A one-time break in the form of an All Savers Certificate has been offered. This means an individual can earn $1,000 tax-free interest or $2,000 for persons filing joint returns. See p. 93 of Lending chapter for comparison of taxable vs. tax-free interest investments.

6. Accelerated Depreciation, or Accelerated Cost* Recovery System. A host of new business tax incentives has been written into the law. Accelerated depreciation is one of your major breaks. This means that real estate other than your residence, which previously took twenty to forty years to depreciate, can now be depreciated in only fifteen years if you so choose. (See the chapter on Real Estate.)

7. Marriage Penalty Relief. New legislation provides some relief to working married couples as of 1982.

8. Taxation on the Profit of the Sale of a Residence. Homeowners who sell their homes now have twenty-four months instead of eighteen months to rebuy without paying tax on the profit of the sale. The amount of profit that can be excluded from taxes by a taxpayer fifty-five years old or older has been raised to $125,000 from $100,000. (See the chapters on Real Estate and Retirement.)

These are only the highlights of the Economic Recovery Tax Act of 1981 as they affect individual taxpayers. The full repercussions of this act will be felt for years to come.

Since the federal government will be pulling in much less revenue, it will have much less money to distribute to state and local governments. You will feel this in your personal finances in many areas: increasingly heavy transportation costs, increased sales tax, probable higher state taxes, increased costs for higher education, cutbacks in already inefficient public education, fewer free or inexpensive services such as

---

*Accelerated cost recovery is the new name for depreciation. However, I have used the more familiar term depreciation throughout this book.

parks and libraries, cutbacks in fire and police protection, less money for environmental protection, and curtailment of programs designed to aid our senior citizens and disadvantaged people. So don't rush out and spend your tax savings because they soon may be eaten up by other increased costs and taxes.

INFLATION

Inflation takes a bite out of all money. It eats away at your salary, reducing the money you have to invest. Then it eats away at the purchasing power of your investment profits. Your savings are also being eroded by inflation.

During the 1970s in the United States, we all learned a new phrase—double digit inflation. This simply means that prices are rising at a rate of 10 percent or more—double digits—over a certain time period. For many years other countries in the world have lived with double-digit inflation, but it was brand new to the United States. In the 1980s, Israel and Brazil are living with triple digit inflation—100 percent and higher!

What exactly does inflation mean? It has a technical definition and a personal meaning for every household. Technically, there are two types of inflation: demand-pull and cost-push.

Demand-pull inflation takes place when a large number of people chase a small number of goods. For instance, 1,000 people are bidding for 500 widgets. Obviously, the widget manufacturers raise the price and still have many willing buyers.

Cost-push inflation, which is what we are suffering through now, occurs when the cost of producing the widgets pushes their prices up.

The result of either type of inflation is rapidly rising prices that you, the consumer, must absorb. The best example of the effects of inflation on a family is the trip to the supermarket or the gas station.

Let's examine how inflation really affects a dollar. The chart on p. 72 shows how the value of one dollar erodes at various rates of inflation. The first example shows how the value of one dollar after one year if the rate of inflation is 4 percent drops to .962 cents. Now your dollar is worth ninety-six cents and two mills. The second example, in the dotted circle, shows erosion of one dollar after twenty years. If the rate of

DOLLAR EROSION CHART

Period	4%	5%	6%	7%	8%	9%	10%	12%	14%	15%	16%
1	.962	.952	.943	.935	.926	.917	.909	.893	.877	.870	.862
2	.925	.907	.890	.873	.857	.842	.826	.797	.769	.756	.743
3	.889	.864	.840	.816	.794	.772	.751	.712	.675	.658	.641
4	.855	.823	.792	.763	.735	.708	.683	.636	.592	.572	.552
5	.822	.784	.747	.713	.681	.650	.621	.567	.519	.492	.476
6	.790	.746	.705	.666	.630	.596	.564	.507	.456	.432	.410
7	.760	.711	.665	.623	.583	.547	.513	.452	.400	.376	.354
8	.731	.677	.627	.582	.540	.502	.467	.404	.351	.327	.305
9	.703	.645	.592	.544	.500	.460	.424	.361	.308	.284	.263
10	.676	.614	.558	.508	.463	.422	.386	.322	.270	.247	.227
11	.650	.585	.527	.475	.429	.388	.350	.287	.237	.215	.195
12	.625	.557	.497	.444	.397	.356	.319	.257	.208	.187	.168
13	.601	.530	.469	.445	.368	.326	.290	.229	.182	.163	.145
14	.577	.505	.442	.388	.340	.299	.263	.205	.160	.141	.125
15	.555	.481	.417	.362	.315	.275	.239	.183	.140	.123	.108
16	.534	.458	.394	.339	.292	.252	.218	.163	.123	.107	.093
17	.513	.436	.371	.317	.270	.231	.198	.146	.108	.093	.080
18	.494	.416	.350	.296	.250	.212	.180	.130	.098	.081	.069
19	.475	.396	.331	.276	.232	.194	.164	.116	.083	.070	.060
20	.456	.377	.312	.258	.215	.178	.149	.104	.073	.061	.051

inflation remains at 4 percent, the figure is .456. That means that after twenty years your dollar is worth only forty-five cents and six mills. Now that the history lesson is over, let's look at a 12 percent rate of inflation. After the first year, your dollar is worth a bit more than eighty-nine cents. After twenty years, your dollar is worth ten cents and four mills. This erosion is what happens to each and every dollar as a result of inflation.

Consumer Price Index and Inflation

There are a number of indexes used to measure inflation in the United States. The most familiar one reported on television and in newspapers is the Consumer Price Index. This measures the cost of the following:

Food and beverages	Other Services and Goods
Housing	Services: Rent for home
Apparel, upkeep	Household expenses
Transportation	Transportation
Medical	Other
Entertainment	Non-durable Goods
	Energy

(In the mid-1980s, there are plans to drop housing from the list and substitute rent for it.)

Each month increases and decreases in these costs are noted and the results are tabulated to figure the current monthly rate of inflation according to the Consumer Price Index.

INTEREST RATES

Charles Dickens wrote, "It was the best of times, it was the worst of times." He could very well have been talking about current interest rates. If you're a borrower, high interest rates are terrible, and this is the worst of times; on the other hand, if you're a lender, high interest rates are a boon, and this is the best of times.

Money, like widgets, is a commodity. During inflation, and even in some deflations, we have high interest rates. More people are chasing fewer dollars, so the price of money goes up. When you borrow money in times of high inflation, you pay more for the privilege. On the other hand, when you lend money, you receive a higher rate of return.

Lending is when you put your money out in return for a given rate of interest. Examples of lending are passbook savings accounts, time deposits, Treasury Bills, and money market funds—all discussed in the next chapter.

There is something reassuring about interest—you invest your money for a given period of time, get paid for it, and when that time is up, you get your original capital back. But all is not peaches and cream. Remember, the purchasing power of your original capital is being eroded by inflation, and your partner, Uncle Sam, is going to tax your interest.

What Moves Interest Rates

The Federal Reserve, the central banking system of the United States, has a major influence on interest rates in the United States. It was first formed to make it possible for banks to borrow money for short periods when there was a run on the bank. A run on the bank takes place when a rumor gets out to the public that a certain bank is in trouble and people run to take their money out. Even banks in A-one shape don't have the cash on hand to pay off all their depositors at the same time, so they have to borrow from the Fed (as the Federal Reserve is called).

The Fed, which is made up of member banks, controls the supply of money. The Federal Reserve is a creature of the government which exercises control of the banks using two important powers. The first is control of the reserve rate. This rate is the amount each bank must hold in reserve of its money on deposit. The higher the reserve, the less the banks have to lend, thus the higher the interest rates.

The second power is control of the discount rate. The discount rate is the rate at which the Fed will lend member banks money. The higher the discount rate, the more interest the banks have to pay, thus the higher the interest rate passed on to you. In these two ways the Fed can control the money supply at a level it believes is healthy for the United States. Naturally, what is healthy is a matter of political and economic argument.

Now you know what it means when the Fed decides to follow a tight money policy. The Fed raises the reserve rate and the discount rate, and right away interest rates shoot up. The prime rate is what banks say they charge their most creditworthy customers, like General Electric or RCA. Prime rate is really a fictional number and nobody actually pays it. We pay *more* than the prime rate, and large corporations pay less. We also compete with the government and large corporations for available money.

When big government and big business go into the marketplace to borrow, they shop at the same store that the general public does. For example, if the government wants to raise money for arms or large corporations want to borrow to buy up other corporations, money for individuals either dries up or becomes incredibly expensive. Money is a limited commodity, and when it's scarce it goes to the highest bidder!

Compound* Interest and Inflation

The chart on p. 76 uses the unit of a dollar to show how money *grows* at different rates of interest. If you have invested one dollar for a year at 5 percent, at the end of the year that dollar will have grown to $1.05. At the end of twenty years at 5 percent interest, the dollar would have grown at $2.65 and 3 mills. If, however, you invest at 12 percent, your dollar will have grown to $1.12 at the end of the first year and to $9.64 and six mills by year twenty.

With 12 percent inflation over twenty years, one dollar erodes to ten cents and four mills. (See dollar erosion chart p. 72.) The chart on p. 76 shows your dollar, invested at 12 percent for twenty years, growing to $9.64. That might seem like a deal but, really, it's not. The purchasing power of $9.64 has declined drastically over twenty years. Twenty years ago you could have gotten ninety-six subway rides in New York City for it; today you get about twelve. Don't forget, Uncle Sam is also going to take his share of your interest in taxes—so cancel a couple of those subway rides. Not a very encouraging picture, is it?

This is only an example. Inflation has never been at the same rate for twenty years running, and nothing is as constant and static as shown on a chart.

TAXABLE YIELDS VS. AFTER-TAX YIELDS

The next two tables show the differences between taxable yields and after-tax yields. Table 1 (p. 78) is for a joint return,

*Compound means interest is paid on your interest, usually daily. For example, 5.25 percent compounded daily gives you an annual yield of 5.39 percent.

COMPOUND INTEREST AND INFLATION CHART

Period	4%	5%	6%	7%	8%	9%	10%	12%	14%	15%	16%
1	1.040	1.050	1.060	1.070	1.080	1.090	1.100	1.120	1.140	1.150	1.160
2	1.082	1.102	1.124	1.145	1.166	1.186	1.210	1.254	1.300	1.322	1.346
3	1.125	1.158	1.191	1.225	1.260	1.295	1.331	1.405	1.482	1.521	1.561
4	1.170	1.216	1.262	1.311	1.360	1.412	1.464	1.574	1.689	1.749	1.811
5	1.217	1.276	1.338	1.403	1.469	1.539	1.611	1.762	1.925	2.011	2.100
6	1.265	1.340	1.419	1.501	1.587	1.677	1.772	1.974	2.195	2.313	2.436
7	1.316	1.407	1.504	1.606	1.714	1.828	1.949	2.211	2.502	2.660	2.826
8	1.369	1.477	1.594	1.718	1.851	1.993	2.144	2.476	2.853	3.259	3.278
9	1.423	1.551	1.689	1.838	1.999	2.172	2.358	2.773	3.252	3.518	3.803
10	1.480	1.629	1.791	1.967	2.159	2.367	2.594	3.106	3.707	4.046	4.411
11	1.539	1.710	1.898	2.105	2.332	2.580	2.853	3.479	4.226	4.652	5.117
12	1.601	1.796	2.012	2.252	2.513	2.813	3.138	3.896	4.818	5.350	5.926
13	1.665	1.886	2.133	2.410	2.720	3.066	3.452	4.363	5.492	6.153	6.886
14	1.732	1.980	2.261	2.579	2.937	3.342	3.797	4.887	6.261	7.076	7.988
15	1.801	2.079	2.397	2.759	3.172	3.642	4.177	5.474	7.138	8.137	9.266
16	1.873	2.183	2.540	2.952	3.426	3.970	4.595	6.130	8.137	9.358	10.748
17	1.948	2.292	2.693	3.159	3.700	4.328	5.054	6.866	9.276	10.761	12.468
18	2.026	2.407	2.854	3.380	3.996	4.717	5.560	7.690	10.575	12.375	14.463
19	2.107	2.527	3.026	3.617	4.316	5.142	6.116	8.613	12.056	14.232	16.777
20	2.191	2.653	3.207	3.870	4.661	5.604	6.728	9.646	13.743	16.367	19.461

Table 2 (p. 79) for a single return. They are to be read the same way.

The top line going across shows the range of taxable income. Drop down to the next line to find your tax bracket for 1982. Continue on down for 1983 and 1984 figures. The percentages from six to thirteen on the left side of the chart are the after-tax yields from investments such as All Savers Certificates and tax exempt municipal bonds.

For example, let's say on a joint return your taxable income is between $24,600 and $29,900. Your tax bracket is 29 percent in 1982. If you were to receive 11.27 percent return on a taxable investment in 1982, it would be the equivalent of an 8 percent after-tax yield. If, in 1983, you received 10.81 percent taxable yield, it would be the equivalent of an 8 percent after-tax yield. Again using the same bracket in 1984, 10.67 percent taxable yield would be the equivalent of the after-tax 8 percent yield.

So don't be swayed by the glitter of high interest. You now have the tools to figure what that interest will mean to you *after* taxes.

ACTIVE INVESTING VS. PASSIVE INVESTING

One of the major themes of this book is the difference between active and passive investments. Active investing requires higher levels of risk tolerance and the rule on this is, "Know thyself." If you can't bear the cyclical nature of active investments, such as stock and real estate, you shouldn't be in them. If you can stand a certain amount of risk and uncertainty, part of your money should be in active growth investments (discussed throughout this book). You must decide for yourself, based on your age, responsibilities, the risk factor in the investment, and your own personal tolerance for risk.

Lending is a passive investment. Once you've placed your money, you don't have to do anything else. You don't have to watch it or worry about it. All the facts are known and the outcome is assured. You just sit back and receive a stream of income in the form of interest on a regular basis.

Ownership is an *active* form of investment. Whether you own your home, a business, or stocks, you must be active and follow up on your investment. If you are passive about active investments such as stocks, you may end up in the same

TABLE 1
Taxable vs. After-Tax Yields
Economic Recovery Tax Act of 1981

Joint Return:

1982 — Taxable Equivalent Yield

TAXABLE INCOME	20,200-24,600	24,600-29,900	29,900-35,200	35,200-45,800	45,800-60,000	60,000-85,600	85,600-109,400	109,400-162,400	162,400-215,400	215,400-xxx
Tax Bracket	25%	29%	33%	39%	44%	49%	50%	50%	50%	50%
6%	8.0	8.45	8.96	9.84	10.71	11.76	12.0	12.0	12.0	12.0
7%	9.33	9.86	10.45	11.48	12.50	13.73	14.0	14.0	14.0	14.0
8%	10.67	11.27	11.94	13.11	14.29	15.69	16.0	16.0	16.0	16.0
9%	12.0	12.68	13.43	14.75	16.07	17.65	18.0	18.0	18.0	18.0
10%	13.33	14.08	14.93	16.39	17.86	19.61	20.0	20.0	20.0	20.0
11%	14.67	15.49	16.42	18.03	19.64	21.57	22.0	22.0	22.0	22.0
12%	16.0	16.90	17.91	19.67	21.43	23.5	24.0	24.0	24.0	24.0
13%	17.33	18.31	19.40	21.31	23.21	25.49	26.0	26.0	26.0	26.0

1983 — Taxable Equivalent Yield

TAXABLE INCOME	20,200-24,600	24,600-29,900	29,900-35,200	35,200-45,800	45,800-60,000	60,000-85,600	85,600-109,400	109,400-162,400	162,400-215,400	215,400-xxx
Tax Bracket	23%	26%	30%	35%	40%	44%	48%	50%	50% →	50% →
6%	7.79	8.12	8.57	9.23	10.0	10.71	11.54	12.0		
7%	9.09	9.46	10.0	10.77	11.67	12.50	13.46	14.0		
8%	10.39	10.81	11.43	12.30	13.33	14.29	15.38	16.0		
9%	11.69	12.16	12.86	13.85	15.01	16.07	17.31	18.0		
10%	12.99	13.51	14.29	15.38	16.67	17.86	19.23	20.0		
11%	14.20	14.86	15.71	16.92	18.33	19.64	21.15	22.0		
12%	15.58	16.22	17.14	18.46	20.0	21.43	23.08	24.0		
13%	16.88	17.57	18.57	20.0	21.67	23.21	25.0	26.0		

1984 — Taxable Equivalent Yield

TAXABLE INCOME	20,200-24,600	24,600-29,900	29,900-35,200	35,200-45,800	45,800-60,000	60,000-85,600	85,600-109,400	109,400-162,400	162,400-215,400	215,400-xxx
Tax Bracket	22%	25%	28%	33%	38%	42%	45%	49%	50% →	50% →
6%	7.69	8.0	8.33	8.96	9.68	10.34	10.91	11.76		
7%	8.97	9.33	9.72	10.45	11.29	12.07	12.73	13.73		
8%	10.26	10.67	11.11	11.94	12.90	13.79	14.55	15.69		
9%	11.54	12.0	12.50	13.43	14.52	15.52	16.36	17.65		
10%	12.82	13.33	13.89	14.93	16.13	17.24	18.18	19.61		
11%	14.10	14.67	15.28	16.42	17.74	18.97	20.0	21.57		
12%	15.38	16.0	16.67	17.91	19.35	20.69	21.82	23.5		
13%	16.67	17.33	18.06	19.40	20.97	22.41	23.64	25.49		

AFTER-TAX YIELDS

TABLE 2

Taxable vs. After-Tax Yields
Economic Recovery Tax Act of 1981

Single Return

AFTER TAX YIELDS

1982 — Taxable Equivalent Yields

Single Return TAXABLE INCOME →	12,900-15,000	15,000-18,200	18,200-23,500	23,500-28,800	28,800-34,100	34,100-41,500	41,500-55,300	55,300-81,800	81,800-108,300	108,300-xxx
Tax Bracket →	23%	27%	31%	35%	40%	44%	50%	50%	50%	50%
6% =	7.79	8.22	8.70	9.23	10.0	10.71	12.0	12.0	12.0	12.0
7% =	9.09	9.59	10.14	10.77	11.67	12.5	14.0	14.0	14.0	14.0
8% =	10.39	10.96	11.59	12.31	13.33	14.29	16.0	16.0	16.0	16.0
9% =	11.69	12.33	13.04	13.85	15.0	16.07	18.0	18.0	18.0	18.0
10% =	12.99	13.70	14.49	15.38	16.67	17.86	20.0	20.0	20.0	20.0
11% =	14.29	15.07	15.94	16.97	18.33	19.64	22.0	22.0	22.0	22.0
12% =	15.58	16.44	17.39	18.46	20.0	21.42	24.0	24.0	24.0	24.0
13% =	16.88	17.81	18.84	20.0	21.67	23.21	26.0	26.0	26.0	26.0

1983 — Taxable Equivalent Yields

Tax Bracket →	21%	24%	28%	32%	36%	40%	45%	50%	50%	50%
6% =	7.59	7.89	8.33	8.82	9.38	10.0	10.91	12.0	12.0	12.0
7% =	8.86	9.21	9.72	10.29	10.94	11.67	12.73	14.0	14.0	14.0
8% =	10.13	10.53	11.1	11.76	12.5	13.33	14.55	16.0	16.0	16.0
9% =	11.39	11.84	12.5	13.24	14.06	15.0	16.36	18.0	18.0	18.0
10% =	12.66	13.16	13.89	14.71	15.63	16.67	18.18	20.0	20.0	20.0
11% =	13.92	14.47	15.28	16.18	17.19	18.33	20.0	22.0	22.0	22.0
12% =	15.19	15.79	16.67	17.65	18.75	20.0	21.82	24.0	24.0	24.0
13% =	16.46	17.11	18.06	19.12	20.31	21.67	23.64	26.0	26.0	26.0

1984 — Taxable Equivalent Yields

Tax Bracket →	20%	23%	26%	30%	34%	38%	42%	50%	50%	50%
6% =	7.50	7.79	8.11	8.57	9.09	9.38	10.34	12.0	12.0	12.0
7% =	8.75	9.09	9.46	10.0	10.61	10.94	12.07	14.0	14.0	14.0
8% =	10.0	10.39	10.81	11.42	12.12	12.5	13.79	16.0	16.0	16.0
9% =	11.25	11.69	12.16	12.86	13.64	14.06	15.52	18.0	18.0	18.0
10% =	12.50	12.99	13.51	14.29	15.15	15.63	17.24	20.0	20.0	20.0
11% =	13.75	14.29	14.86	15.71	16.67	17.19	18.97	22.0	22.0	22.0
12% =	15.0	15.58	16.22	17.14	18.18	18.75	20.69	24.0	24.0	24.0
13% =	16.25	16.88	17.57	18.57	19.70	20.31	22.41	26.0	26.0	26.0

shape as if you paid no attention to a leaking roof in your home.

Ownership, otherwise called an equity position, has generally fared well as a strategy during periods of inflation. Home ownership, for example, a most typical and favored form of investment, has well outpaced the general inflation rate. Government policy encourages ownership and risk capital. In return for investing in active risk ownership, the government rewards owners with a load of special tax benefits.

Women, when they invest, are most likely to lend, which is passive. Generally, however, I advocate active investing— equity positions—as the best way to make money. However, during periods of great economic flux, I tend to want to keep my assets liquid. That means the greatest portion of my otherwise uncommitted cash at this time is in short-term lending instruments. When this period reverses itself, even temporarily, I will be able to pick up some ownership investments at bargain basement prices.

In an inflation, when money is losing value, go into equity ownership positions. In a disinflation (restoration of the economy to conditions prevailing before an inflationary period), be a prudent woman. Move out of equity assets and go into a conservative posture with such investments as money market funds, bank lending instruments, short term AAA bonds, etc. This will put you into position to take advantage of the spectacular deals and rebates offered by merchants and vendors and of softening real estate prices. Money that you don't invest remains in safe harbor during the fluctuations and gyrations that disinflation brings. While speculators do well in an inflation, prudent women are the wise ones in a disinflation.

Before you choose where to put your money, you should know the full range of investments and their basic principles. The next section deals with both active and passive investment instruments and will help you to comfortably make investment strategy decisions to suit your own needs.

5

Lending

When you put your money into a bank, you call it saving. You are, in fact, *lending* the bank your money. You are the lender, the bank is the borrower, and the interest is payment for the use of your funds. You may be saving, but that's not what the bank's doing. It is using the money borrowed from you at one interest rate to lend out at a higher rate.

I used to advise my clients to stay away from lending investments except under special circumstances, such as an immediate need for a stream of income. However, in periods of high inflation and high interest rates, though you'll never get rich from lending, I now believe it *is* the best and most prudent place to rest your money.

Women tend to invest most of their money in lending instruments because it seems such a logical and lucrative thing to do. After all, you get to save your money for a specific period of time and then—*Voilà!*—you not only get your money back but also a bonus in the form of interest. Sounds good, right? But let's investigate more closely.

Unless you invest in a very *high-yield* instrument, your interest, after taxes, could be well below the rate of inflation. Remember, too, when you get the money back, its buying power has been eroded by inflation.

If you lend out $10,000 for a year and at the end of that year you get back $10,000 (forget the interest for a minute), you have indeed *lost* money because with inflation you get back less valuable dollars. For example, if inflation is at the rate of 10 percent, the dollars you get back can only buy $9,000 of goods.

$$\$10,000 - 10\% = \$9,000$$

Now let's bring in the interest. If you receive 10 percent

interest for lending, it looks like you broke even. The equation is $10,000 − 10\%$ inflation factor = $9,000 + 10\%$ interest = $10,000. You haven't broken even, of course, because you're probably going to have to pay taxes on that $1,000 worth of interest!

The Long and Short of It

Banks and savings and loans no longer lend for long periods of time because they got creamed by doing so. They are holding thirty-year home loans at 6 percent, 7 percent, and 8 percent and have to pay their depositors double-digit interest on everything but ordinary savings in order to attract customers.

The most important piece of lending advice I can give you is NEVER LEND LONG. By long, I mean no more than a year or two. Though long-term instruments offer a higher rate of return than short or intermediate ones, don't buy them. Remember, do not *ever* lend for a long period unless you have word from on high that inflation has permanently abated. You could end up with a time deposit paying you 9 percent for thirty months when 14 percent is the going rate on other lending instruments.

So Why Lend?

One good reason is that lending money provides a stream of income to live on, and most people need this at some point in their lives. I first needed it when I started Moneywise because I was unlikely to make money in my first year of a new business. I sold some real estate to acquire the cash necessary to start the business. What money I didn't need for Moneywise I put into money market funds and took my interest monthly to give me an income.

Lending, as I've mentioned, is also a good way to ride out periods of high inflation. When you can't afford real estate and the stock market is zany, lending is the only way to go.

Lending is also convenient for small investors. During periods when interest rates are high you could even get ahead. And at retirement, when you are no longer looking for growth and you've made whatever fortune you are going to make, lending offers security as well as income.

Lending is attractive because it is a low risk, highly liquid investment. The liquidity of lending investments is useful in unexpected emergencies such as the loss of a job, unusual medical expenses, or appliance breakdowns. All lending instruments are liquid—some can be sold, some can be traded, and some can be cashed in. A big advantage of time deposits and U.S. Treasury issues is that they can be borrowed against and/or used as collateral.

BANK AND SAVINGS AND LOAN INSTRUMENTS

1. Savings Accounts. Once upon a time there were savings accounts where people put their hard-earned savings and received interest that outpaced or at least kept pace with inflation. Savings accounts now pay between 5.25 percent and 5.5 percent interest; and this is taxable. What else can I say about savings accounts? Sure, they're insured by the FDIC. They are also guaranteed to lose you a bundle. With inflation ripping along you'll probably lose at least between 4 percent and 6 percent on the real value of your money.

2. Time Deposits. In the chapter on Banking, I list many of the names of time deposits, such as certificates of deposit, T Bill-plus, six-month money market certificates, and the like. All have certain common denominators. You buy these instruments for a fixed length of time at a fixed rate of interest, and most are insured by FDIC or FSLIC.

Time deposits by any name also have some pitfalls that you should be aware of. Check them out! For example, most time deposits do not compound interest. When you buy a certificate of deposit you get to check one of four little boxes that ask if you want your interest mailed to you monthly, quarterly, semi-annually, or at maturity. Take your interest monthly. If it isn't compounding what is it doing?

Banks must keep your interest on full reserve and can't loan it out to make a buck. You're not making interest on your interest, and neither is the bank. Get your interest out of any instrument that doesn't compound. If you have a CD that doesn't compound, be sure to tell the bank that you want the interest monthly. Invest the interest where it will compound. After all, money, like rabbits, is meant to multiply.

Remember that with time deposits, if you need to get your money out because of an emergency, you'll have to pay a substantial early withdrawal penalty. The bank was counting on your money for a set period of time, so if you renege you'll have to pay. The penalty, however, is tax deductible.

There are some good, new time deposit deals for people with limited cash. One of my favorites is the Small Savers Certificate, which requires an investment of from $100 to $500. Banks, credit unions, and savings and loans offer these for a term of thirty months at a fixed rate of interest. The interest rate can be quite high, and accounts are fully insured. Generally, these pay the highest interest you can earn on small savings. The disadvantage is that there are early withdrawal penalties. Different banks pay different rates on Small Savers. These can differ as much as 3 percent so be sure to shop for the best deal.

Another nice new instrument for small savers is called a Repurchase Agreement (Repo), sold by banks and savings and loans. The minimum investment is usually $1,000 and ties your money up for from eight days to eighty-nine days. Repos pay a high fixed rate of interest. Moreover, *some* banks will repurchase (Repo) your investment before the maturity date at full value plus interest, thereby eliminating early withdrawal penalties. Shop banks to see how they handle Repos, what interest they pay, do they repurchase, and what are their minimums. Repos are not insured by FDIC or FSLIC. This *could* be a problem if you're dealing with a small bank or savings and loan. Should they go belly-up, you could lose some of your money.

3. Commercial Paper and Bank Paper. Commercial paper is sold by banks for a small handling charge. The minimum is at least $25,000 and sometimes more. You may think you'll never have such a large sum at one time to invest. But think ahead to the possibility of an inheritance, life insurance settlement, or profit from the sale of your home. Commercial or bank paper might come in handy at these times.

When you buy commercial paper you are lending money to a large corporation such as General Electric for a fixed time at a fixed rate. Maturities are generally short—anywhere from one to 270 days. Bank paper works exactly like commercial paper, only you're lending to a bank. The interest on these instruments varies and fluctuates with the economy, and it's not possible to know if it is higher or lower than the interest of other lending instruments unless you check it out at the bank.

4. All Savers Accounts, Tax Savers Certificates, etc. Under the Economic Recovery Act of 1981, the government has allowed a one-shot, tax-free, one-year savings certificate. Inter-

est is based on 70 percent of the one-year U.S. Treasury Bill yield and varies with Treasury Bill interest. These certificates became available on October 1, 1981 and will continue to be available until January 1, 1983.

All Savers certificates are available in units of $500. Up to $2,000 of the interest earned on these accounts are excluded from federal income tax for married couples, $1,000 for single people. Some states do not tax this interest, others do.

MONEY MARKET FUNDS

Remember the saying, "Everything I love is either immoral, illegal, or fattening?" Well, I can tell you one thing I love that is none of these things—money market funds. These are pools of money—your $5,000, your neighbor's $2,000, etc. —all put together in a professional fund managed by anybody from a stockbroker to Sears. They buy short-term jumbo certificates of deposit, short-term government obligations, commercial and bank paper, and so on. Because of the vast amount of money in each transaction, they command very high rates of interest, and these earnings pass on to you. Economist William L. Silber told Congress, "Money market mutual funds are one of the few unadulterated benefits to emerge for households during the inflation-plagued 1970s."

Money market funds are usually run by stock brokerage firms. Each has its own minimum for joining, which might range from $100 to $5,000. In a typical fund, you deposit your money with your broker on *day one*. Then on *day two* the broker buys your shares in the fund. Interest is paid daily, and you can withdraw any amount you need by calling your broker—you'll be able to pick up a check for the amount you've withdrawn the following day. Most funds give you checks, so you can draw on the fund with the ease of a checking account. Usually the check must be written for $500 or more.

There is no commission when you buy and none when you sell. Because of this, if you do not already have an account with a broker, some brokers may be less than thrilled to open a money market account for you. However, in each brokerage firm there are always new brokers who believe that if they provide this service today, you may be a client tomorrow. So look for a young face or ask for a new broker to start your account.

Interest on money market funds changes every day. The financial section of your paper carries a weekly column giving the week's average yield and the last thirty-day average yield of all the funds. Unfettered by Regulation Q, which has limited the interest banks can pay, these funds are giving the first decent break to the little saver.

Money market funds are available to suit almost every taste. There are funds that invest exclusively in government securities, in tax-free municipal bonds, in foreign currencies, and so on. There has been some concern that money market funds invested partially in commercial paper might be hurt if a major company failed, which would then cause a ripple effect through other funds holding commercial paper. These are the highest paying funds. There have been no defaults on them so far, and they are my favorites. But if you are a great worrier, stick with the funds that invest only in government securities.

Hilary, an older client of mine, came to me for help. She's a widow living on her interest income, which just was not enough. When I looked where her money was placed, I found that she was getting a return of only 6 percent on the money she had lent out. By switching her to a money market fund, her income was practically tripled! Hilary and her friends now see me as the great guru of the financial world. (See Appendix for a list of money market funds and minimum investment amounts.)

Caution: Banks and savings and loans do have their own high-interest instruments—the $10,000, six-month money market certificate. These are not money market funds but are insured by the FDIC. They guarantee the current interest rate for six months—good if interest rates go down, bad if the reverse is true. However, having to tie up the large sum of $10,000 for at least six months leaves the banks' money market certificate out of the running competitively with the cheaper, highly liquid money market funds.

FEDERAL ISSUES

United States Treasury Bills (T-Bills) are the most marketable fixed income security in the world, and as such have become an international currency. T-Bills can be sold before they reach maturity, can be borrowed against, used as collateral, and, like the Cuisinart food processor, can do just about everything but make love.

T-Bills are sold in minimum denominations of $10,000. You can buy a three-month, six-month, or a twelve-month bill. T-Bills are purchased at a discount. Example: Say you buy a twelve-month bill paying interest at about 13 percent. You pay your $10,000 up front, and the Treasury mails you your interest check the same week you buy your bill. So, really, your $10,000 bill costs you $8,700. At the end of the year you cash in your bill and get your $10,000 back.

The interest you receive is *free* from state taxes, and your interest of $1,300 can be reinvested immediately to bring your effective rate to more than 13 percent.

T-Bills can be bought at your bank or a brokerage house for a small service charge. They can also be bought at the Federal Reserve building, if you have one in your city, or they can be ordered by mail. Their price is set at auction every Monday.

There are Federal Reserve Banks in the following cities:
Atlanta, Georgia
Boston, Massachusetts
Chicago, Illinois
Cleveland, Ohio
Dallas, Texas
Kansas City, Missouri
Minneapolis, Minnesota
New York, New York
Philadelphia, Pennsylvania
Richmond, Virginia
San Francisco, California
St. Louis, Missouri

Twenty-four other large cities have branch offices where you can also buy T-Bills. The cities with branch offices can be found listed in your library in the Federal Reserve Bulletin.

Buying a T-Bill at the Federal Reserve will save you the service charge that banks levy to buy one for you. It will also involve standing in line at the Federal Reserve for a long time and using gas to get there. Check on bank or brokerage house charges to decide what's best for you.

A word of warning: T-Bill accounts sold at banks and savings and loans are *not* Treasury Bills. A T-Bill-plus account is also based on treasury rates, but it is *not* a Treasury Bill.

I could cheerfully throttle the man who thought up the word "treasury" for use in bank instruments. The vast difference is that Treasury Bill interest is paid up front and is not taxed by the state. If you live in a state that has a state tax, this can make quite a difference. You buy Treasury Bills (T-Bills) *directly* from the federal government. It is the federal government and *not the bank* that is borrowing from you when you buy a bill. All other instruments with the word "treasury" in them are misleading and downright phony—*watch out*! Only a Treasury Bill, is a Treasury Bill, is a Treasury Bill. All other so-called "treasury" accounts are bank instruments and time deposits with fancy names.

The U.S. Treasury also sells Treasury notes and bonds. Notes can be bought to mature any time from one year to ten years; Treasury bonds mature in more than ten years. Notes and bonds have the built-in problem of all long-term fixed-rate investments: They pay a fixed rate, and so if the rates go up on new issues, your old instruments's resale value goes down.

An example: I inherited Treasury bonds due to mature in the year 2000. These bonds were paying only 9½ percent. There are newer bonds paying a good deal more than that. I sold my bonds at a loss—two-thirds of their face value—and reinvested in a higher yield short-term instrument. (See the following section.)

If you live in a state with an income tax, Treasury Bills, notes, and bonds are not taxed by the state and may be a good deal for you.

BONDS

Traditionally women have been advised to invest in bonds. The reasoning behind this was that bonds were considered extremely safe, unspeculative, and provided a stream of income. However, I always advise my clients to get out of bonds and stay out because I believe them to be a very poor investment and, in periods of high inflation, extremely risky. More people have lost money in bonds than at the race track!

Stocks and bonds, like love and marriage, are always mentioned in the same breath. They are *not* the same thing. They are only traded at the same store—your corner brokerage house.

When you buy a bond you *lend* money to the issuer and become a creditor. This is unlike a stock, where you become a partner. The issuer of a bond may be the federal government or one of its agencies, a state or local government, or a corporation. Bonds come in all denominations.

There is a double whammy when you hold bonds during periods of inflation. You can lose on the interest and get clobbered when you sell. A client of mine, Clydel, was holding $7,000 worth of corporate bonds (see section on Corporate Bonds) paying 7 percent interest. Seven percent wasn't bad in 1974, when she purchased the bonds, but in the early 1980s it was terrible. She decided she couldn't tolerate receiving such a low rate of interest when money market funds were paying in the neighborhood of 15 percent, so she sold her bonds. She took a bond blood bath. In order to make her 7 percent bonds salable, they were discounted at the market by 50 percent so that the yield to the buyer would be 14 percent. Clydel had lived with a below-market interest return from 1976 to 1981, and when she sold her bonds she did so at a $3,500 loss.

Clydel could have held her bonds to maturity in the year 2004. Her loss would have been even greater. Not only would she have had a terrible interest rate for thirty years but the purchasing power of her original $7,000 would have been disastrously eroded.

Bond Rating

All bonds on the market are rated by Standard and Poor's and Moody's. These two major rating services do not necessarily agree with one another but they come very close.

The most secure bonds are rated Aaa by Moody's and AAA by Standard and Poor's (they like capital letters). The bond rating then goes down:

Standard & Poor's	Moody's	Quality
AAA	Aaa	Prime
AA	Aa	Excellent
A	A	Upper medium
BBB	Baa	Lower medium
BB	Ba	Somewhat speculative
B	B	Very speculative
CCC	Caa	Very speculative
CC	Ca	Default
C	C	Default

If you insist on bonds, it's best to stick with bonds whose rating is A or better, to avoid any risk of default. Bonds with lower ratings do pay higher interest in order to attract buyers, but also carry far greater risk. Remember, the higher the rating, the more you pay for the bonds.

There are short term bonds that are issued for five years or more, intermediate bonds issued from ten to fifteen years, and long term bonds issued for fifteen years or more. If you invest in a short term bond you'll get interest for five years and a return of your capital at the end of that period. If you have a longer term bond, the same system holds true.

Most bonds are traded through a brokerage house. Like stocks they go up and down in price but for different reasons. As interest rates go up, bonds go down in value and vice versa.

Let's take the example of a $10,000 bond issued by Moneywise for five years paying 10 percent. You buy it on the day it's issued. A year later you decide to sell, but during that year inflation has risen and new bonds are on the market offering 12 percent interest. In order to make your bond salable, it will have to be discounted (sold at a lower price) to bring the buyer 12 percent. If, on the brighter side, interest rates have dropped and new bonds are only paying 8 percent, you can get a premium on your bond. A buyer will be willing to pay you more than $10,000 for your bond.

If you hold your $10,000 Moneywise bond for five years, and inflation is running at 10 percent a year, your $10,000 bond's value will be eroding at the rate of 10 percent a year or more than 50 percent in the five years. To add insult to injury, you will be taxed on the interest you earn.

I have older clients holding bonds at 4½ percent and 5 percent who cannot bear to discount their bonds to make them marketable. They can't stand to face the monetary loss. What they don't want to see is the loss there already.

Tax-Free Municipal Bonds

Tax-free municipal bonds are bonds issued by cities or towns, territories or states, government agencies such as port authorities and local government agencies. They are all tax exempt by the federal government and by the state government if you are a resident of the state that issues the bond.

During the sixties and seventies they were a good deal for wealthy people whose unearned income was taxed at the rate of 70 percent. However, the glitter of tax-free municipals for these wealthy citizens has been tarnished by the Economic Recovery Tax Act of 1981. With unearned income being taxed at the same rates as earned income, the benefit of the tax-free municipals has decreased. Even though their tax-free interest may look attractive, when it comes to selling them you could lose part of your principal as you'll have to compete against newer, higher yield bonds. Also, with cities falling on harder financial times, you run the risk of having your bond rating downgraded or even going into default. Put your money elsewhere, pay the tax man, and you'll sleep better at night! (For comparison of tax-free vs. taxable yields, see p. 93.)

Some municipal bonds are insured by the Municipal Bond Insurance Association or the American Municipal Assurance Corporation. If you have an insured bond you are insured against default. If the issuer goes belly up, you get your money back. You are *not* insured against the fall in price of a bond due to fluctuating market conditions.

Corporate Bonds

There are many types of corporate bonds.

1. First Mortgage Bonds. These bonds are secured by a mortgage on the fixed property of the corporation (equipment, land, etc.). These bonds are often the highest grade bond because they have a claim to the corporation's earnings and assets.

2. Debenture Bonds. These bonds are secured only by the full faith and credit of the company that issues them. They're like an I.O.U.

3. Convertible Debenture. These bonds offer the buyer the right to convert the debenture to a given number of common stock in the company under specific conditions.

Which is the best bond to buy then if you must buy a bond? There is no pat answer, although I'd rather own a debenture in A.T. & T. than a first mortgage bond in Braniff Airlines! If two companies are equally sound financially, the first mortgage bond offers more security.

Zero-Interest Bonds

This is the latest in bond offerings. Zero-interest bonds come in both corporate and tax-free municipal styles. These bonds pay no interest until maturity. Instead they are sold at

sharply discounted rates that compensate the buyer for giving
up current income.

A corporate zero-interest bond with a $1000 face value
might be offered at $335 due to mature in eight years. The
hooker here is that, although the investor gets no interest
until maturity, the IRS taxes you as if you were receiving the
interest annually. Remember, too, that the money received
in eight years is liable to be seriously eroded by inflation.

A bond is only as good as the company issuing it. So if you
are tempted by these bonds, be sure to stick with AAA rated
businesses. These types of bonds might be useful for children
who are in the zilch tax bracket.

With the tax-free municipal zero-interest bonds you do not
have the disadvantage of having the IRS tax your interest.
One example of this type of bond is one underwritten by
E.F. Hutton that offers $5000 to $10,000 bonds for a mere
$2000 or $4000, respectively, with a period of maturity of 33
years.

Wow! at maturity, you get back 25 times as much money as
you put in. Remember, however, that you are betting on the
purchasing power of the dollar thirty-three years hence.

Hint: Never put these tax-free municipal zero-interest bonds
in your IRA or Keogh plan. That money is already accumulating tax deferred.

COMPARING LENDING INVESTMENTS

Once you know what you need in terms of liquidity and
how long you can commit your money, the main question
remains—how can I get the most bang for the buck?

The only way to figure this is to sit down with paper and
pencil and work with the possibilities.

The following example demonstrates how to analyze three
different lending instruments to determine after-tax yield.

LENDING ANALYSIS

Cash Needed for Investment. You can open a saving/lending
account for as little as $10. You can lend any sum of money
you wish. There is always someone willing to borrow.

Risk: Very low risk factor if you don't buy bonds and don't
lend long.

Return on Investment. Between taxes on interest and the
erosion of the dollar due to inflation, your real after-tax

AFTER TAX YIELD ON $10,000 INVESTMENT

Tax bracket	Money market fund @ 17%, or $1,700 annually AFTER-TAX YIELD	12-month certificate of deposit @ 15.75%, or $1,575 annually AFTER-TAX YIELD	All Savers certificate @12.14%, or $1,214 annually AFTER-TAX YIELD	
			Single	Married
20%	$1,360	$1,256	$1,171.20	$1,214
30%	1,190	1,102.50	1,149.80	1,214
40%	1,020	945	1,128.40	1,214
50%	850	787.50	1,107	1,214

As you can see, if you are in the twenty percent bracket, the All Savers certificate produces the lowest yield. In the thirty percent bracket, it is still better to pay taxes. In the forty percent bracket, the All Savers certificate begins to look good. In the fifty percent bracket, an All Savers certificate is quite a bargain indeed!

return will probably be low or show a loss of capital. If inflation is low and interest rates high, your after-tax return will be excellent.

Liquidity. Money market funds are totally liquid. U.S. Treasury issues and bonds can be sold. Bank time deposits and U.S. Treasury issues can be borrowed against and used as collateral. Bank time deposits can also be withdrawn with penalty.

Active or Passive. Passive.

Age. At any age when a stream of income is needed. Important for older women as a source of low-risk investment.

6

Real Estate

During the 1970s, she was the hottest item in the country. No matter where she was or how she looked, everybody wanted her. She was expensive to get and expensive to keep, but her value kept going up and up so no matter what the cost, she was well worth it!

She's the same hot item in the eighties only she's just too expensive now. And even the old ways of having and holding her have changed.

What is she? She is a home. Her name is house or condo or co-op, and she's getting harder and harder to get and keep.

Every day was the Fourth of July in real estate in the seventies. House prices skyrocketed, and real property was very much in demand.

What happened during the seventies was that a house stopped being just a home. Real estate became the investment vehicle of *choice*. In 1973–74 with the formation of OPEC, inflation began escalating rapidly, instead of creeping up slowly. The dollar started buying less and less, the stock market took a nose dive, and there was a tremendous flight from currency. A house, a building, a piece of land, each had intrinsic value; getting out of shrinking dollars by investing in something real was the intelligent response of the public. Cost-push inflation was making new home building more expensive (cost of material and labor *pushes* prices up). Demand-pull inflation drove real estate prices even higher (demand, without an adequate supply, pulled up the price) on every existing and new unit.

The investing public understood that with cost-push and demand-pull inflation, the house you saw yesterday could only cost more tomorrow. You didn't need economic terms for inflation to understand that lumber and bathroom fixtures were going higher because wages were going higher to pay for food and shelter, which was going higher to pay for wages and new technology. And the cost of money was going higher because it was so much in demand, because . . .

When lumber, bathroom fixtures, and labor go up, so do the other materials needed to build a house. The demand for houses bid up the price, and dollars rushed into American real estate from the four corners of the world. Investors demand political security, and the United States is without a doubt the most politically stable country in the world. Europeans, Asians, South Americans, and Arabs along with Americans were buying homes, land, and buildings. Two houses, three houses, as many as you could afford, became the best speculative investment.

In came the eighties with the incredible high cost of money. Out went the thirty-year fixed-rate mortgage. In came high interest on dollars invested in lending instruments. Out went the flight from currency into real estate. In came a whole new ball game, and in the eighties a house may once again become shelter from the elements—a home.

Property Ownership

Ownership of real estate has traditionally come to women through inheritance, the acquisition of it has been passive. Ownership itself is an active form of investing and is an excellent way to accumulate capital and avoid the erosion of net worth in inflationary times. Women are now learning to take an active role in capital accumulation!

In colonial times, only men who owned property could vote. A property owner had a stake in the future, and it was believed that he was the type of man who could be counted on to make wise and intelligent choices—a man who had a stake in the community. He had shown himself prudent by accumulating the wherewithal to buy property. The founding fathers believed in democracy, all right, but by God you still had to have standards!

Property has a mystique older than gold and jewels. A large school of sociology has investigated the need for territory both in humans and animals. A whole body of law has grown up around the idea that a person's home is his castle. People may act within their own property and defend their own property in a manner different from how they may act outside their property.

Property has romance. When the good land on the East Coast could no longer provide enough room for land-hungry Americans, they went to the unknown West to look for land. There was no danger too great, no mountain too high, to quench the thirst for land.

From Marco Polo to today, adventurous people have dreamed of new land that could provide riches and satisfy the dream of owning. Now outer space and the oceans provide the stuff of dreams.

Large numbers of people are no longer needed to farm America, and most of us now live in cities; but the love of land remains with us. The desire to own our own home, to put down roots, is still part of the American dream.

Women and Home Ownership as Investment

Historically, women have been able to own their own homes in only three ways: widowhood, spinsterhood, or family inheritance. Before ECOA, that statement pretty well held true. Now ever-growing numbers of women are making enough money to buy their own homes.

Emotional satisfaction aside, *is* home ownership a good investment for a woman alone? The answer is an almost unqualified yes! One, you are almost sure to have a hedge against inflation since real estate prices have been kept well ahead of inflation in the last decade. Nobody can guarantee they will continue to do so, but with the continuing high cost of building material, labor, and land, it is hard to see why a home should not continue to appreciate at a reasonably good rate.

You also have the chance to write off the interest you pay on your mortgage from your income tax, thereby sheltering other income you have. Real estate taxes are also deductible from your federal income tax.

Generally, my advice to women is to explore every avenue open to home ownership before investing money anyplace else. In a very inflated housing market (Los Angeles, San Francisco, Washington, D.C., for example), this advice is open to modification. Let's face it, if a woman earns $1,500 per month, it's ridiculous for her to shell out $1,200 of it for a house payment. But, in many other places home ownership should be a major investment option for any woman.

There are myriad complex psychological as well as financial reasons why women shy away from buying a home. Let's explore some of these.

One of a woman's biggest hangups may be in how she perceives herself as a potential homeowner. Women have probably always thought of a home as a package deal: husband, kids, dog, house. This represents the cultural lag that is always with us. For instance, the U.S. Census Bureau reports that women are marrying at a later age and divorcing more frequently. The notion that a husband is the provider of shelter is in serious need of reexamination. A woman owning her own home does *not* preclude husband and kids. Really, it enhances her security and increases her financial independence.

Some women probably feel that if they buy a home for themselves then they'll be buying themselves a lifetime alone. A home of one's own might be read as a statement that a woman intends to remain single! It is indeed a declaration of independence, and this may, in fact, frighten some men. True, but so what! If we, as women, avoid working toward financial independence because it's unfeminine, we're going to find ourselves stuck in our traditional low-pay, low-status, second-class position! And that's definitely *not* what we want, right? Right.

Besides, there are growing numbers of *smart* men who appreciate women who can take care of themselves. Since, statistically speaking, women will spend many years without a spouse (later marriage, divorce, widowhood), it can only be considered a giant plus if a woman has the wherewithal to own that roof over her head.

Fear of ownership is a major problem for women to overcome. Traditionally, any money that women had to invest has been funneled into passive lending investments. Home ownership is an *active* investment, and this may be scary for women to contemplate. It's okay to be scared at first. It's natural. *But*, it's better to be a little scared and have a roof of your own than not scared at all and be stuck with a leaky roof and a petulant do-nothing landlord. Owning your own home is the best single investment you can make, and it's worth a bit of anxiety!

According to the National Association of Realtors, single women have become the fastest growing segment of the home buying market. A bright young woman stockbroker that I know encourages all prospective women clients to buy a home for themselves if at all possible before sinking one thin dime into the stock market!

Okay. You have cleared your head enough to consider buying a home. Statistics and the best advice are surely on your side. *Now*, what to do?

RESIDENTIAL REAL ESTATE

What kind of a home do you think would best suit your needs, your lifestyle, and the needs of your family? The definition of what a home is has changed radically in the last ten years. A home may still be a house on a lot with grass in the front and trees in the back. It may also be a condominium, a cooperative, a mobile home, or even a houseboat.

The different types of housing in demand today reflect large changes in society itself. A major change is in the growing number of singles and young marrieds who do not plan on families, the increased number of people who have divorced, and the large number of widows who live alone. This particular group is not interested in the traditional large home, near good schools, in a quiet neighborhood, with a nice lawn, and near parks. They are more interested in security. With increasing crime, people may feel safer living in buildings that provide security—everything from closed circuit TV with doors and windows wired to security companies, to the less expensive but still reassuring feeling that there's a neighbor a thin wall away if you need help.

With cheap fuel a thing of the past, most people do not want to live far from their work, from good transportation, or from where children go to school. Nor do they wish to put aside an ever increasing sum to heat or cool a large home. With a steadily increasing number of women in the work force, the lovely home in the suburbs, empty during the day, has lost much of the appeal it had twenty years ago. (However, if the number of baby showers I'm attending is any indication, the more traditional family home might be in heavy demand again!)

Types of Residences

1. A House. A single family dwelling on a lot. A house is still the favorite form of home ownership in America. It provides a chance to raise flowers and to fight without the neighbors hearing. Unlike other forms of ownership, you

have control over all improvements and decor, and can decide when and if you wish to make those improvements.

2. Condominium. A divided, designated unit in a dwelling of two or more units with an undivided interest in the common areas, such as halls, elevators, and swimming pool. Each unit has its own mortgage.

Financing a condominium is exactly like financing a home. What you are purchasing as property is different. I own one unit, a *divided* interest, in a building of thirty-nine units. I have my own mortgage plus a monthly assessment to pay for the upkeep of the common areas. If I don't pay my monthly assessment, the Board of Directors, fellow owners elected by the Homeowners Association, will foreclose on me under the same laws that lending institutions would use if I failed to pay my mortgage for a certain number of months. The HOA is made up of all thirty-nine unit owners. The elected Board is made up of five hard-working unpaid saints! The HOA has certain powers, the Board has certain powers, and the condominium itself is a non-profit corporation and must meet all the requirements under the California Department of Corporations.

All condo owners are comrades in arms, a fraternity of survivors. If one bought one's condo brand new, there is a special sense of having been on a shake down cruise together.

A condo is a little cosmos of the world. Small wars rage, feuds develop and factions plot, a few souls do all the work and worrying, while love blooms and dies. Every condo has a card carrying crazy, an odd couple, a busybody, a slob, and a cleaning maniac. After a year or so, one stops noticing in much the same way one doesn't *really* listen to one's own mother. I love the drama of it all, and now I would actually miss the people I dislike. I guess a condo is a bit like a family.

When I close my door to my unit I am mistress of all I survey. What I survey is what I bought, the air space enclosed by my walls and the paint on my walls. The interior walls are mine, but I may do nothing to the common walls that belong to me—only to the degree I do own 1/39th undivided interest in them. Oh, I can decorate and hang pictures and light fixtures, and even build interior walls and cabinets. If the toilet leaks, however, it must be adjudicated as to whether it is my leak or a leak coming from a pipe in the common area. I always hope for the latter, since the bill will then be paid by the monthly assessments fund and not by me.

3. Co-op. An *undivided* interest in real property. It works much the same way in practice as a condominium with some major exceptions.

When you buy a co-op you buy into a stock company and own shares in that company, prorated to the size of the unit. Rather than each unit owner having a mortgage, usually the entire co-op has one blanket mortgage, and you are responsible for that mortgage in proportion to the amount of stock you hold in the cooperative. Your monthly assessment in the co-op covers your share of maintaining the common areas plus your mortgage payments. A new development in financing is individual mortgages for co-op owners, identical to condo financing.

The Board of Directors of the co-op retains the right to decide to whom you may sell your unit. This received wide publicity when Pat Kennedy Lawford and former President Nixon both were turned down by the Board of two New York City co-ops. A co-op owner is usually only able to lease his unit if the Board gives its permission.

Most of these very important differences stem from the condominium being a *divided* interest in real property and the co-op being *undivided*. From a financial point of view, the co-op is a much less desirable asset unless it carries an individual rather than a blanket mortgage. With a blanket mortgage, a woman would be unable to decide the size of the mortgage she wants. She would be unable to place a second mortgage because her interest is undivided and therefore unmortgageable. She has no control over when a new mortgage would be negotiated or what she would have to pay if the co-op decided to remortgage.

Being unable to sell to whom one chooses might lose you a very good sale. Not having the unrestricted right of renting out your co-op could also put you in the terrible position of either having to sell when you don't want to or leaving an empty apartment that costs you money.

The condominium, an improved form of ownership, first came from Puerto Rico and is used widely in the western part of the United States. The older form of co-op ownership is found in the East and is very common in New York City.

YOU AND/OR A REAL ESTATE BROKER

Some women are naturally good negotiators. They can buy and sell houses as easily as they change dresses. But for most of us, negotiation comes hard and particularly so when we are selling a home we have loved or buying a house we've fallen in love with. When you're selling a property for income the dollars and cents have to make sense, but selling one's own home is a very emotional issue.

Your real estate broker is a vital member of your team of professionals. Finding the right real estate agent is very much a question of chemistry. Is the agent respected in the community? The answer may be yes, but if the chemistry is wrong, that agent isn't right for you.

Agents make the major part of their living by listing houses for sale. When you list with one, the agency knows that selling your house puts commission money in the bank. When an agent comes for a listing he or she has a tendency to tell you what you want to hear. You'll be shown comps, a list of comparable houses in your neighborhood that have sold in the last six months. You'll be able to see how much they sold for and get a good idea of what you should get. If the broker is good at her job (most real estate salespeople are women), she will suggest you offer your house for more than you can expect to get, to leave room for negotiation. This is because buyers hate to pay the asking price. They want to feel that by making you lower the asking price they've gotten a deal!

If a broker is too hungry for a listing, she may well tell you your home is worth more than it really is. This is obviously an attempt to get you to sign a listing with them. The danger to you is if your home is listed at an unrealistic price, buyers will be scared off.

Take, for example, a house that an agent knows should sell for $100,000. By listing it and advertising it for $150,000, they discourage potential buyers of a $100,000 house from inquiring. Common sense tells these buyers that you won't knock one-third off the price in negotiations. You'll lose your real customers, and those buyers willing to pay $150,000 will give your home short shrift having seen homes that are *really* worth $150,000.

A listing is a contract between the seller and an agent. It is for a given length of time. The contract gives the agent the exclusive right to sell your property during that specific length of time at a specified price. There is also within the contract an agreed upon commission to the agent if a sale reaches closure.

The commission paid to the agent is her compensation. It

is negotiable. Some brokers won't negotiate and will only work for the traditional rate in their area. This may range as high as 10 percent or as low as 3 percent. Only in buying and selling dwellings does the question of the commission loom large. In the sale of commercial and industrial real property, the agent usually works for a set fee.

Should you negotiate your broker's commission? I don't know. A good, hard-working, honest, intelligent broker will probably get you as much money as the market will bear. It is possible that by knowledge and diligence, she will bring you an offer that more than makes up for the higher commission.

On the other hand, I, as a licensed real estate broker in California, know wonderful women who do excellent jobs *and* negotiate their commission.

I would suggest interviewing a few agents after checking on their experience. Friends can be helpful and might recommend somebody they've worked with and liked. After interviewing, go with your gut feeling.

During the sale of a house you have one job. That job is to keep the house spotless and sweet-smelling at all times. For obvious reasons, this is necessary. It's also a pain!

Your broker works for you. You are the client. Brokers, like every worker, will do a better job for someone they like, so it pays to be a considerate client. In general, brokers will give you good advice. However, don't ever forget that they need to sell the property to make a commission.

If a house doesn't sell in a reasonable time (the word "reasonable" depends on market conditions such as supply and interest rates), talk to your broker. She will probably suggest something you can do to make your home more attractive, and she'll probably suggest dropping the price. She may well be correct. Keep in mind, however, the arithmetic of it.

Let's take, for example, a 6 percent commission on a $100,000 house. After it's paid, and possibly split with another agent, and then each agent splits with their offices, the agent will usually end up with about 1.8 percent of the selling price of the home. If an agent suggests a $5,000 reduction in the sale price, you will be getting $5,000 less, but the agent's commission will only go down by $90. An extra few days on the job just isn't worth $90. Dropping the price for the agent means little, but for you it means a lot.

The importance of trusting your agent is obvious from this

example. If you find the relationship is not good after a while, level with her and fire her. An agent and client live in each other's pocket during the time a house is for sale. Her ability to negotiate is crucial to you. Being honest and tough is her business. You might not want her over for a drink and a chat, but her very tenacity and toughness may be very good for your bank account.

BUYING A HOUSE—STEP BY STEP

The kind of home that you dreamed about will rarely be available in today's high-priced housing market. You may be earning three times what your father earned and be able to buy a house only one-third as desirable as he bought. House hunting can be a depressing job, causing you to feel angry, inadequate, and undeserving. You are not alone! More people are settling for much less than they thought they would.

Saturdays, Sundays, and evenings, your search for a home has you rushing about, following up leads and ads and calls from your broker. Try always to remember that value in real estate is defined with three words—location, location, and location! The least expensive house on the most expensive street is an ideal location!

Finally you settle on a house (or condo or co-op apartment).

Remember, there are two basic rules of real estate:

1. GET EVERYTHING IN WRITING—He said, she said, have no place in real estate!

2. EVERYTHING CAN BE NEGOTIATED—I once sold a house where the family watchdog was *included* in the price of the house.

Going to Contract

The next step is to submit a written contract for the purchase of the house, spelling out the price you're willing to pay and how you're going to do so (see Financing section). Also included in your bid are those things that are to remain in the house and become yours. For example, the refrigerator, stove, washer/dryer, and Tiffany bedroom lamp may pass to you with the house. Your offer should include the right to have a building inspector of your choice check the roof, plumbing, electricity, heating system, and all appliances. Your offer should be contingent on the fact that all of the above are satisfactory. Pest inspection is mandated by many states. Be sure that you have a pest report on your prospective property.

If the seller refuses your offer, you will probably receive a counter offer. If this is unacceptable to you, you make what is called a counter to the counter offer. Somewhere along the line, you and the seller probably reach an agreement. By following state law and local custom, you arrange to pass the title of the property from the seller to your hands.

Title of a property, which is the unbroken chain of ownership since the time of the first property owner, must be clear when it passes to you. Clear means without recorded debts or encumbrances. A title company will search the title and issue a policy of title insurance to guarantee that the title you receive is clear.

From the time your offer is accepted until the deal is closed and title passes to you, the seller will require a deposit, earnest money. This is to show that you are earnest about buying the property. It is held by a neutral third party to be applied to the purchase price when the deal closes. (Tip: be sure this deposit is in an interest-bearing escrow or trust account!)

Financing

Once your purchase offer is accepted by the seller, you and/or your broker must look for mortgage money. A mortgage is defined by Webster as a claim on property given as security for a loan to the lender.

The word "mortgage" is familiar to almost everybody. The horrible, mean banker foreclosing the mortgage on the family farm, usually at Christmas, the story of the happy couple burning the family mortgage, paid off at last—these are all part of folklore.

In many western states, including California, we don't use a mortgage. We use an instrument called a trust deed. There are a number of legal differences between a mortgage and a trust deed, but there is one major financial difference. If you don't pay on your mortgage, the holder of that mortgage must give you as long as a year in some states to reinstate.

Reinstate means pay up! The amount of time you have to redeem *does* differ from state to state, so check. During that time you may live on the property. If you don't reinstate yourself at the end of the period specified by your state, the holder of the mortgage *must take you to court for foreclosure* (to take over your home and sell it).

With a trust deed it's different. The clock starts ticking when you miss your first payment, and at the end of ninety days the holder of the trust deed can deny you the right of redemption. The lender will then publish notification of sale for twenty-one days and then will sell. No court action is necessary. In real estate jargon, we refer to the trust deed as having the power of sale.

When you enter the marketplace for mortgages, what a potpourri of things you will find! In today's world of expensive money, shopping for the right loan has eclipsed shopping for the house itself!

Hail and farewell to the thirty-year mortgage. It was born in 1929 during the Depression and died in the tight money market of 1980.

The savings and loan industry was created to supply long-term home mortgages. Savings and loans, as well as banks, discovered unhappily that during periods of high inflation they were holding the wrong end of the stick. In their portfolio of outstanding loans today are mortgages paying an interest rate of as low as 6 percent! By contrast, they are having to pay you as high as 15 percent to put your money in their lending instruments. Obviously, this is no way to run a railroad.

When I bought my condo four-and-one-half years ago, I took out an $83,000 mortgage at 9 percent for thirty years. My monthly payment (rounded off for convenience) is $633 and change. If you figure that every additional percent would bring my monthly payment up by around $100, let's see what happens as interest rates climb:

      9% on $83,000 = $ 633
     10% on $83,000 = $ 733
     11% on $83,000 = $ 833
     12% on $83,000 = $ 933
     13% on $83,000 = $1,033
     14% on $83,000 = $1,133
     15% on $83,000 = $1,233
     16% on $83,000 = $1,333

My bank is stuck with my $633 payment for the next twenty-four years. Furthermore, I have money in that same poor institution in a six-month certificate paying 14 percent interest!

Alternative Financing, Creative Financing

Alternative, or creative, financing rose out of the ashes of the thirty-year mortgage. Alternative financing combines the buyer's money with the equity of the seller.

It arranges, in a multitude of ways, to provide for the purchase of a home at an initial cost lower than current market rates. Watch out for those words "initial cost." Under almost all the new mortgage alternatives, costs can accelerate rapidly after the first few years! Creative or alternative financing has successfully shifted the entire risk of inflation from the lending institution to the homeowner.

No matter *how* you decide to finance your home, you'll still have to qualify for the loan. When you apply for your mortgage the lending institution checks your credit and requires a full financial statement from you. You stand naked before your banker, your assets in full view.

In olden days (five or six years ago), lending institutions felt that you should spend no more than 25 percent of your family's monthly income to pay off your mortgage; since ECOA a wife's income must be fully counted when figuring the family income. Using this rule of thumb, the lending institution decided how much it would lend you. Lenders now are more realistic. They have come to realize that the old formulas just won't work, and are looking without disfavor on families planning to spend 33 percent to 37 percent of their monthly income for mortgage repayment. (Research indicates that if inflation continues, Americans will be paying an even larger share of their income for shelter.)

Creative financing accounted for only about 15 percent of home loans in 1979. Now, the National Association of Realtors says creative financing accounts for 75 percent of all home loan transactions and is climbing. There are as many as thirty new varieties of home loans. But first, let's look at the good old dinosaur, the 30-year fixed-rate mortgage. These are now given at an interest rate well above the going rate of mortgages. For example: You may be able to find a fixed rate-mortgage at 17 percent to 19 percent. The National Association of Realtors says that 90 percent of first-time homebuyers in America could *not* qualify for a $50,000 mortgage at this rate. The thirty-year home loan is doomed to extinction. The few left are rare and costly.

The most common varieties of creative financing are as follows:

1. Owner-Will-Carry. In this case the seller plays the part of the bank. You give him or her a down payment, say 20 percent of the total price, and he or she carries the mortgage at below market rates.

Example: Total price $80,000
          Down payment $16,000 (20% of total)
          Mortgage $64,000 held by seller at 12%
          Interest to seller
          on mortgage $ 7,680 per year or
                            $ 640 per month

The seller is usually willing to carry for from five to ten years. In the above example lurks a snake-in-the-grass, typical in many owner-will-carry deals. First, you are paying the owner *interest* only and at the end of a specified period you must pay back the entire $64,000 in a balloon payment. Second, this means you eventually will have to journey into the unknown marketplace for refinancing, which may be more chaotic and difficult than it is today.

2. *Wrap-Around Mortgage*. This is another owner-will-carry type of mortgage and one that is hard to find. The example is similar to the previous one, only in this case the seller has a $20,000 mortgage at 8 percent. He or she will wrap the mortgage given to you around the mortgage he or she already has. However, you will not have the full advantage of the 8 percent mortgage. Part of the seller's profit comes from charging you 10 percent for the $20,000 he or she has at 8 percent and 12 percent for the remainder.

Example: Total price $80,000
          Down payment $16,000
          Mortgage $64,000 includes

$20,000 @ 10% = $2,000 per year, or $166.66 per month, and $44,000 @ 12% = $5,280 per year, or $440.00 per month.

Total—$7,280 per year, or $606.66 per month. Many banks, if they are informed of this arrangement will not go along with it. If they are *not* informed and find out later, there could be trouble. Have a lawyer check your contract.

*   *   *

Remember, the same snakes stand ready to bite at the end of this term of contract!

3. Assumable Mortgage. A 1982 Supreme Court ruling released Federally-chartered savings and loans from having to allow new buyers to take over the seller's mortgage at the old (and often low) rate. However, some state-chartered savings and loans are still required by law to allow assumable mortgages. In the above example for wrap-around mortgages, if you could have assumed the original 8 percent mortgage, instead of the $2,000 payments per year you would have only paid $1,600 per year. As you can imagine, the state-chartered savings and loans wish to get rid of *all* laws pertaining to assumable mortgages.

4. Shared Appreciation. In this type, the bank gives you a fixed-rate mortgage at bargain interest. When the house is sold, the bank takes an agreed upon chunk of any profit. The snake-in-the grass here is that the bank stipulates *when* the house will be sold. If, when that time comes, you do not want to sell, you must pay the bank an agreed amount of the fair market profit on your house. Again, if you can't come up with the money, it's back to the chaotic marketplace for refinancing!

5. Variable, or Adjustable Rate Mortgage. This is offered by many lenders. Monthly payments are tied to prevailing interest rates. Depending on the contract, the variable rate may have a cap (no more than a 4 percent or 5 percent increase per year) or, as is common now, no cap. Without a cap, you can't even guess what your monthly house payment will be or how high it may go. Some adjustable rate mortgages will guarantee a rate for the first two to five years; others will not. These are *very* complicated loans. They should be shopped for, compared, and used with extreme caution. Be sure you understand what prevailing interest rates are and what they mean. Different banks have different interpretations of this idea. Prices are indexed to various prevailing rates such as six-month, one-year, or three-year Treasury Bill rates, the Federal Home Loan Bank Board Index (FHLBB), and so on. Ask your banker to explain, when you consider a variable rate mortgage.

6. Negative Amortization. The borrower gets a mortgage below the going rate and the difference between the bargain rate and the going rate is tacked on to the principal of the loan. Let's get back to our example of the $80,000 house:

Total price $80,000
Down payment $16,000
Mortgage $64,000 @ 12%
= $7,680 per year, or $640 per month.

Prevailing rates are 17 percent so the mortgage is 5 percent below this. That 5 percent of $64,000, or $3,200, is tacked onto the principal. So in the first year you are indeed paying 12% on $64,000. In year two you are paying 12 percent on $67,200. Then next year, $67,200 x 5% = $3,360. Add that to $67,200 and you have $70,560. The principal continues to creep up year after year after year. You are only paying off a tiny amount of what you *originally* borrowed. It's quite possible that when the time comes to sell, you will owe more than the house can be sold for!

7. Graduated Payment. This form of mortgage usually carries a fixed interest rate, but the monthly payments are not fixed. They generally start low and increase each year for a certain period of time, usually five to ten years. Payments are then fixed for the life of the loan.

The early low payments are not large enough to pay the actual interest owed. So the unpaid interest is added to the unpaid balance, creating negative amortization. After the payments graduate to the fixed amount, the higher monthly payment is then sufficient to cover interest *and* principal, so that the loan is paid off in the traditional fashion.

8. Five Percent Down with Forty Years to Pay. This latest wrinkle is a result of slackening federal regulation regarding mortgages with balloon payments due after a specific period of time. It permits savings and loans to accept a 5 percent down payment on a forty-year loan, with the principal due at the end. This is brand new. Federal regulation used to require 20 percent down and thirty years to repay on this type of mortgage.

Monthly payments would fluctuate with interest rates, exactly like a variable rate mortgage. However, it is likely that you would be paying a lower dollar amount because little or no part of your payment would be principal. Another possible twist on this would be a fixed payment amount for ten years and a variable rate for the subsequent thirty years.

9. Zero-Interest Mortgage. This type of financing is not

really a loan at all. Rather, it is the newest and in some ways the ultimate in creative financing because it involves no interest payments. This new approach is not available everywhere yet, but it probably will spread because it has great appeal to some people.

Here is how it works: a buyer puts anywhere from 20 percent to 50 percent down on a home. Then the buyer must pay off the balance of the house in from three to seven years, depending on how the deal is structured. No interest is charged. For example, on a $100,000 home or condominium with 30 percent down and five years to pay, the monthly payments amount to $1167. This is only slightly higher than if the buyer had a thirty-year mortgage at 17 percent with 20 percent down.

The drawbacks to this type of mortgage are the large down payment and that you lose the opportunity to pay off your mortgage in ever-cheapening dollars. Houses sold with a zero-interest mortgage often have a padded price which can run as high as 25 percent above market value.

Almost all of these loans can be had in combination, such as adjusted rate graduated payment mortgages. The tables that follow on pp. 111–113, demonstrate some of these possibilities, and bring home dramatically how fluctuating interest rates affect your pocketbook.

All the examples use a principal balance of $70,000 with thirty years to repay.

Traditional Fixed Rate Level Payment Mortgage

Principal: $70,000 Term: 30 years Interest: 14%

End of Year	Interest Rate	Monthly Payment	Total Principal Payment	Total Interest Payment	Total Paid	Outstanding Balance
1	14%	$829.41	$ 163	$ 9,790	$ 9,953	$69,837
5	14%	829.41	1,098	48,666	49,765	68,902
10	14%	829.41	3,301	96,228	99,529	66,699
15	14%	829.41	7,720	141,574	149,294	62,280
20	14%	829.41	16,581	182,477	199,058	53,419
30	14%	829.41	70,000	228,590	298,590	-0-

Rate Capped Variable Rate Mortgage

Principal: $70,000   Term: 30 years   Cap: 5% Overall Rate Increase

End of Year	Interest Rate	Monthly Payment	Total Principal Payment	Total Interest Payment	Total Paid	Outstanding Balance
1	14%	$ 829.41	$ 163	$ 9,790	$ 9,953	$69,837
5	18%	1,051.23	723	55,690	56,413	69,277
10	17%	996.67	2,051	115,527	117,578	67,949
15	19%	1,100.40	4,612	178,369	182,982	65,388
20	10%	1,098.70	11,143	237,251	248,393	58,857
30	19%	1,098.70	70,000	310,238	380,238	-0-

Variable Rate Mortgage, No Cap

Principal: $70,000   Term: 30 years   Cap: None on Interest or Payments

1	14%	$ 829.41	$ 163	$ 9,790	$ 9,953	$69,837
5	18%	1,051.23	723	55,690	56,413	69,277
10	17%	996.67	2,051	115,527	117,578	67,949
15	20%	1,152.83	4,360	181,097	185,457	65,640
20	21%	1,187.97	10,581	242,079	252,660	59,419
30	21%	1,214.23	70,000	328,716	398,716	-0-

Payment Capped Variable Rate Mortgage

Principal: $70,000   Term: 30 Years   Cap: 25% on Payment Increases

1	14%	$ 829.41	$ 163	$ 9,790	$ 9,953	$69,837
5	18%	829.41	-7,954	57,719	49,765	77,954
10	17%	1,036.76	-18,014	129,984	111,970	88,014
15	20%	1,295.95	-30,623	220,350	189,727	100,623
20	21%	1,619.94	-29,513	316,437	286,924	99,513
30	21%	2,081.42	66,559	466,746	533,305	3,441

Fixed Rate Graduated Payment Mortgage

Principal: $70,000   Term: 30 years   Fixed Rate: 14%

Graduation Period: 5 Years

Graduation Rate: 7½% Annual Increase in Payments

1	14%	$ 645.77	$-2,188	$ 9,937	$ 7,749	$72,188
5	14%	862.40	-7,015	52,025	45,010	77,015
10	14%	927.08	-4,552	105,188	100,635	74,552
15	14%	927.08	387	155,873	156,260	69,613
20	14%	927.08	10,293	201,592	211,885	59,707
30	14%	927.08	70,000	253,127	323,127	-0-

Variable Rate Graduated Payment Mortgage

Principal: $70,000 Term: 30 Years Rate: 24%, No Cap

Graduation Period: 1st 5 Years

Graduation Rate: 7½% Annual Increase in Payments

End of Year	Interest Rate	Monthly Payment	Total Principal Payment	Total Interest Payment	Total Paid	Outstanding Balance
1	14%	$ 645.77	$ -2,188	$ 9,937	$ 7,749	$72,188
5	18%	862.40	-16,880	61,890	45,010	86,880
10	17%	1,336.97	-21,149	141,516	120,367	91,149
15	20%	1,546.45	-18,052	229,474	211,422	88,052
20	21%	1,593.58	-9,707	311,277	301,570	79,706
30	21%	1,628.81	70,000	427,495	497,495	-0-

Closing

Before the house deal closes, do a walk-through inspection to be sure the seller has kept the house and grounds in the same condition as when you bought the house. You wouldn't believe some of the things some sellers try to take with them: toilet seats, moldings, giant oak trees, wood for the fireplace, and every last geranium bush on the property!

Closing is a time when title passes from the seller to the buyer. Be aware of closing costs. These include the prorating of all current real estate taxes, the cost of title and fire insurance, the cost of the escrow (all searches, notarizations, fees, and paperwork involved in the purchase), and other sundry items that differ from state to state. Closing costs usually run anywhere from one to two percent of the purchase price and can be an awful shock to the system if they have not been anticipated.

Closing costs are usually split in traditional ways between buyer and seller. However, they can be negotiated.

Holding Title

When you've found your financing, you'll then have to decide on how to hold title so closure can take place. No matter how your state traditionally effects closure, be sure to use a real estate lawyer to check all papers, titles, and contracts!

The simple English meaning for "holds title" defines who owns the property and under what laws. There are several ways to hold title:

1. Joint tenancy and/or tenant by entirety.
2. Tenants in common.
3. Sole and separate property.
4. Community property (only in states that have community property laws).

Brokers, when they make a deal, almost always ask how you want to take title or how title should be vested. Both questions mean the same thing. Tell the broker you don't know because, believe me, you *don't* in most cases! How you take title is a question for real estate lawyers and your accountant, not for you or a broker.

Under the Economic Recovery Tax Act of 1981, the old rules no longer apply and the ramifications of holding title have become very complicated. There are tax considerations, estate considerations, financial ramifications, and emotional issues involved in each choice. Investigate this area with your professionals, and make an informed choice based on what is best for you. How you take title doesn't have to be decided until closure is imminent.

If you are married and are buying a home or income property with your own money, I strongly suggest you buy it as your sole and separate property. There may still be some states where women can't do this, so check with a lawyer.

Holding property in your own name is vital to your security. In case of a divorce, there could be no dispute over who owns what. If yours is a second marriage, you and your present husband may have different heirs. You may want to leave your property to your own children or to charity. The most important thing is that you retain control of what is yours.

If you buy property as a single woman and then marry, there are many ways of showing love and devotion to your husband. Changing title is not one of them. Giving up any interest in your property smacks of a business deal and not necessarily love.

A few of my clients have told me that their husbands resent their holding sole and separate property, seeing this as less than a full commitment on the part of the wife. Not one of these marriages has lasted. I don't believe the sole and separate property did in *true love*. I suspect the motives for the marriage! Happily, most men seem to have an understanding of their wives' needs to remain independent, and the issue doesn't arise. Many men also have sole and separate property, and keep it that way when they marry for the same reasons I suggest you do.

When to Buy

Even with high interest rates, the right time to buy is the minute you can afford to. When houses aren't selling, it's a buyer's market. A buyer with a down payment who can qualify for a loan is a rare bird and can drive a mighty hard deal with an anxious seller.

In the last half of the 1970s we had a seller's market. Everybody wanted a house, so the sellers were asking top dollar and getting it.

Isn't it wiser to wait for rates to come down? No, it's a poor idea. The moment there is a real break in the rate it will become a seller's market again and the price of homes will shoot up. If you buy with an adjustable rate mortgage, your payments will go down when the rate breaks. Drive a hard bargain when people are eager to sell and you'll have a home and a profit when the market turns again.

OWNING VS. RENTING

Owning your home is a good deal, with or without the spectacular appreciation (increase in value) that homeowners realized in the 1970s. Say I pay $600 per month on my mortgage and you pay $600 per month for rent. At the end of one year I have equity in my home, a nice tax deduction, as well as a place to live; you have only had a place to live. Even if my house does not appreciate I still have an advantage over you. Furthermore, my house would have to *depreciate* a great deal in one year for our situations to be financially equal.

The table below compares buying a $100,000 home and renting a $700-per-month apartment. In the example, a $20,000 down payment was made and an $80,000 mortgage was taken out for thirty years at 15 percent. Our renter invested $20,000 in a money market fund paying 16 percent. The house appreciates at 10 percent per year, and the tax bracket for this example is 50 percent.

Buying vs. Renting

Total cost	$100,000
Down payment	20,000
Mortgage	80,000 @15% for 30 years
Interest (first year)	12,000
Property tax	2,000
Rent	700 /month

First Year:	Buying	Renting
Gain		
Appreciation of house	$ 10,000	—
Interest, money market fund	—	$3,200
Interest, tax deduction	$ 6,000	—
Property tax deduction	$ 1,000	—
Total gain	$ 17,000	$3,200
Expenses		
Mortgage interest	$ 12,000	—
Property tax	$ 2,000	—
Utilities	$ 2,000	$ 2,000
Insurance	$ 400	$ 225
Repairs, upkeep	$ 1,000	—
Rent	—	$ 8,400
Tax, money market interest	—	$ 1,200
Closing costs (1st year only)	$ 1,500	—
Total expense	$ 18,900	$ 9,825
Net gain or loss	−1,900	−6,625

Five Year Summary: Inflation is figured @ 10% except for mortgage, which remains constant.

Gain	Buying	Renting
Interest	—	$ 22,007*
Tax deductions	$ 35,000	—
Appreciation	$ 72,040	—
Total gain	$107,040	$ 22,007
Expense	$ 94,466	$ 50,260
Net gain or loss	$ 12,574	$−28,253

---

*Money market interest is normally compounded daily. It has been compounded annually for this chart. Therefore, the net loss to a renter would be slightly less.

Note: A little known fact: Homeowners stand a better chance to obtain a federal student loan for their kids than renters. The government sees "poor" homeowners as being deeply in debt because of their mortgage. The renter is considered to be debt-free and therefore not in need! If this sounds crazy and illogical, there's nothing wrong with you. It is crazy and illogical—a little like something out of George Orwell's, *1984*.

Tax Benefits

Despite all the problems with financing, home ownership is still the best investment you can make. The main advantage of this is in our tax laws, which allow interest payments and real estate taxes to be deducted.

The following example is a $100,000 home with an $80,000 mortgage assumed at a fixed rate of 15 percent for thirty years. For purposes of illustration, a fixed rate must be used. The principles, however, remain the same for all the different kinds of financing.

Total mortgage: $80,000 @ 15% = $12,000 interest for the first year.

You can deduct your interest payments based on your tax bracket from your federal income tax:

20% bracket = 20%, or $2,400.
30% bracket = 30%, or $3,600.
50% bracket = 50%, or $6,000.

These interest deductions dramatically bring down the real cost of your house payments. You still must have the money to meet your payments twelve months of the year. But April *can* become the sweetest month.

Happily, your state real estate taxes are tax deductible from your federal return, using the same formula as for interest deductions. Closing costs are also deductible in the year they are incurred.

For those people with income generated mainly from work done in their home, there is another nice tax break. You can depreciate those rooms in which you work. Depreciation means that your property becomes incrementally less valuable with age and use. The government lets you write off on your taxes this decrease in value, even though we all know that in the real world the property is probably getting *more* valuable. Who said IRS was of the real world?

Note: You can do nothing else in these rooms but work or you lose your qualification to depreciate.

I tend to be paranoid about this rule of the IRS. Can my exercycle be in my office? What if I take my portable TV into the office at 9:30 P.M.? I've solved my problem by having my secretary in my downstairs office, my research assistant in my upstairs office, and depreciating only those two rooms. I write in my bedroom but I also sleep there, so I can't claim I use it *only* for work. I consult in my dining room. But I also eat there, so it isn't depreciable. So I depreciate where work is done for me, but I don't depreciate where I work if I also do other things in that space.

There's a big tax break for people fifty-five or over who sell their home (see Retirement chapter). In order to qualify for this break, you must have lived in the house for three of the last five years. Up until 1980, the first $100,000 of profit was exempt from taxation. With the passage of the 1981 Economic Recovery Tax Act, this figure has been raised to $125,000. The rest of the profit, if any, is taxed at the low, long-term capital gains rate.

All income property, from rental of a second home to a shopping mall, can be depreciated on your tax return. In the past, depending on the material used to construct your building—brick, stucco, toothpicks, it could have been depreciated over twenty to forty years. Under the Economic Recovery Tax Act of 1981, those people lucky enough to own income property have been given a special break in the form of rapid depreciation. The *entire* building can now be depreciated in just fifteen years. This is a major break for real estate investors, and makes owning income property even more attractive than it was before. (See section on Income Property.)

SYNDICATION/LIMITED PARTNERSHIPS

Since many women don't have adequate money to invest in real property, syndication, also called limited partnerships, is important. Syndication and limited partnerships are one and the same in real estate. Women with limited capital, but who want the benefits of a real property investment, can become owners.

Ethical syndicators work only with sophisticated investors who know the benefits and risk of such an investment. By reading about how this form of investment works, you will become a more sophisticated investor!

Syndication is not organized crime but a way to invest in a real property. Syndications can work in one of a hundred different ways, so we'll just look at how they work in principle. The many things you'll need to know for your own protection will be listed.

A real estate syndication is a group of investors who decide to pool their money and buy property together. By doing this, they can get into a much larger deal than they could afford as individuals. Syndication also gives a person a chance to have all the benefits of ownership. Syndication is the most passive form of real property ownership. Its very passivity can be of great advantage to busy people or people who like real estate investments but don't like the management that such an investment involves. Syndication at its best is more of a profitable fun affair than a marriage.

Syndicators, the people who put the deal together, tend to be lawyers, accountants, builders, or real estate brokers. They have the know-how and are often looking to place clients' money. They are also the most likely group to be offered a deal.

The Deal

When the syndicator has found an interesting deal, a written prospectus will be put together showing pertinent information, such as a description of the property, often with pictures of the building. If it's a deal involving the development of raw land, there will be a map and a description of needed improvement such as sewers or grading of the land. The prospectus will also include the cost of the project, the maintenance of the project, and the financing on the project. There should also be projections for holding the property, and each year's expenses should show the effects of inflation. Obviously, gardening, roofing, garbage pick up, management, etc. will cost more each year. A projection without an inflation factor is the sign of an amateur or a crook.

The goal of many syndicators is to find property that can be improved and then resold at a profit. Another idea behind syndication is to find a deal that will improve property by proper management and maintenance and to hold the property for income, tax breaks, and appreciation.

Every professional prospectus should show the worst possible script and the syndicator's evaluation of how good the deal would be if it went sour. It should also show a realistic script of what might be made if all goes well as planned.

The syndicators I'm writing about will not make a public offering. To make a public offering, you must be registered with the Securities and Exchange Commission, which costs a bundle.

The syndicator approaches monied people or people like myself who deal with money. There are legal restrictions on the number of people that can be approached and the number of people that can be brought into a syndication. In some states there are limitations on the type of people that can be brought into a syndication—sophisticated investors only, for example. The syndicator is looking for people to invest their money to purchase property *or* to build property *or* to purchase raw land for a project.

A syndication takes title as a partnership. The syndicator is the general partner (there may be more than one), and the investors are the limited partners. The syndicator may also be an investor, in which case he may be both a limited partner and a general partner.

The general partner is in almost total charge of the deal, its management, and its eventual sale. Naturally, he or she must make annual accounting reports to each limited partner and for tax purposes provide them with a K-1 form (the 1040 of partnerships). He or she bears full liability. The limited partners have no managerial duties, no decision making rights about the project, and are limited in liability. They can only lose up to the amount they invested.

The general partner, in a well-drawn syndication agreement, leaves the limited partners two main powers:

1. By a majority vote, they can remove the general partner and elect a new one.

2. The general partner is forbidden by the limited partners to do any major refinancing that would in any way water down the investment of the limited partners.

So, all right already, where's the money in all this? I'll hedge again and say it depends on how the syndication was set up in the first place. Let me give some examples.

My Life in Syndication

I'm in two syndications at the moment, and for about ten years I was in one that I sold. Let's look at all three.

The share of the syndication I sold is the easiest deal to understand. The developer and general partner had a piece of industrial land by the airport. He wished to put up a warehouse and rent it out to a major company (known in the trade as a Triple A tenant). He knew the land cost and already had a tenant, but didn't wish to tie up his own money in the project. He guaranteed in writing to his investors a 12 percent return on their investment plus all the tax breaks. In the event that the building was sold, the split of profits was described in the partnership agreement. The developer/general partner would get 40 percent of the profits and the limited partners would get 60 percent prorated to the amount of their investment. The developer did the work of putting the deal together (packaging), constructing the building, and managing it. He also did the unusual thing of guaranteeing a return on his personal signature. Had the deal gone bad, he would have had to come up with what he guaranteed out of his own pocket. Since he was a very rich man with an excellent name in the field, the deal was rock candy mountain for the limited partners. Many of them had invested with him before. Actually it took pull to get into something as sweet as this!

The philosophy behind this syndication was to build, rent, and hold. In continuing inflation, the tenants had to pay more rent each time they renewed their lease. The building became more valuable and the general partner, after paying out 12 percent to his investors, was able to keep a tidy sum for himself. The best deal in all business is when everybody wins; and this was exactly that sort of situation.

The second syndication I was involved in was brought to me by a real estate broker who had found a condo on the beach south of Los Angeles, in a very good location. The condo was underpriced and the financing was good. She wanted ten people to come in as limited partners. She had needed $75,000 to buy the condo, part for the down payment, and part to be held in reserve for an expected negative cash flow. In a negative cash flow, more money goes out than comes in. We knew we could rent the condo, but the rent wouldn't cover the debt burden (mortgage payments) and the syndication would have to reach into its collective pocket to cover whatever shortage there would be. Not only did the rent not cover the mortgage, but we also had to consider property taxes, maintenance, and a possible vacancy.

The broker decided to divide the needed $75,000 into units that investors could purchase at $5,000 each. Since we were limited to ten people, some investors bought more than one unit.

What kind of craziness is this, buying something as an investment that doesn't even pay for itself? The people who bought in weren't crazy at all, at least not the ones I knew.

They were women with good salaries who didn't want to have more income. More income could easily lead to being kicked into a higher tax bracket. They were looking for tax breaks offered by ownership and appreciation on the property. When the syndicate was formed, it was decided we would sell in two years unless the market was bad at that time. The original cost of our luxurious beachside condo was $245,000. It is on the market now for $415,000, two years later. The huge appreciation is real because it was bought at a low price for the area, its location is superb, and it's the only beach condo for sale in its immediate area.

The general partner took 30 percent of any profits as her share for packaging, renting, and maintaining the condo. The limited partners will receive 70 percent of the profits on a prorated basis.

Let's look at the math.

Example:	Selling price	$375,000	(You don't get the
	Minus purchase price	245,000	asking price.)
	Profit	$130,000	
	Minus money back to limited partners	75,000	
	Profit	$55,000	
	Minus 6% commission	8,400	
	Profit	$46,600	
	Minus 30% share of general partner	13,980	
	Profit	$32,620	

Divided by fifteen units = $2,175 per $5,000 invested.

We pay a capital gains tax on the property, which is lower than ordinary income tax. The tax shelter we had by writing off the interest payments on a prorated share and depreciation, since this is commercial property, adds to the profit.

This small syndication brings up a vital issue for women. Syndicators abound but they are mostly interested in big deals needing large capital. Syndicators like to talk to investors with $100,000 or so to put into a deal. Women, seldom having this kind of money, rarely get a chance to invest in syndications. The small units of $5,000 each gave women with a small amount of extra capital a chance to participate in the profits and tax advantages of real property ownership. Women professionals should be encouraged to put together smaller syndications in which women *can* participate. There's a very good market out there.

The other syndication I'm now in has a different goal. A syndication was put together to buy a medical building in a nearby community. Again, the price was right and the location perfect. There are seven hospitals within a twelve-mile radius, one right across the street. In California, doctors may not have offices in their homes but must rent in a commercial building. A building where all the tenants are M.D.s is called a medical building.

The one we bought needed upgrading and some modernization. Most of the leases are going to expire within the year. With the upgrading and inflation, the doctors are going to have a hefty rent increase. Plan one is to hold on to the building and collect rents and tax benefits and depreciation. Perhaps in a year or so, we'll apply to the city to turn the building into medical condos. (Office condos are becoming very popular.) If we get a permit, the general partners will go through all the necessary paperwork the state demands before a building can be converted. When this is done, we may sell the whole package to a converter. Either way, holding or selling, is a good investment. It's a good investment because using either script and very conservative figures, we'll all either have a good monthly return on our investment from rent or do nicely on a sale.

Warnings

Syndication does look like a good way to make money, but watch out: Here's why:

1. The woods are full of crooks with promises like drops of goodies in a chocolate chip cookie. Look at the syndicator's track record. Find out if he has any other kind of record.

2. Have an accountant look at the figures.

3. Have a lawyer look at the partnership agreement.

4. See where you'd be if the worst possible script took place.

5. Never invest without looking at the property. Pictures may be worth a thousand words, but how do you know the picture is not of a different property?

6. Never invest money you can't afford to lose in a syndication. Oh, you will holler a lot if you lose, but don't invest a penny that once lost might affect your lifestyle.

7. Always have an outside accountant do the books. A dishonest general partner can skim money from the books without even having to think about how—all the ways are centuries old.

8. Don't go with a syndicator who promises you anything. The exception to the rule is in the first example. The only promise a general partner can honestly make is that as a limited partner you can only lose the amount you've invested.

9. Remember, when you sign a partnership agreement, it's like signing anything else, you may end up in court.

10. Never look to make the last dollar in an investment. Look for a reasonable deal.

11. Remember, everything in real estate is negotiable.

12. Remember, everything in real estate should be in writing.

13. Understand what you want from a syndicator. Do you want to hold for income? Are you looking mainly for appreciation? Are you most interested in tax advantages? Let your accountant or lawyer know what you're aiming for so he can see if what you want is indeed the thrust of the syndication.

14. Read all contracts even after your professional has okayed them. It may be all strange to you in the beginning. Ask for an explanation of ANYTHING you don't understand! Ask again, and again, if you don't understand the explanation. You're paying to learn! Your aim is to become a knowledgeable woman in investing. The first time you may need a lot of help. The second time you'll be surprised by how much you know.

INCOME PROPERTY

Owning real property is an *active investment*, whether it be your own home, another home, an apartment house, a store, or a factory. Plumbing breaks down, roofs leak, things need painting, appliances age, foundations sink, grease wears into driveways, and furnaces blow up and die. Not all at once, you understand, but real property needs tender, loving care, a watchful eye, injections of money, and some amount of time. If you need to hire a manager, do so. That salary is deductible as an expense.

Let's say you own a second home as an investment and rent it. (This is only an example, and the figures here will be too high in some areas of the U.S. and too low in others.) You bought the house ten years ago as an investment for $50,000, putting down 20 percent cash.

Cash down $10,000
Mortgage $40,000 at 7% for 30 years = $266.13/mo.
Rent $ 400 per month

The rent of $400 minus the $266.13 mortgage payment would give you $133.87 per month clear, or $1,606.44 a year clear, or put another way, 16 percent return on your $10,000 down payment. Of course, there will be real estate taxes and maintenance, so we have to figure further.

Let's say real estate taxes are $450. This brings your profit down: $1,606.44 − $450.00 = $1,156.44. You receive 11.5 percent on your $10,000 down payment. Now it gets interesting!

There are lovely tax benefits on the interest you pay on your mortgage. During the first years of any mortgage you are paying almost all interest to the bank and only a wee bit on principal (the sum you borrowed). As you are making payments of $266.13 a month x 12 months you are paying $3,193.56 a year. Of this let's say $3,000 is interest and the rest principal. Okay, you can deduct the interest from your income taxes using the same formula we used before. In the 25 percent bracket, deduct 25 percent, or $750.00. In the 50 percent bracket deduct 50 percent, or $1,500.00

Since real estate taxes and depreciation are deductible from your income tax, these deductions will bring the real rate of return (profit) on your investment to quite a bit more than the 11.5 percent we were looking at before the tax break.

In the real world, what's happening to your rental house? It is getting more and more valuable with inflation and you are able to charge more and more rent. Your investment is getting better and better. With your interest write-off, your real estate tax write-off, and the depreciation, you're sitting in the catbird's seat. Of course, you had expenses, income taxes on rent, some period of vacancy, and some inconvenience when tenants wanted things done immediately, but you have a good investment.

So let's look at your rental after 10 years:

Cash down $10,000
Mortgage payment $266.13/mo.
Rent (inflation, remember) $650.00/mo.

The total: $650.00 – $266.13 = $383.87 montly income, or 46 percent annually on your down payment of $10,000. As we saw before, repair and maintenance would lower this figure, also ever-present real estate taxes that might or might not have gone up. To offset this, there are still all the tax breaks of deducting the interest on your mortgage, your real estate taxes, and depreciation. A little jewel of an investment, wouldn't you say?

In this example, we have a picture of how all real estate works. Whether you own a single family house for rental, a duplex, a triplex, an office building, a vast shopping center, or an industrial building, the principles are the same. There are goodies in each type of investment that make each one slightly different, but the *principle* of how the money is made in real estate remains the same.

Management Companies

Commercial real estate has been very profitable and still is in some parts of the country. It involves a lot of active management. If the project is large enough it will need a manager or a management company. They will deal with maintenance problems and tenant problems, and you will deal with the management only.

Management companies run from good to very bad. You should have an outside accountant audit the books for any possible skimming.

Industrial Buildings—Paradise Regained

The most trouble-free investment in real estate is an industrial building. You usually have only one tenant and you have a net lease. A net lease means the tenant pays for all repairs and maintenance, plus any increases in real estate taxes. Traditionally, the owner is only responsible for the roof— repairing it or replacing it. The word "net" means that all the monies coming out of the property are yours (and the government's, naturally).

TAX TIPS

Selling and Trading:

On a mortgage, as I have said, the first twenty-four years of payments are mostly interest, and that interest is a way of lowering your taxes. After a while, however, interest and principal payments become about equal. You begin to lose some income tax advantages, and as time goes on this increases. Your ability to depreciate your property also may change. So most investors, in consultation with a real estate lawyer or a CPA, start to think about selling, refinancing—(market conditions permitting), or trading. If you sell and invest in new property or trade up to a more expensive property—very popular now, you can start all over again, tax breaks and depreciation all shiny and new to your financial advantage. Your accountant is the professional who will help you make this decision.

If you sell commercial or industrial real estate you can't defer taxes. Capital gains are paid in the year you sell. The only way to defer taxes on commercial or industrial property is to trade them, not sell them. If you trade property, it must always be like for like, residential for residential, commercial for commercial, industrial for industrial. Yes, you can trade homes if you wish, but you do have the other option of deferring for twenty-four months and then buying.

Trading is difficult, and the laws pertaining to tax-deferred exchanges change all the time. To learn more about trades, consult a real estate broker. If you do decide to trade property you own, your accountant should review the deal to be sure it falls within the tax code #1031 for tax-deferred exchanges.

Remember, *there are no tax-free exchanges*. You hear and read the expression tax-free. There is also a market for science fiction, and tax-free exchanges belong in that genre. You can have tax-deferred exchanges. But as we all know, death and taxes are inevitable, so don't get your hopes up about avoiding taxes forever.

REAL ESTATE ANALYSIS

Cash needed for investment: Anywhere from $5,000 to millions.

Risk: Paying too much for real estate or buying in the wrong location can raise your risk factor. However, owning always carries a risk factor.

Return on investment: Today, a return of nine percent or ten percent plus all tax advantages is excellent! But as the economy changes, these figures may be too optimistic or overly conservative. Buying and selling can get expensive as the costs involved in real estate transactions are high.

Liquidity: Not liquid. Can be borrowed against under certain conditions.

Tax advantages: Excellent.

Active or passive: Active, as is all ownership, but passive if invested in syndication.

Age: Best for investor between ages of twenty and sixty or for knowledgeable investors over sixty years of age who can afford some risk.

7

Stocks and the Stock Market

Let's listen in on a conversation between two Wall Street aficionados:

"The decade of the eighties is the decade for stock!"

"Why?"

"They're underpriced, that's why! They've been down so long they gotta go up!"

"Excuse me, didn't Newton's Law go the other way?"

"Stocks are the only good buy, with real estate so high and gold so crazy. Besides, the Dow will be at two thousand by 1990."

"Ya, I know, I heard that one in 1960 and 1970, and the Dow can't stay over one thousand for more than twenty-four hours."

"But the market loves the Republican party!"

"Ya, goes down twenty points the day after President Reagan takes office."

"Buy auto stocks now, particularly Chrysler, it's got to go up!"

"Hm, Newton would spin in his grave! Why not just buy Penn Central and be done with it. No cliffhanging in that stock. It went so far down, it's blown away right into receivership."

Okay, what does all that jazz mean? It means that the market consists of perennial optimists, called bulls, and perennial pessimists, called bears. Both are right some percent of the time. The stock market moves according to a strange concoction of the interpretation of news, passion, hope, and despair. There is no formula, no foolproof method of predicting what the stock market will do. The only way to effectively work the stock market is to understand it and then follow it closely.

What Is Stock?

The dictionary defines stock as "the capital of a company or corporation, divided into portions or shares of uniform amount, which are represented by transferable certificates (called stock certificate or stock). The holder of one of these is considered a part owner, rather than a creditor, of the company."

When you buy stock in a company you become a partner in that company. Though you are not an active partner, you are in an ownership position. That means stocks are an *active* investment. If you don't want to follow the stock market and keep abreast of the news and how it will affect your stocks, you'd be wiser to invest in stocks through mutual funds, discussed later.

Why There Is Stock

Corporations issue bonds in order to *borrow* money from the public. But they also issue stock. This means they *sell* pieces of their company to the public as another way to raise money.

Let's look at a fictitious company to get an idea of what we're talking about. Say I start a business and sell stock in it to my friends. My company is called Moneywise and its function is to service clients, mainly women, as a financial consulting firm. I have the moxie and the know-how but, unhappily, not the capital. I have figured that I'll need $100,000 for start-up costs, running expenses, salary, rent, and public relations. I don't have a rich backer, but a few financially successful friends of mine believe Moneywise could make money for them and want to invest in the company.

First, I incorporate and issue stock at $20 a share. I have $30,000 of my own so I buy up 1,500 shares. I do this because I want to retain as large an interest as possible in my own company. I have $70,000 left to raise. Seven friends have decided to buy in. Each will buy 500 shares at $20 each.

When Moneywise shows a profit, we pay each stockholder a dividend. I say "we" because I'm no longer a me, I'm a we. My seven friends (now known as shareholders) are partners in Moneywise.

If, as a sentimental gesture, I give one share of stock to each of my daughters, they are also partners and will have a prorated share of all profits.

My shareholders now have a very big interest in the success of Moneywise and they will carefully oversee its management. The selection of a board of directors might look like this: Moneywise stockholders get together and elect me and two of their own to be members of the Board of Directors. They also elect a lawyer, a CPA, and a businesswoman, all from outside the company. As members of the Board, our job is to be sure that Moneywise is running well *and* well run.

Once a year all the shareholders will get together and vote on the Board of Directors. If they don't like the way Moneywise is going, they can elect a whole new Board. The shareholders have one vote for each share of stock they own, and if they dump me by using my own kids' two votes I will be very sorry for being sentimental! Of course, I *am* the major stockholder and so have the largest voice.

Okay. This story tells you the basic principle of how all stock companies work. There are no mysteries involved here.

Now, let's look to the future when Moneywise has grown, expanded, made money, and expanded again. Now we want to open branch offices in San Francisco, Cleveland, New York, Minneapolis, and Chicago. My stockholders are ecstatic, but we have a problem. We don't have the money to expand into a national market. We're in need of capital again, much more capital than we ourselves can raise. Our company decides to qualify to sell stock to the general public on the stock exchange. By doing this we'll raise the money to expand. You, the stock-buying public, can now become new partners in Moneywise. As stock buyers you should be aware of the different types of stock and what each means.

Common and Preferred Stocks

When people talk about stocks, they are usually talking about common stock. Common stock is the basic instrument of the stock market. Common stockholders assume the greatest risk, generally exercise the greatest control, and may gain the greatest reward in the form of dividends and capital appreciation.

Common stockholders have voting rights in the management of the company. That obviously means they have some control. If they band together they can throw out the management or at least give it one hell of a scare. Common stockholders assume the greatest risk, since they are the last

to be paid if the company goes bankrupt and the last in line
to be paid dividends if the company is in trouble. However,
they gain the greatest rewards if the company is successful,
because their dividends increase as the company's profits
increase. Also, their stock value goes up.

Preferred stock usually pays a fixed rate of dividends. In
case of liquidation of a company, bond holders are paid first,
preferred stockholders second, and common stockholders last.
Preferred stocks move up or down not on company performance but rather, on the prevailing interest rates throughout
the country. As interest rates go up, the price of preferred
stock goes down, and vice versa. This can best be shown by
example:

Let's say a preferred stock is paying a return of 10 percent
and interest rates are at 15 percent. The price of this preferred stock has to go down because nobody with any financial sense would buy a fixed-rate security paying 10 percent
when they could get a different instrument at 15 percent.

Some preferred stock can be converted to common stock.
These are listed as preferred convertible.

How the Stock Market Works

There are three major stock markets: The New York Stock
Exchange (NYSE), located in New York; The American Stock
Exchange (AMEX), located in Chicago; and the Over-the-
Counter Market (NASDAQ), located everywhere. Over-the-
counter stocks sell through the wire services and can be
bought through any stockbroker.

There are also many smaller, regional exchanges, such as
the Boston, Cincinnati, Midwest, Pacific, Philadelphia, Salt
Lake City, and Spokane exchanges. These are linked electronically by a system called the Intermarket Trading System.
Your broker, therefore, has instant access to any market.

The New York Stock Exchange is located on historic Wall
Street in New York City. This exchange, with its highest
quality listings and stringent standards, is the giant in the
world of stock trading.

What happens when you walk into your broker, plunk
down your money, and order ten shares of say, M&M? As an
example, we'll take a tour of the New York Exchange.

We enter a trading floor about the size of a football field.
Teletype booths are located all along the edge of the floor,

and that's where your order will be first received. The phone clerk gives your order to his floor broker to execute. The floor broker represents your brokerage house, and he has paid an enormous amount of money for the job of doing so. His seat on Wall Street is a costly one but also highly lucrative!

The floor broker goes to one of twenty-two trading posts located throughout the Exchange. About ninety different stocks are sold at each post, their names displayed on cards above the post. There he or she will find other traders milling about.

A rule of the Exchange is that all buying and selling must be done out loud in public. No transactions can be done in secret, and all transactions must be completed between the hours of ten A.M. and four P.M. Eastern Standard Time on Monday through Friday.

The floor broker will announce his or her offer out loud, usually in an abbreviated jargon. Within moments, a trader accepts the bid. The transaction is made, and both buying and selling brokers make their own notations. Your brokerage firm is then notified, and arrangements are made to transfer ten shares of M&M to you. Normally, this entire transaction (except for the exchange of stock certificates) takes two or three minutes!

Stock Prices/Stock Splits

The price of any stock offered for sale on the market is determined by several factors, such as company earnings, product desirability, and the economy in general. However, the single most determining factor in setting stock prices is whether or not the investing public is interested in a particular stock. If a lot of people want a piece of a company, its stock prices will rise. On the other hand, if a lot of people decide a company is a bad risk and pull out of it, the price of its stock has nowhere to go but down! If your floor broker gets to M&M trading post and finds a crowd clamoring to sell or buy, the price of your stock will be affected.

Stocks that sell for high prices (say $150 per share) become unwieldy. Stockholders complain that it's difficult to sell their shares because of the high cost. When this happens, companies declare a stock split. For example, $150 will then buy ten stocks instead of one. Your $150 share will be converted to ten $15 shares. This will make it easier to buy and sell to the general public.

Growth or Income

Some people buy stock expecting that the company they invest in will grow and become increasingly successful. If this happens, the price of the stock will rise. Thus, they'll be able to sell their stock for substantially more than they paid for it. This stock is called growth stock.

Picking stocks that have a good chance for success is a national pastime. We are all familiar with some of the more dramatic former growth stocks, such as IBM and Xerox. Though they may continue to grow slowly, their huge adolescent spurt is over.

There are fortunes to be made if one could foresee the IBMs of the future. But growth is a tricky business. A well managed, financially sound company with a new and exciting product might look like a good candidate for growth. However, there are risks. The public may simply not want its product, or a better version comes out simultaneously, or a recession occurs and this company is destroyed by economic conditions. On the other hand, this product could turn out to be as exciting as the Xerox machine!

While some people buy stocks for their potential growth value, others invest in order to receive a stream of income. *Only rarely can you find a stock which produces growth as well as a good income.*

The stream of income from a stock is received in the form of dividends. A dividend is payment distributed to a company's shareholders; the amount is decided on by the Board of Directors. Dividends vary with the fortunes of the company and also with the cash-on-hand position of the company. Dividends can be omitted if business is bad or if the Board of Directors decides to invest in expansion or new equipment. Fixed dividends on preferred stock can *also* be deferred. In all cases, before common stockholders can receive any dividends, all dividends owed to preferred stockholders *must be* paid. Dividends can be thought of much like rents in real estate. The stock itself can be compared to real property.

Appropriate Investing by Ages and Stages

Each stage in a woman's life presents different financial responsibilities. Marriage, kids, college expenses, divorce and/or widowhood, and retirement will dictate how much risk a woman can take and how much security she needs.

The financial needs of a twenty-five-year-old single woman are very different from those of a fifty-five-year-old grandmother. While a young, single woman should be going for growth in the stock market, a middle-aged woman should be trading off her growth stocks for the security of good dividend stocks. If you're going to lose in the market, it's better to do so when you're young and can absorb any losses. Having to rebuild your portfolio in your fifties can be frightening and very difficult.

Every woman should carefully analyze her financial goals according to her current situation before buying a stock. Why are you buying that stock and what do you stand to gain or lose? Are you buying it to finance your child's college education or to encase her little mouth in braces? Do you need the money right now or do you want it to grow and pay off later? These are some of the kinds of questions you must ask yourself.

My daughters are grown and are self-supporting. One daughter even earns more per year than I do! I must constantly remind myself that long-term growth investments are not for me. My goals are to travel and to be a little self-indulgent. I'm not interested in any stock that will pay off in ten years—I want it now! I *am* saving for retirement but any excess is for today.

Below is a list of stock recommendations for the different ages and stages in a woman's life:

AGES AND STAGES	STOCK RECOMMENDATIONS
Young and single	Growth stocks
Young and married	Growth stocks
Thirty-plus	Growth stocks and some income stocks if needed
Forty-plus	Evenly divided between growth stocks and income stocks
Over fifty	Mostly income stocks

All of these recommendations are, of course, subject to modification according to your own needs and income bracket.

TYPE OF STOCK	SAFETY	GROWTH	INCOME
BLUE CHIPS Stock of a major company.	Very safe, reliable. Examples: AT&T IBM	Very slow; some capital appreciation over the long term.	Varies from low to moderate, but steady and quite safe.
CYCLICAL STOCKS Stocks of companies that are tied to business cycles and that respond to economic conditions.	So-so; if the economy is stable, stocks are safe. They can be damaged by inflation and during periods of recession. Examples: auto and building industries.	Some growth potential; most companies are already established.	Can be excellent.
DEFENSIVE STOCKS Quality stocks that are recommended during bad markets.	Quite safe; reliable. Examples: pharmaceuticals utilities	Very slow; some growth potential though most companies are already established.	Moderate to good, but steady and safe.
GLAMOUR STOCKS Any stock that's very attractive at the time.	Can be quite risky; usually volatile. Examples: oils and gambling stocks were once glamorous.	Can be quite substantial.	Usually very low.
GROWTH STOCKS Any stock that has grown more this year than last and is expected to continue to do so.	So-so; varies from reasonably safe to very risky. Demands caution when purchasing and then constant watchfulness. Examples: Fremont General & Xerox in its day.	Can be very substantial.	Usually very low.
SPECULATIVE STOCKS Stocks believed to have great potential for quick growth.	Very risky. Can cause serious tension headaches, so be careful. Examples: genetic engineering high technology	Capital appreciation can be very substantial if you choose right.	Usually very low.

So if you turn fifty-five, find yourself rich and comfortable, you can certainly keep your money in growth stocks to leave to your fine young grandchild!

MARKET PERFORMANCE

Dow Jones Industrial Average

The Dow Jones Industrial Average is the most popular method for analyzing the market. Whether it's any good is unimportant. Everybody interested in the market, both here and abroad, watches the Dow, talks about the Dow, dreams about the Dow, jumps off high buildings because of the Dow. If everybody responds to the Dow, then you, too, must follow it. If it is an imperfect theory (and it is), it is at least a super-psychological indicator.

The Dow Jones market theory is based on the performance of the Dow Jones industrials' average. Thirty stocks make up this list. This theory purports that the market is in a basic upward trend if the Dow Jones average advances above a previous important high. When the average dips below this high, it is regarded as a basic downward trend. The Dow does not predict how long any trend will continue. The Dow is not a method of forecasting and it was never meant to be. It is a widely held misinterpretation that the Dow has a crystal ball within its theory! Any theory by its very definition should have some predictive use. Since the Dow Jones theory does not, it's best to think of it strictly as a performance indicator.

The world is presented each business day with the closing Dow Jones average. You can hear it on radio news, TV news, or read it in your local paper. For investors everywhere, the closing average is an obsession. They would no more go to bed without undressing than go to bed without knowing how the Dow closed. Why this is I don't know, but then I feel the same way. If you are invested in stock or are interested in investing, you better join us crazies or you might be sorry!

The Dow Jones closing average is found each day by adding up the gains of its thirty stocks, subtracting the losses, and dividing by thirty. If gains outnumber losses for the day, the Dow Jones goes up. If losses outnumber gains, the Dow goes down.

Hardly anyone can name the thirty stocks that make up the

Dow Jones list. These change somewhat from year to year.
Because I love little bits of obscure information I have listed
them below as they are in 1982:

Allied Corporation   International Harvester
Aluminum Company   International Paper
American Brands   Manville Corporation
American Can   Merck
American Telephone &   Minnesota M&M
  Telegraph   Owens-Illinois
Bethlehem Steel   Proctor & Gamble
DuPont   Sears, Roebuck
Eastman Kodak   Standard Oil of California
Exxon   Texaco
General Electric   Union Carbide
General Foods   United Technologies
General Motors   U.S. Steel
Goodyear   Westinghouse Electric
Inco   Woolworth
IBM

The Market and Inflation

The stock market is one place where professionals (lawyers,
CPAs and others) advise women to invest their money. True,
some people have done well with growth stocks but on the
average it has been a terrible place for a person with
little knowledge and no desire or ability to be an aggressive
trader.

The Dow Jones Industrial Average has gone up only 19.5
percent since 1913, or less than one-third of one percent a
year measured in constant dollars. Constant dollars is an
abstract idea of a dollar, a dollar that always has the same
purchasing power. It's a dollar whose power is unaffected by
inflation or devaluation. Don't you wish you had some?

Stock growth has hardly kept pace with inflation. Actually,
the market has been a disaster, as measured by the Dow.
Some stocks naturally have made millions for those who were
in at the beginning. IBM and Xerox are examples of this type
of stock. But I'm talking now only of those stocks measured
by the Dow.

All right, so much for the growth of these thirty stocks.
What about dividend income? The chart on p. 139 shows the

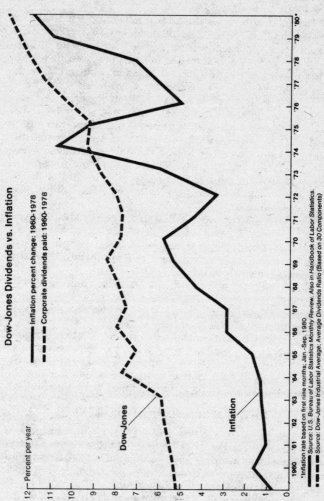

Dow-Jones Dividends vs. Inflation

Inflation percent change: 1960-1978

Corporate dividends paid: 1960-1978

Percent per year

Dow-Jones

Inflation

*Inflation rate based on first nine months: Jan.-Sep. 1980
Source: U.S. Bureau of Labor Statistics Monthly Review. Also in Handbook of Labor Statistics.
Source: Dow-Jones Industrial Average; Average Dividends Ratio (Based on 30 Components)

annual rate of inflation as compared to the annual rate of dividends on the Dow Jones.

The solid line shows the rate of inflation since 1960. The broken line shows the rate of dividends since 1960. Dividends have consistently been higher than the rate of inflation, except for 1973–74, when inflation outpaced dividends. This drastic rise in the rate of inflation occurred with the formation of OPEC! Remember those gas lines?

To take a broader view, let's look at Standard & Poor's Composite Index of 500 common stocks sold on the New York Stock Exchange. Standard & Poor's is one of the two largest and most prestigious firms in the field of securities statistics and research. The other tops in the field is Moody's Investment Service, but I usually think of them more in terms of bond rating. Standard & Poor's also rates quality of bonds, has a stock market index, and a mutual fund with a good performance record.

The S&P market index of 500 stocks covers about 86 percent of the total value of all Big Board (New York Stock Exchange) stocks. Since it is a much larger sample of stock than the Dow Jones it is a more accurate picture of what is happening in the market.

Here, too, we see that dividends have kept pace with inflation.

However good dividends are, they are *also* a taxable stream of income and offer no guarantee of growth.

From this we must conclude that the market has paid good dividends for the last twenty years but has been very poor in growth performance. So, as a stream of income it rates reasonably high, but for capital accumulation this was not the place to be. I'd rather be in Philadelphia!

IS THE MARKET RIGHT FOR *YOU*?

Before jumping into the stock market, you must assess your financial position. For instance, if you own your home, are adequately insured, have savings in a good lending instrument, and want to invest some excess money, the stock market is probably a good place for you.

There are also many happy apartment dwellers who do not find home ownership attractive. The stock market offers them a chance for ownership and a piece of the action of American industry, where they can buy into lawn mowers and never have to push one.

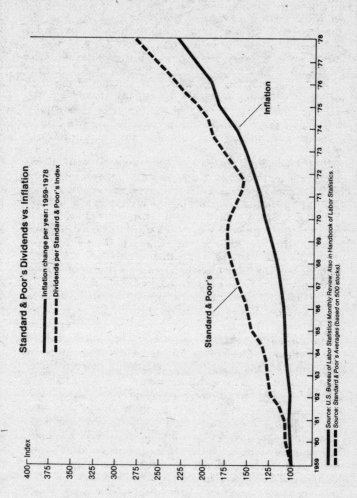

Standard & Poor's Dividends vs. Inflation

— Inflation change per year: 1959–1978
- - - Dividends per Standard & Poor's Index

Inflation

Standard & Poor's

Source: U.S. Bureau of Labor Statistics Monthly Review. Also in Handbook of Labor Statistics.
Source: Standard & Poor's Averages (based on 500 stocks).

Index

400
375
350
325
300
275
250
225
200
175
150
125
100

1959 '60 '61 '62 '63 '64 '65 '66 '67 '68 '69 '70 '71 '72 '73 '74 '75 '76 '77 '78

There are two things a person should have in order to play in the stock market: excess cash and excess calm. It's fairly easy to figure out how much cash you have to invest. By the age of twenty-five you should also know if you are a professional worrier. Are you going to run to the paper every day and cheer your gains or mourn your losses? Are you going to lose sleep over every paper loss? Or rush out and spend every paper profit? Are the ups and down of a fluctuating market going to blight your life? If so, stay out of the stock market. One should watch the market like the tides of the ocean and know that change will occur, for that is its nature.

If you decide you have the personality and the cash to enter the stock market, you must then analyze your financial goals:

1. If you want a stream of income from the market, you must compare dividends of any stock with interest from lending investments such as T-Bills or money market funds. (See Chapter 5.) During periods of high interest, you will probably do better to invest in high interest instruments rather than in the market. As we have seen, stock dividends *have* outpaced inflation. However, they do not compare to the yield you can get in the money market funds these days. They could once again be a competitive place to invest for a stream of income. As economic conditions change, so does the market.

2. If you want growth from the market, then you'll get little or no income. What you will get, if you choose the right stocks, is capital accumulation and some excellent tax breaks when you sell. For example, say you buy one hundred shares of Power Lawn Mowers for $10 per share. Your initial investment is $1,000. Several years later, the Continental United States is visited with a crabgrass plague! Every patriotic citizen rushes out to buy a power lawn mower to save his family and his country from the dread crabgrass! Bingo, your stock shoots up to $30 per share, and you've tripled your initial investment. So you decide to sell and take your profits. You've made money, and the tax man wants his share. However, your profits will *not* be taxed as ordinary income. Rather, you'll receive a special tax break from the U.S. Government in the lowest form of taxation, capital gains. This is how the government rewards you for taking the risk of ownership. Your stock may not triple in just a few years, but as long as it continues to grow you will make money.

Benefits and Tax Breaks

Besides offering financial benefits either in the form of dividends or capital growth, there are several other good reasons to use the stock market as an investment vehicle:

1. The stock market is fun, educational and creative, and it doesn't take much money to play. While lending is like a snapshot, the stock market is a first-run movie! Your decisions make things move. Your judgment is called into play, and your gut feeling about when to get in or out is rewarded. You work for your money and, as in any creative work, it can be very satisfying.

2. You reap the rewards of ownership when you have your very own piece of the rock! And remember, ownership is the only path to accumulating any kind of real money.

3. When you need cash in a hurry, for whatever reason, stocks are liquid and can be cashed in quickly. There's always a ready market for stock, open every day except weekends and national holidays.

4. Stocks can be used as collateral for bank loans or additional stock purchases. They are considered a perfect form of collateral because they are so liquid.

5. Stocks offer protected exposure. This means that if you invest a dollar you can never lose more than that dollar.

6. Stock sales are taxed at the capital gains rate, and under the Economic Recovery Tax Act of 1981, the low capital gains tax rate has been made even *lower*. Therefore, there are more advantages to those with the most money to invest; the law was written this way to encourage and reward those with the wealth to invest their capital in corporate America.

For example, say you sell your Power Lawn Mower stock for $3,000 realizing a $2,000 profit. According to the tax reform act, capital gains are taxed as follows:

1. The first sixty cents, or 60 percent of every dollar, profit is not taxed at all. Only forty cents, or 40 percent of your gain, is subject to taxes;

2. This 40 percent will be taxed on a sliding scale with a maximum of 50 percent if you are in the 50 percent tax bracket.

So, 40 percent of your $2,000 profit is $800. If you are in the 50 percent tax bracket you pay 50 percent of this $800 in tax, so that your maximum tax on $2,000 profit is $400. The lower your bracket, the lower your tax will be.

Remember, in order to receive capital gains treatment, you must hold your stock for at least a year and a day.

STOCKBROKERS/SALES PEOPLE

A stockbroker may be a genius, a gentleman or a gentle-woman, and a scholar to boot! He or she may be a drug abuser or into porn. They are just like everybody else in town, only they sell stock. Like most salespeople they live on commissions, and if they don't sell, they starve. They work out of one of the many offices of the stock brokerage houses. The stock companies with wonderful preppy names like Merrill Lynch, Pierce, Fenner and Smith, Inc., Dean Witter, Reynolds, or Shearson, Hayden, Stone are all members of the New York Stock Exchange as well as of all the other exchanges.

Stockbrokers must be twenty-one years old and citizens of the United States. They are bonded by their companies and licensed by the Securities and Exchange Commission (SEC), the federal regulatory agency that controls and polices the stock market.

The process of becoming a stockbroker differs from firm to firm, but all brokers must take their SEC test in New York City and receive some training in market analysis and accounting. They are trained and hyped, supported and educated, nursed and watched by their firms until they are ready to fly, at which point they go from salary to commission. The large firms may keep a broker on salary for as long as two years. Brokerage firms make a huge investment in their new sales people and *not* for reasons of charity.

Commissions—Ins and Outs

When you buy or sell stock you pay a commission to the broker. The broker splits with his company on a contracted basis. Commissions can be negotiated if you're buying or selling in large amounts. Actually, commissions are always negotiable by law, but your broker won't tell you that! If you try to negotiate on small purchases you will fail. Why? Because the broker will not wish to set a precedent with you and because it is really not worth his time.

There is an inherent conflict of interest between stockbrokers and clients, and brokers worth their salt will tell you so. If you want your broker to take care of you, he will, but only after he has taken care of himself first. He will try to sell you the instrument that pays the highest commission.

I make brokers sound like greedy, awful people. Most of them aren't, but remember that they're not social workers nor are they your mother. Stockbrokers, (just like working mothers), are working to make the most possible money for themselves.

Some brokers say they don't like doing business with women and that they can't make money from women. They claim we are uneducated, don't know what we want, and that we are worrymongers, calling them for reassurance every time the market goes bumpety, bumpety, bump. I suppose this is sometimes true, but it doesn't do any good to blame the victim. Women are new to the financial world and will get shrewder *and* richer in time.

Tip: Buy stock in round lots if possible, it saves money on commissions.

Round lots are multiples of one hundred and odd lots are any amount less than one hundred shares or other than multiples of hundreds.

Examples: Two hundred shares are a round lot, 201 are odd.

One hundred shares are a round lot, twenty are odd.

Discount Brokers

Discount brokerage houses are the fast food franchises in the stock market. You can "have it your way" at these houses because they serve only one function: They take and execute stock buy and sell orders. If you know exactly what you want you can get it at discount houses for a very low commission. In order to provide this service, discount brokers *do not*:

1. Provide any financial research.
2. Review your personal needs.
3. Balance your portfolio.
4. Discuss pros and cons of a particular stock. These houses are strictly drive-ins and make no attempt to be anything else!

Good Guy Broker

What makes a good broker and how do you find one? A good broker is one who:

1. Brings information on the market to your attention.
2. Gives the pros and cons on a stock.
3. Gives information on the past performance of the stock and its earnings history.
4. Doesn't pressure you.
5. Keeps in touch with you during business hours, never calls at night!
6. Calls with bad news as well as good news.
7. Follows orders even if he or she feels they know better about what's good for you.
8. Never tries to churn your account (churning is getting you to buy and sell, usually on a hot tip, in order to generate commissions); and most important
9. Knows what your goals are, whether growth or stream of income, and works accordingly.

How do you find such a paragon? By interviewing as many brokers as you can until your gut instinct tells you that you've met a person you feel you can trust. In a small city or town your choice may be limited. The good news about a broker is that once you've found a good one, you can take him with you whenever you move. Since buying or selling is done by phone and checks go through the mail, your broker can be in Cleveland, while you can reach out and touch God in Sante Fe.

Bad Guy Broker

A client of mine, Patricia, a professional musician, came to me for a financial consultation. She made $6,000 last year from her music and received $450 a month child support, which was to stop in six months when her child became eighteen. She had one super asset from her divorce settlement, a large well-located home. She didn't want to sell or rent this until her child was in college. She invested in silver coins, gold South African coins, and a high yield bond fund. Since her total capital to invest was about $12,000, she had decided to try to make a killing with high-risk investment.

I explained to her that she might as well go to Las Vegas. By putting her money either on red or black, she would have had better odds than she did at present. She didn't have enough capital to be speculating on metal. As to her high yield fund, she thought it contained stocks and not bonds. She had the prospectus with her and right on the front it said it was a bond fund with bonds rated Baa or less. Her broker had given her the prospectus, but she hadn't read it; and if she had, she didn't know what a Baa rating was. (Bonds and their ratings are discussed in the Lending chapter.) Her broker, who works at a nationally respected brokerage house, had screwed her royally. He had put her into a terrible investment for her, but had made the best possible commission for himself.

Pat could have read the prospectus. She could and should have asked questions! She had invested in things she didn't understand. She did everything to give the other guy the edge, and he took it!

What to Ask Your Broker

Say you decide to put $5,000 in the market. When you talk to your broker, he or she will ask you about your goals. Are you most interested in growth or dividends? Your broker might then suggest a stock. Here is a list of issues you should take up with your broker in order to find out why he or she thinks a particular stock is for you.

Check on:

1. The past record of earnings per share.

2. The p/e ratio as compared with other stocks with good past records (p/e ratio is explained later).

3. Whether the stock is likely to grow in the present economy. Example: Recreation vehicle stock is not going to do too well in a recession when people are careful of every dollar. RV's are very unpopular in a gas crunch!

4. Whether the company makes a good product that is desirable and acceptable by the public. Example: The abacus is out and the computer is in!

5. Whether there is a record of good management.

6. How the company compares to the competition in size, products, marketing, and management.

7. Whether the stock is in an industry that is growing. Example: Services and products for older people are growing as the demographics of the country change to an older population.

8. Your broker should give you the Standard & Poor's

information sheet. This gives you a comprehensive picture of the company you are interested in.

STOCK STRATEGIES

Stocks and Pickles or Ice Cream

Why are you buying that stock? Is it for the dividend (income) or for growth (capital accumulation)? Remember, no stock will ever offer both. A craving for pickles and ice cream doesn't even work for a pregnant woman—one or the other but definitely not both.

If you want income, you and your broker should pick a stock with a past history of paying good dividends regularly. This is a conservative approach and one that I recommend. Most charts and books touting the market will show how much money you could make if you bought a stock and perpetually reinvested the dividends in the same stock over many years. Well, if you're young, make a lovely salary, and have no financial obligations that can't be met from your income, those charts and statistics are for you. However, many women count on dividends to supplement their income, and for many older women, the dividends are their major source of income.

When you buy for income you should definitely invest in stocks for the long haul. Short-term trading cuts deep into dividend income as commissions in and out take their bite. When dividend income is what you're looking for, don't fret if your stock goes down in price and don't celebrate when the stock goes up. Your income will probably remain the same. Fluctuations in the market are something you should get used to. The broader, almost cyclical fluctuations are hard to live with but will affect dividends much less than you would expect. Watch out, however, for a Penn Central or a Chrysler!

When a dividend check comes, it goes into the bank; and rather than the joy of perpetual reinvestment you have the joy of paying your bills! So if you need income, tell your broker. Then make your broker prove that what he or she suggests really is an income-producing stock.

My favorite stock strategy is a good example of bargain hunting. It's called fishing the bottom. The stock market *hates* the high cost of money, and in times of tight money stock prices go down. When they get low enough to be a real bargain, I fish the bottom and usually pick up a deal on my equity positions.

Psychologically, it's very hard to buy a stock when it's on the way down. Think of it as being on sale. You have no trouble buying a dress that has been marked down by one-third or even one-half. It actually feels good and virtuous to do so! Try to keep this image in mind when buying stocks in a down market. Fishing the bottom can be a sound financial strategy rather than just another chapter in the perils of Pauline. You may not hit the rock bottom, but in a bad market a good broker should steer you to some real bargains!

Choosing a Growth Stock

If you want stock that will grow, then you want a stock that will rise in price. For example, you want to be able to sell the share you bought at $20 for $40 and make a killing. Good luck!

The strategy for winning in this game is to buy at the bottom and sell at the top. For that you need more luck than brains and next year's stock quotes from your local crystal ball.

What stock does one pick for growth? Look at a new company that you feel will grow or an established company that might change due, perhaps, to deregulation, new products, or increased demand by one group of people for its product (more babies, more older people, etc.). If you want safety, go for safety. If you want dividends, go for dividends. But if you want growth, don't ask for safety or anything but scant dividends. You can hardly expect to eat your pickle and have it too!

How can you be sure a growth company will grow? You can't. Neither can all the brokers, chartists, or technical analysts from here to Bombay! If they could they'd all be rich rather than the working stiffs that they are.

This does not mean you shouldn't risk a certain amount of your capital. Figure out what you can tolerate to lose and go for growth, because that's one good way to capital appreciation.

Look at the world of the eighties and you'll see a growing demand for the earth's goodies, those disappearing supplies under the earth of gas, oil, coal, minerals. Look at the earth and a growing population that needs food and drugs, transportation and services. Look at what grows out of the earth that is limited. Look at the oceans and their potential harvests. Look at the high tech (technology) stock and then bet on who'll make synthetic fuel first or come up with a breakthrough in the computer world. These are probably the best bets for the 1980s.

Hedge Your Bets

Most people buy stock and forget it. I even had one client who came to me with $80,000 worth of stock in a brown paper bag. The stock and the bag had been given her by her grandmother!

When you buy a stock you should decide how far down you'll ride it before you sell and how far up it should go before you take some profits. In personal relationships, there is a moment when you say, "I never want to see you again" or "I like you, let's have dinner." This is also true in the marketplace.

After you've decided when you want to stop losing (for me, I never let a stock lose more than 15 percent of what I paid for it—stock bought at $10 per share is dumped when it goes down to $8.50!) and when you want to take your profit, then you have two more choices.

1. You can spend all day at your broker's office watching the market on his electronic board and selling or buying when you've reached your goal, or

2. You can give your broker an order.

There are several types of orders that you can leave with your broker: a market order, a limit order, a good-till-cancelled order, a stop order.

A market order is just that! Buy or sell at market, right now, hurry up, and chop chop! You own one hundred shares of M&M and they are selling at $10 each, so you think you'll get $1,000 from the sale. It may not work that way. Other people who own M&M are also buying and selling, and it's first come first served. By the time your order is executed the price may have changed. Your order will then be sold at the new price. If M&M, Inc. has a lot of stock that is traded frequently, you'll find the price you get is often lower or higher than you expected.

When I feel I should sell, the feeling comes from nerves deep down in my gut. My hands begin to shake and my voice gets one octave higher. I want out! One-half or one-quarter of a point doesn't make any difference to me, because I'm not a big stockholder. If I'm selling, I'm selling for a reason that makes sense to me. I'm a sell-at-market fan! Most professionals will disagree with my emotional approach, but there isn't a market tool better for me than my gut feeling. I also buy at market for the same reason.

You can tell your broker an exact price that you wish to get when you sell or pay when you buy, but this means you may sit around quite a while before you can buy or sell what you want. Therefore, a *limit order* is a good idea. You tell your broker your outside limit, and then he can negotiate around that. A limit order really says I'm willing to pay between $10 and $10.50 for M&M, Inc. or I'm willing to sell M&M Inc. for between $10 and $9.50, if that's the best you can get for me. The broker will try to get your price, but again, it's always possible he or she will get less on a sale or pay more on a buy because of the orders ahead of you and the movement of the stock. The higher the price of a stock, the more leeway you must give your broker. However, always be specific. If you are new in the market, follow suggestions from your broker about reasonable limits to be set. As you gain experience it will become easier to count on yourself.

A good-till-cancelled order is a buy or sell order that remains in effect till you cancel or the order is executed, whichever comes first. This is another useful device, but not to be used by people with short memories. You'll be sorry if your broker calls in six months to say you've just bought $5,000 worth of Crippled Creek Hooch at $25 a share. You *were* in a gambling mood when you placed a good-till-cancelled order six months ago, but you might not be feeling that way now.

A stop order is given to buy a stock at a set price above its current market value or sell at a set price below its value. This is like an insurance policy. The stock you want can't go too high without the stop order working to get it for you. The stock you want to sell, at some point, can't fall too far before your stop order triggers a sale. This is very useful if you are back-packing in the woods. A stop order is usually used for short sales, which we'll deal with later.

When you buy a stock, you must pay for it within five working days. If you sell, you must deliver your stock within five working days. Many people prefer to keep their stock at the brokerage house, where it is held in the name of the broker. This is called "holding your stock in street name." Others keep their certificates in a bank vault or a brown paper bag! I recommend holding your own certificates in a safe deposit box—it's safer. If you lose stock certificates, they can be reissued, but the rigamarole is so time-consuming and painful, the correspondence so vast and slow, the lesson so painfully learned, that no one will do so twice.

Widows and Orphans Stocks—Watch Out!

There are certain stocks that traditionally have been sold to widows and orphans. What does a fifty-six-year-old woman have in common with a seven-year-old orphan? Nothing at all, actually, but both are *perceived* as needing protection.

Lawyers, CPAs, and stockbrokers are usually male, and when asked for investment advice by widows or divorcees are usually ultra-conservative. This conservatism can stem from a desire to protect women in a nice masculine way or from a desire to cover their own professional asses—probably both.

After all, if they give advice that is speculative and that advice turns sour, they are liable to be sued! And courts tend to rule in favor of the poor widow lady, since the professional is considered knowledgeable and should have known better.

The way out of this dilemma for gun-shy pros has been to put women without a husband to protect them into the safest possible investments. So what if they're terrible? They *are* safe and conservative, and no court would fault the advisers.

The stock groups that are usually picked are utilities and blue chips. The utilities are indeed safe, but their earnings have been below what bank passbook accounts pay, and you know how awful that is. Utilities have not grown much, so besides paying meager dividends they offer almost no chance of capital accumulation. Utility companies are big borrowers, and during periods of high inflation with high interest rates these companies suffer. If interest rates come down, utilities *could* become a good buy again. (Utilities stocks have received advantageous tax treatment and under the new tax laws they have made them much more attractive than in the past! They are also paying higher dividends and deserve to be watched.) We will always need power, and the utilities will probably always pay their dividends, unless something dreadful happens.

Nothing, not even utilities, is ever without some risk. My

mother had stock in General Public Utilities, the company that owns Three Mile Island. When the nuclear generator leaked at Three Mile Island, so did the stock. By the time she sold she had lost 75 percent of her investment. All the utilities suffered from this ghastly accident, even those that had no nuclear holdings.

Blue chips are very expensive, with a high p/e ratio. These companies have already done their growing, and so future growth will be very slow. They provide only a small return on invested capital and have poor growth potential.

Only brothers seem to give their widowed or single sisters worse advice than some professionals! In my business, I've run across some really weird ideas. Inevitably I find my client's *brother* suggested this weird idea. I have no notion why brothers give consistently awful advice nor why women trust their brothers' advice so blindly. Of course, my own brother, Jeremy, is wise and has my best interests at heart. I'd *always* listen to him—he's different. Do you think that herein lies the trap?

EVALUATING STOCKS

How to Read the Financial Page of Your Paper

The front section of your daily paper contains news stories that move the market. The business section reports on how the market moved. The news section is read and digested by people in the market trying to understand how the politics of today will affect the economy of tomorrow. News makes the market, and the market consists of people reacting to the news.

Sports lovers *never* miss reading the daily sports section of the paper, and stock market followers *never* miss the financial news. The business section of your paper will give you all the news that happened yesterday. In it you'll find where your stock opened and closed and if it lost or gained in price.

Stocks are not listed by their proper names but by an abbreviated code that doesn't necessarily make sense. Fremont General Corp., an over-the-counter stock, has the code of FRMT. When you buy a stock, remember to ask your broker the code so you can follow it in the paper. Each stock is listed under the market it trades on: New York Stock Exchange, American, or NASDAQ (Over-the-Counter).

DAILY NEWSPAPER STOCK TABLES

NEW YORK COMPOSITE TRANSACTION									DATE (DAY, MONTH & DATE, YEAR)		
12-Month		Stock	Div.	Yld.	P/E	Sales (in 100s)	High	Low	Close	Net Chg.
High	Low										
30-1/2	21-1/8	ConEd.	2.96	9.9	6	z457	30-1/8	30	30	-1/8
100	68-3/8	ConEd.pf	6	6.2	1	1	97-1/8	97-1/8	97-1/8	+1/8
50-3/4	33-1/2	LeviSt	1.65	4.3	8	289	38-1/8	38-3/8	38-1/2	-1/4
91-1/2	42-3/8	StdOOh	2.40	4.5	7	1563	53-1/2	52-3/8	53-1/8	+5/8

High and Low (12-Month): Highest and lowest price paid per share for the year to date.

EX: Levi Strauss reached a high of $50.75 and a low of $33.50 per share this year.

Stock: Name of common stock in abbreviated form. Notation of pf after the stock name designates it as preferred stock. CVpf means convertible preferred. Each stock has its own fixed abbreviation. EX: LeviSt is Levi Strauss Company and StdOOh is Standard Oil of Ohio.

Dividend (Div.): The rate of annual dividend for a share of stock based on estimates from previous quarterly payments. EX: ConEd pays $2.96 in dividends per share of stock.

Yield (Yld.): Percentage of return per-year. Found by dividing the current price of a share of stock into the current annual dividend rate per share. Ex: StdOOh − 2.40 (Div.) ÷ 53.125 (closing price) = 4.5% yield.

Price/Earnings Ratio (P/E): Price of one share of stock is divided by the earnings per share for a twelve-month period.

Sales (in 100s): Total number of shares traded during the day. Does not include odd lot shares. Letter z in front of this number indicates it is the actual amount of shares traded. EX: ConEd traded exactly 457,000 shares for this date.

High and Low: Highest and lowest price per share of stock for the day.

Close: Last price of a share of stock for the day.

Net Change (Net Chg.): Difference between closing price today and yesterday.

Note—Warrant (WT): The letters WT following a common stock name stands for warrant. This keeps securities at a set price for set time as an inducement for investors.

Note—ConEd is Consolidated Edison, LeviSt is Levi Strauss, StdOOh is Standard Oil of Ohio

Your business section will give you yesterday's Dow Jones industrial average, the high and low the industrial reached, and the closing figure. It also gives the volume of the entire market, which is the number of shares traded during the day.

Volume is fascinating to watch. If I saw nothing else in the paper but the volume, I could make a good guess about the front page. If the volume was thin (not much activity), I'd know that nothing dramatic had happened in the world. When something big happens—an election, war or peace, unrest in a foreign country, famine or flood, or a change in the prime rate—the volume of shares traded is heavy. Thin at this time would be less than thirty-five million shares, moderate is between thirty-five million and forty-seven million, and more than fifty million is heavy. The biggest day in the history of the market was more than ninety million shares. This was in reaction to advice to investors from Joe Granville, famous market analyst and tipster, to pull out of the market before it collapsed!

Your business section will also print any changes in regulations. My morning paper has a headline saying, "High Court Eases Rules on Mutual Funds." This news is very good for banks and could affect bank stocks. There are a couple of stories on mergers and takeovers. Mergers are effected when one company becomes part of another company, a marriage of two firms. Takeovers are an attempt by a company or an individual to buy out an unwilling firm, and is considered rape by the unwilling party. But if the price is right, it may end in a merger. Takeovers are usually nice for stockholders as the company trying to take over will offer stockholders a fat profit for their vote. Rumors of a takeover bid usually send a stock way up. If the rumor is fake or the takeover fails, the stock zaps down.

The paper also has information on durable goods. They dropped last month by 2.2 percent, while transportation equipment orders fell by 7.2 percent. The Department of Commerce attributes this to problems in the auto and shipbuilding industries. If you own stock in these industries, it might be affected by this news. You may also conclude from this news that there is more trouble ahead for the economy in general because bad news tends to generate a ripple effect on the whole economy.

When newspapers attribute the fall or rise in the Dow Jones to high interest rates, they are only giving their best guess. You and I know that the fall of the Dow Jones is because more people are selling than buying and thus driving prices down. When the Dow Jones goes up, more people are buying stock than selling and thus driving prices up. People buy or sell on their emotions and perceptions, and that's what makes the Dow Jones go up or down!

If you find your paper is not adequate for you, subscribe to *The Wall Street Journal*. Not only does it have all the financial news, but it also provides excellent coverage of all news. If you make a serious investment in the market, *The Wall Street Journal* is a must! (It's also tax deductible.)

Price/Earnings Ratio

A tool used to evaluate a stock is the price/earnings ratio. The P/E ratio shows you the price of the stock in relation to the earnings of the stock. For example, Hot Air, Inc. is selling for $50 per share and its annual earnings per share are $10. $50 ÷ $10 = 5. Hot Air has a P/E ratio of five—it is selling for five times its earnings. If Hot Air has other things going for it, it's a good buy.

Some of Wall Street's sages say never buy any stock with a P/E ratio of more than seven. Other sages have given advice at one time or another to buy stocks with a P/E of sixty-five or even a crazy ninety-two. Sony P/E was ninety-two in 1972, during its peak growth period, and fell to seventeen in 1980. Walt Disney was seventy-six in 1972 and eleven in 1980.

People have made and lost money on stocks with P/E ratios ranging from as low as seven to as high as ninety-two. Sometimes Wall Street's sages are right and sometimes they're wrong. P/E ratios are only clues to stock values. The economy and the perceptions of the investing population are the true determinants of stock market behavior.

Company Earnings vs. Dividends

Earnings of a company have little or no direct relationship to dividends. Let's look back at Moneywise, Inc. as it grows. For the first few years of the company's life, all profit was plowed back into the company to buy computers, to pay for more consultants, and to buy the office building we had been renting. At our annual stockholders' meeting, we decided to keep the profit to expand the business rather than pay out dividends. So, while our profits increased every year, we paid out *no dividends*. When we became listed on the stock exchange (remember this is fantasy), we knew we had to show some dividend payments or nobody would buy. So here's the rub. We, as a business, had been solely interested in growth. Now we needed money from investors to expand, and so must pay out profits in order to attract buyers.

Many companies with bad earnings or even a loss will continue to pay dividends. Some companies will dip into reserves to do this or perhaps sell off assets. Remember, then, you can't judge a company solely by its dividends!

The Company Report: Fact or Fiction?

When you're evaluating a stock for income or capital accumulation, you should briefly check the company's annual report. It looks like a magazine, glossy and multi-colored. It has excellent graphic designs, but unless you're a CPA it's not going to mean too much. The company's president has a message to the stockholders in the front of the report, and the message is always cheerful. Example: "Even though nobody bought our cars this year, next year promises to be a banner year for U.S. autos because," etc. The bad news is on the last pages, which show earnings, profit and loss, assets, liabilities, and so on. Unless you know how the company manages its books, its annual report is only worth a glance because it's too damned technical and may contain more fantasy than fact. Only stockbrokers who follow that particular stock closely can perhaps make some sense out of it. Remember your broker is a salesman *not* a math whiz. Neither he nor she is *an insider* in a business with insider information! Your glance is really only a gesture, but in good conscience you must glance!

If there were any perfect tools for the lay person to use when buying stock, we'd all be winners in the market. All one can really do is better the odds in this biggest of all crap games.

Prophets, Chartists, Technical Analysts, Tips, and Tipsters

There are as many stock market theories as there are child-rearing theories. They're interesting and diverse. However, most only stand up for a day or two! Sophisticated stockbrokers don't bother with these theories, and neither should you.

Prophets prophesize the future, while chartists chart the past history of stocks looking for mystical configurations that foretell the future. Technical analysts practice an art rather than a science. Tips from tipsters work well if everybody believes them, but if people don't believe, if people *really* don't believe, like Tinkerbell, they die.

There is too much information available each day for anyone to absorb. All this information and news affects the stock market. A war, a drought, a frost in Florida, a change of government in Iran, a rumor that a world leader is sick—the market will react to these events sometimes by going up and sometimes by going down.

Let's pretend that a world leader in an unstable country is rumored to have cancer. You know that a popular Communist leader is in the wings waiting to take over. You also know that a neighboring state is ready to go in to prevent this from happening. Pineapples are the major cash crop of this trouble spot, so you naturally figure pineapple juice is going to be scarce during the coming trouble. If pineapple juice is scarce it's bound to go up in price, so a major pineapple juice company is the place to put a wise buck. You've reached the right conclusion! But it won't do you any good unless other people agree with you! If they have reached a different conclusion, the market will move with them because the market moves with the majority.

Technical analysts say the price of a stock is determined, not by the financial performance of the company, but rather by how strong the demand is for its stock. Simple. If a lot of people want a stock, the price of that stock will rise.

Tips are inside information. Just as we are all equal in the eyes of God, so are we all supposed to have equal information when we buy or sell stock. Nobody is to have the inside track, and the Securities and Exchange Commission (SEC) has the job of enforcing this law. Your broker is never supposed to give you inside (not public) information to induce you to buy or sell stock. This works pretty well for small buyers, because they don't deal with the kind of brokers that would have inside information.

For example, let's look at large bankers who do business with huge companies. If the company wants a loan, the banker gets a look at its books. If a company wants an extension on a loan, the banker will find out the reason. If a company is having trouble or doing very well, the banker will know long before you do. Although banks can't take a position on stock, except for bank stocks, bankers *can*. When a banker starts to unload a stock because of bad news, or to buy because of good, the banker's broker has some interesting inside information, and so do his favorite customers *and* all of his favorite relatives.

The Weysong theory of stock analysis is based completely on insider buying and selling. Weysong uses a federal report called *Official Securities Transactions,* and follows the buying and selling of company insiders. When six or more insiders buy over a period of a month or so, the stock is recommended. When at least four insiders sell, it is a signal for other stockholders also to sell.

Major scandals involving illegal inside trading and the sale of inside information have come to light over the last few years. With cutbacks in SEC regulations and reduction in the numbers of SEC enforcement officials, illegal manipulation of the market is likely to increase.

Well, so much for being equal! When we trade stock we're playing with the big boys and girls. Believe me, by the time you figure out it's time to go home, they've long ago left the playground.

Does this mean that you should not be in the market? No! It *does* mean you should avoid the chic and the trendy. Don't buy wow-wow stocks. By the time you hear what you should buy, the big kids are already selling and taking the profits. The rich may get richer, but don't let it be on your money!

OTHER WAYS TO PLAY

Foreign Investments

Many Americans have become interested in investing overseas. Almost every major stock brokerage firm has a foreign investment division. My favorite the most glamorous name is Drexel, Burnham, Lambert's Global Management Division. One hundred years from now we may have Intergalactic Management where your piece of the rock may be on Pluto!

In the 1980s, the most popular foreign areas of investment are: Japan for its computers, Australia for its oil and vast untapped supplies of natural resources, England for its oil, and West Germany for its stable productive capacity. France used to be popular for investing until the election of the current Socialist government, now busily nationalizing banks and basic industry. Nationalizing may solve France's economic problems, but it's terrible for American investors who need profit to thrive.

France and Mexico are examples of the dangers of foreign investing. Political unrest, economic instability, devaluation of currency, and high overseas inflation rates are all risks to be faced when buying overseas. We face some of these same risks in the United States, but we're part and parcel of our country's changes and so are better able to evaluate them.

We are also familiar with U.S. products. We may not know if General Foods stock is going up or down, but we *do* know it'll be here tomorrow. If GF comes out with new no-cal fudge brownies, you can probably go with your hunch that this will be a big seller. As a woman, you have a vast subliminal knowledge of local markets and local products. But what do you know about products in West Germany?

The United States attracts a great deal of foreign money because it is considered the most politically stable country in the world. Many Europeans are willing to trade off potentially higher profits in their own country for the stability in this country.

Only relatively sophisticated investors should put their money in foreign stocks. There's a good profit to be made abroad, and it's an area of investment worth serious consideration as you become familiar with markets in general. If you do feel the time is right to invest abroad, be sure to go to a large brokerage firm and deal with brokers with specialized knowledge in the area of foreign investments.

Mutual Funds

Another way of sharing the risks and rewards of investing is through mutual funds. These funds grew up with the same goal as investment clubs: Get a group of people together and pool your dough. (See Chapter 1 for how to set up an investment club.) Because mutual funds are so big, your money is spread into many groups of stocks giving you diversification. Diversification is one of the best hedges against serious loss.

For example, if all your money is in M&M and the stock goes down, that's big trouble. If you are in four or five stocks and one goes down, that's only little trouble. By investing in mutual funds, you spread the risk.

Mutual funds did very poorly in the mid-seventies, and many people were hurt. The funds had started out in the sixties with heavy investment in highly speculative stock. When the bad market of the early seventies hit, they got clobbered. Fortunately, they've seen the error of their ways, reformed, and are doing quite well now.

There are different types of funds for people with different objectives. There are growth funds and high dividend funds and funds that are a mixture of both. There are specialized funds that invest in only one industry. This strikes me as crazy, because then you would have all your eggs in one basket.

There are load funds (you pay to get in) and no-load funds (you pay a small sum each year to cover operating costs). The important thing when you invest in a fund is to be sure that its goal is the same as yours. Also, check its past performance to be sure it's a profitable fund.

There are certain giant funds, like the Templeton Fund or the Dreyfus Fund, that are headed by financial wizards. They are dependent on their wizards, and as long as the wizards are around the fund leads the market. These have been good places to put money, but no one can guarantee the future.

Investing in a mutual fund is the most passive form of ownership the market offers. However, if you have only a little knowledge and neither the time nor the inclination to follow individual stocks closely, this just might be the ticket for you.

You should ask your broker for the stock guide put out by Standard & Poor's. Here you can find detailed information about some of the funds and their objectives. *Barron's National Business and Financial Weekly* publishes *Quarterly Mutual Fund Records*. Back issues can be found in the library.

The no-load funds are sold directly by the fund and not through a broker. So don't ask your broker about them, because he can hardly be objective!

Mutual funds can also be a good first step in investing. After you've been in the funds a while, if you want to fly on your own you'll have some background in the ups and downs of the market. Mutual funds also give the small investor a chance to get in the market bit by bit without having to pay extra commission for buying odd lots—three shares here or four shares there.

The major drawback of mutual funds seems to be that like

the dinosaur, they are slow to move. If the market is poor, they cannot unload their stocks and get into other money instruments because they are basically committed to the market.

There is one way out of this. That is to find front-end load funds that permit you to switch from one kind of fund to another within the fund *family* without commission. The fund family is a number of funds under the same management. Your broker will be able to discuss with you the performance and management of the different family funds. For the average investor, I think this is the very best route.

Buying on Margin

There is more than one way to buy a stock. If you are a new investor or a conservative investor, stay away from the methods described now. Actually, I am uncomfortable with some of the fancy footwork involved in alternative ways of playing the market.

Buying on margin, however, does not make me uncomfortable because it is simple leverage—I'm using other people's money again! Buying on margin differs from buying with cash in that at least part of your transaction is done with money or securities *borrowed* from your broker. Naturally you must give your broker some collateral. The Federal Reserve Board specifies the maximum amount you can borrow, and your broker will charge you interest just like a bank.

Before 1934 you could buy stock with a tiny down payment. That's really what margin is, a down payment. This allowed people to overleverage; and when the crash came in 1929, this practice brought disaster to thousands and thousands of investors. In 1934 the rules of the market were changed so that the market could never again crash as spectacularly as it did in 1929.

Margin requirements change with the Federal Reserve policy. The Federal Reserve acts in what it perceives to be the best national interest. In times of recession, margin requirements will be lower to stimulate the market (you can borrow more). If things get overheated in the market, margin requirements will go up (you can borrow less).

For example, let's say you bought 2,000 shares of M&M for $20,000 in 1978. By 1980 your investment was worth $40,000, a gain of 100 percent. Now let's buy the same thing on margin. Instead of putting up $20,000, you only put up $13,000 and borrow $7,000 from your broker. When you sell the stock at the end of 1980 for $40,000 and repay your broker the $7,000 you borrowed, you will have grossed $33,000 on a $13,000 investment, or a gain of 246 percent. You will have paid your broker interest of over $2,000. But, so what!

Things unfortunately can also go the other way. If the stock goes down, you would lose part of your $20,000 and owe the broker $7,000 *plus* interest. Ouch!

When the stock you bought on margin goes down, you will get a margin call. This is a request from your broker for more cash or securities because your equity (ownership) in your margin account has fallen below the minimum standard set by the stock exchange or by your brokerage house.

I remember being on margin and getting margin calls. They came as mail-a-grams in white envelopes with blue lettering. I was a poor candidate for being on margin when I didn't have the money to support my habit. So, when I got my mail-a-gram I had to sell. Since the stock was down, I also had to take a loss. I had been right to think the stock would go up eventually, but I had been wrong to think I could afford to be on margin. One woman leveraged is another woman overleveraged!

Selling Short

Selling short, or shorting the market, is done when you believe a stock is going down. You plan to take your profit, not from a rise in the price of a stock, but from a fall in price.

Just as you borrow money to buy stock on margin (going up, please), so you borrow stock from your broker to go short. You decide M&M is going down, so you borrow one hundred shares from your broker and *sell* them for $3,000. A year later you can buy one hundred shares of M&M for $1,500. The difference between what you sold the borrowed stock for ($3,000) and what you had to pay for the stock ($1,500) to repay the broker is your profit. In order to do this, you must have collateral with the broker for the value of the borrowed stock and you must pay interest on what you borrowed.

There are two problems with selling short. The first and most obvious is the stock can go *up*. That means that at some future time you will have to buy it at a higher price in order

to deliver it. For example, you may have to pay $4,000 to buy
M&M and then deliver it to your broker to cover the stock
you sold at $3,000—not so good. In theory, your loss is infinite
till you cover (buy the stock). The stock you've shorted can go
up and up and up. If you are long in the market you can only
lose what you put in, but if you're short you can lose much
more.

There is a second problem, which is psychological. The
average person is optimistic when buying stock and enjoys
the idea of it going up. It's hard to stay short, and good
brokers will tell you so.

My first husband and I went short on a stock years ago
because we had some inside information. A friend of ours,
the daughter of the chairman of the board of a national
company, told us that her father's firm was losing money and
the annual report would show discouraging news. We shorted
the stock, and it went down like a little darling as soon as the
annual report came out. We stayed short as long as we could
tolerate it psychologically, and then took our profits. We
could have made more, but it was too hard to maintain a
short position.

I think shorting is best left to the pros and to investors who
can afford a big risk.

Commodities

The commodities market is for speculators who bet on the
future cost of anything from interest rates to pork bellies.
They place their bets by writing contracts and trading them.
Jane Bryant Quinn wrote, "The main job of individuals in the
futures market (commodities) is to lose money to professionals. One common estimate is that 74 percent of individual
trades result in losses."

If you want to know how to bet in the commodities market,
find a book on the subject because I won't explain it to you.
You can get better odds at the tables in Monaco or Kowloon,
while enjoying a foreign climate and widening your horizons!

Options

An option is the right to buy (call) or sell (put) a fixed
amount of a given stock at a specified price within a limited
amount of time. The person buying a call is hoping the stock will
go up, the person buying a put is hoping the stock will go down.

This is done by writing a contract that costs only a small amount of money. The stock must move enough to cover the cost of the contract, the broker commission, and various fees that must be paid to exercise the contract. If you don't exercise a contract because the market hasn't moved or because it moved in the opposite direction, the price paid for the option is a dead loss.

As I've said, a call is a hope that the stock will go up, a put is like shorting the market in the hopes it will go down. Writing a call can be a useful investment tool, but to me a put is just a bet and again is best left to the pros.

Writing a call option on stock you own can increase your return on that stock. Only some stocks have options, and for this example let's pretend M&M is one of them. You bought 500 shares of M&M a year ago, for which you paid $10 a share. M&M is a growth stock and pays no dividend, but it's worth $20 a share today. You decide you want some money out of your M&M stock so you have your broker write five option contracts on your M&M stock. Your contract says that you will sell your M&M stock to the person who buys your contract (calls) in six months for $25 a share. The person who buys your contract believes M&M will be well above $25 a share, so he's happy to pay you a premium to have the right to buy at this figure. Your call is out of the money, that is, at higher than present market value.

The premium for M&M is four points for each option. Each point represents $100, so four points is $400 × 5 options, or $2,000 in your pocket, no matter what happens. Now if M&M doesn't go to $25 a share in six months the person who bought your call will let it expire and not buy from you. If, however, M&M has moved nicely and is at $30 a share, you will have to deliver it at the contracted price of $25 per share.

Options are for short periods, three, six, or nine months. They are only written in multiples of five, that is, the call can only be written for $5 (or $10 or $15) above market. The premium, however, can be for any amount the market will bear.

Most options are written on growth stocks, because they have the potential of real movement. American Telephone and Telegraph, Xerox, or the large blue chip stocks just don't move that much or that fast.

Last-Minute Tips

1. Buy on the rumor, sell on the news. The market goes up on *rumors* of good news. And by the time the news is actually out it has already been discounted, and the market tends to go down.

2. By the time you get a hot tip, it will probably burn. When you get a tip, it's very old news to the big investor. If you buy along with all the others who got the tip, the pros will already be selling.

3. Don't fall in love with a stock, get a dog instead. You should buy or sell using judgment as well as your gut feelings.

4. A glamour stock that every broker says to buy, is almost always overpriced.

5. Avoid the chic and fad industries. Chic and fads fade quickly. Look what happened to bellbottom trousers and the Edsel!

6. Avoid new ventures. Ninety percent of new businesses go bankrupt.

7. Avoid high-priced growth stocks. They've probably reached their full size and are too expensive.

8. Avoid heavy industry blue chips. They are too tied into the business cycles. People will always have to eat, but U.S. Steel can be killed by foreign competition.

9. Avoid fancy footwork! Don't buy options, except calls. Don't buy commodities. These offer no growth potential, have very high transaction costs, and are very risky.

10. Don't buy something because a technical analyst says so. In my opinion, they're great on history but they can't really predict anything.

11. Never try to get the last dollar when selling. Nobody can guess what the top dollar will be; and if you ever do guess right, it's just luck and not genius. Remember, bears make money, bulls make money, and pigs get eaten—pigs try for the last dollar.

12. Practice the golden rule of finance: Know thyself! Nobody can be as interested in you and your welfare as you. Know what you want from an investment, and find the best possible people to work with you.

STOCK MARKET INVESTMENTS ANALYSIS

1. Cash needed for investment. Anywhere from $20 to millions.

2. Risk. Growth stocks are more risky than established stocks. Dividend stocks have less risk than growth stocks but little chance of capital appreciation. Stocks must be bought wisely by working with a good broker, but you have no control over whether it's a good market or a bad market. Buying well and holding good stock will bring a better return than frequent trading.

3. Return on investment. Good dividend stocks have historically outpaced inflation. Growth stocks may grow or may not grow. Growth stocks will give you little return but may give you capital appreciation.

4. Liquidity. Very liquid. Stocks can be sold, can be borrowed against, or can be used as collateral for loans.

5. Active or passive: *Active* as with all ownership.
                    Less active if in mutual funds.

6. Age. Good for all ages. Younger women should have growth stocks as well as dividend stocks. Older women who are going to retire or women totally dependent on dividends for income should only be invested in good dividend stocks.

8

To Collect or Not to Collect

Picture this scene, if you will. Beautiful furniture in a stately room lit only by magnificent silver candelabras. On the walls hang the Masters, the rich pink flesh tones of Renoir, a rough and virile Christ by Rouault, the stark bisected lines of Mondrian. The seated couple drink wine from glasses of exquisite cut Waterford crystal, the dark woods of their Louis Quinze furniture reflecting the centuries of care given to these rare and beautiful pieces. The muted colors in the priceless Oriental rug are complemented by the Italian leather binding on the first edition books in the glass enclosed cases. Her jewels are classic, creamy pearls with a single pear-shaped diamond fastener, diamond earrings, and one large square-cut sapphire on her long aristocratic fingers.

She is surrounded by the best *things* the world has to offer. Her setting shows taste, appreciation of beauty, and the time and care spent collecting. It also shows money, lots of money!

The rich and powerful have always enjoyed the best goods and services the world has to offer. Traders and crusaders have brought home from the marketplaces of the world the finest and most precious goods they could buy or plunder. The wealthy, the titled, and the Church have been patrons of the arts and custodians of beautiful things for centuries.

Today, most of these treasures are in museums throughout the world for all to enjoy. The art treasures of the world not in museums are owned mostly by the very rich and by corporations, the new patrons of the arts. Because great art, furniture, and jewels are scarce and in demand, they are costly. They will always be costly, because only a few of the world's artists and artisans turn out timeless objects of beauty.

Collectibles—Love Them and Leave Them

The collecting of beautiful objects satisfies both the eye and the spirit. However, only when all creature comforts have been satisfied can money be diverted to beauty.

I am a lover of collectibles. My home is full of as many as I can afford, and my daughters have been collecting for years. I'm fond of jewelry, and treasure the pieces I've bought for myself as well as those sentimental things I've received as gifts. I love looking around at those objects that came from my parents' home, were part of my childhood, and are now part of my adult life. There is a wonderful sense of continuity in my home that is starkly absent in the outside urban environment.

When I die, if my children like the things I've collected they will integrate them into their homes. If they don't care for them they will sell them, auction them, or give them away to charity. I doubt very much if they'll get much money for them. I can't afford the best, the rarest, the one of a kind, so there won't be much of a market for what I've collected. But I've loved and enjoyed my things, so they haven't been a bad investment after all!

Unless you are very wealthy, the joy of owning beautiful things and passing them on to loved ones is the best you can hope for when collecting. As financial investments, collectibles are risky and the return on them is usually negative.

COLLECTING—A POOR INVESTMENT STRATEGY

Sterile Assets

Collectibles have been touted as an investment hedge against inflation. If the world isn't producing any more of an item, then the theory is that there's only one way for the price to go—up! Well, as we shall see, that ain't necessarily so!

All collectibles are sterile assets. This means that they do not produce any income nor do they provide a tax shelter. The money you have tied up in sterile assets could be working for you elsewhere. And with today's high interest rates, collecting for investment purposes is a losing proposition. For example, your silver set for twelve may be worth $6,000. That money could bring you a return of about $900 a year if placed in a money market fund or time deposit account.

Unless you love what you've collected very much, you'd be wiser to put that money out to work.

The ever-increasing cost of insuring collectibles against fire, theft, and catastrophe is high and must be figured in as part of a collectible's maintenance costs. Expenses for storage in a safe deposit box or vault and preservation of furniture, art, or furs are also figured into investment costs. All of these costs, hidden or obvious, must be considered when you sell, before you can know whether you've made a profit on a given item.

Wheelers and Dealers

Another problem with using collectibles as a form of investment is that of finding a reputable dealer. This can be as frustrating as finding a needle in a haystack. Check with the giants: Sotheby, Parke, Bernet, or Tiffany. These are the largest, most reputable, and, surprisingly, often the cheapest.

Beware of media scams touting the glories of particular limited edition items, such as plates, glassware, and coins. These unscrupulous outfits limit their editions to the exact number of orders they receive! The resale value of these collectibles is usually *less* than what you paid for it—if you are able to sell them at all!

I Can Get It for You Retail

When you buy a collectible (a silver set, some wonderful etching, or a fine old piece of furniture), you're most likely to buy this at a retail price from a reputable dealer. If you know enough about art or antiques, you might buy at auctions. In any and all cases, you will be buying *retail*. When you or your heirs sell, you will sell at wholesale prices. This means that in order to realize a profit, what you sell must have appreciated enough to equal the original purchase price plus upkeep, insurance, and the ravages of inflation. If you bought something for $100 in 1972 and sell it in 1985 for $150, you've lost money because the purchasing power of the dollar you receive in 1985 is much lower than the dollar paid out in 1972.

This means that when you come to sell, you can only hope that your collectibles will be still in vogue, still in demand, and able to command top dollar. The finest, the very best, the flawless, the complete collection, the one of a kind, the masters' signature pieces are the only ones that can bring real money. The good or the second best will not. In the case of collectibles as an investment, the best is the enemy of the good.

To Market, to Market

Another serious problem with collectibles is that the market is basically disorganized. If you live in a small town or small city, you may have a difficult time finding a dealer who specializes in buying what you collect. You will have to ship your collectibles to a large city if you want them to be auctioned off. To make such arrangements is costly and time consuming.

As with all markets, timing is everything. If you must sell something to raise cash fast, you can almost bet that the market will be awful at that moment. It's an unspoken rule, like the one that says the bread will always fall jam side down.

NOTHING BUT THE BEST

The Complete Collection

My sister collects beautiful little silver boxes. She loves them for their workmanship and luster. They are in her home to be touched, admired, and loved. They also add to the charm of the decor. Each one has a story: "This one was bought on my last trip to England in a little shop in New Bond Street. That one was designed by, . . ." etc.

There is no doubt that the boxes have appreciated in value. Each box is by a master silversmith. Each box is a period piece. Each box is the finest of its kind. Each is rare. They are a collection of the *same* type of objects and, as such, would be worth more than a collection of different types of items.

Complete or carefully edited collections, such as all first issue Israeli stamps, political buttons, or nineteenth century Amish quilts, are as valuable as the one-of-a-kind collectible. If these types of collections are for sale, they need very special buyers, people interested in very special things. Very special people can be hard to find, and they make a very narrow market.

Furniture

Only the very finest furniture in the best shape will bring money when sold. All other furniture, no matter how attractive, is considered secondhand junk.

Furniture that has been in the family for generations is not necessarily antique just because it's old. There are many good books in the library on antique furniture from France, Italy, and England. Other books will tell you about the beautifully crafted furniture made in America.

Silver Flatware

Silver has become extremely costly to buy. You have to be very fond of a bride to even think of giving her a gift of silver. One teaspoon can run well over $50.00. Selling it is quite a different story. Unless the silver is old, of high quality, from Germany, France, or Holland, and made in the fifteenth, sixteenth, or seventeenth centuries, it is probably only worth the weight of the silver itself. The names Tiffany or Jensen or the description "Georgian" pale in significance when the silver is bought by dealers only by the weight of the metal.

Silver flatware can be handed down from generation to generation. Its beauty and *sentimental* value increase with time. It is *not*, however, a good investment.

Stamps and Coins

Only the best and the rarest stamps and coins will appreciate. Also, there is more value to those collectibles if you have a complete collection. An example would be the first issue of each stamp printed by the government of Monaco. Individual stamps and coins can be traded through stamp and coin clubs, but single items are usually worth little or nothing. There are always stories of an extremely rare stamp or coin that brings a fortune at auctions. Winners of the Irish sweepstakes are also given much publicity. In both cases, it's big news because it is so unusual.

It takes time and money to build a stamp or coin collection. People who collect coins or stamps as a hobby have great fun, but they do not consider it a financial investment. It's just as well they don't, because it isn't. Rare stamps have some portable value, but they cost a lot to buy and it's hard to find a good market for them when you want to sell. Again, beware of ads from private mints selling coins or special commemorative limited issues of coins and stamps. Remember, they issue exactly as many as they can sell.

Furs

The minute you put on your new fur coat it becomes a secondhand garment. The only market for it is a store that sells old clothes. Wear it, have it warm you, look glamorous in it, enjoy it. Its only real investment value is pleasure. Remember some of the best investments in life produce no income. Do not confuse emotional investments with financial investments. Most of the very best things in life never pay off—in money!

Art

Buy the best artists and then only their major works, because only these will appreciate regularly and substantially. The masters of the past are well known today, and their works are terribly expensive. There is a fortune to be made if you can spot the masters of the future and buy their paintings now before they've been discovered. There are a few people who will indeed make money this way. But these future richies are not psychic, they're just people who are buying paintings by young artists, paintings they love and want to live with. Only a handful of these artists will be the greats of our time. The odds are terrible if you invest with the hope you're picking a new Picasso. Buy what you love and enjoy yourself. If your art appreciates, it will be an extra bonus.

Only the very rich can buy originals of the masters of the past. If you covet a Breughel, a Vallotton, or a Matisse, there are wonderful posters of their works. My home is full of posters, and I feel surrounded by works I love but could never afford. I also have unimportant paintings that are very important to me.

If some of my unimportant pictures *were* to appreciate, and I wished to sell at an auction, the commission would run between 10 percent and 25 percent. If I sell to a dealer, he will buy them at 35 percent to 50 percent below the current retail price. In both cases, any profit will be diminished by these fees.

DIAMONDS AND JEWELS

Excellent quality diamonds and colored stones such as rubies, sapphires, and emeralds, have appreciated very well over the last fifteen years. Remember, the usual two caveats apply in the case of jewels, as in all other purchases of collectibles as investment:

1. You must buy at retail and sell at wholesale prices.
2. You should buy *only* from the most reputable dealer.

If you buy jewels for investment, buy only the stone. The setting may be beautiful and most certainly expensive, but when you come to sell it's only the stone that has any value.

There are two types of diamonds, jewelry grade and investment grade. The investment grade is flawless and is used in some very expensive jewelry. Investment grade diamonds are scored by clarity, color and cut. A one-carat stone of either grade sells for between $2,000 and $35,000 wholesale. The difference in price depends on the clarity, color and cut of the stone. If you are buying for investment rather than pleasure, buy *only* investment grade stones.

However, the smallest investment grade diamond now would be about $2,500. This sum would buy a ½-carat diamond of the least desirable investment grade.

Diamonds are only valuable because we all agree they are. Some diamonds are more valuable than others because we all agree that a diamond that is colorless and flawless is worth more than a diamond that is yellow with a flaw. But let's face it, what's so glorious about a colorless, sparkling stone?

The Gemological Institute of America (GIA) is a nonprofit private corporation that provides research, training, and expertise to the jewelry industry. The European Gemological Laboratories (EGL) is also recognized worldwide. The majority of diamonds under one carat are certified by the EGL. While neither organization will appraise a stone, they will certify its physical qualities.

Diamond buyers should *always* insist on a grading certificate from either the GIA or the EGL, since diamond industry sources estimate that investors were duped out of $100 million in 1978 alone. The world has certainly not gotten more honest since then.

Colored stones are considered by many experts to have a better chance for higher appreciation. Prince Charles gave

Lady Diana a sapphire ring surrounded with diamonds. I don't think Prince Charles is worried about appreciation. Europeans, however, have always preferred colored stones for jewelry and frame them with small diamonds.

Diamonds and colored stones are considered to have good investment potential for the following reasons:

1. Dwindling supply and increased demand almost always result in higher prices. However, the increased demand is neither assured nor steady.

2. They can be an anonymous asset. This means that you can sell them privately and not report the gain to the government. You can also pass them on to your heirs without their having to pay inheritance taxes to the government. This way of avoiding taxes can work only if the jewels are not insured and no records have been kept on them. I am not advocating tax evasion. It's illegal! But as long as we have taxes, some people will try not to pay them.

3. Precious stones are proof that good things come in little packages. They are indeed the most concentrated form of wealth.

4. Diamonds and jewels are portable. If you wish to cross international borders with your wealth and liquidate them abroad, there is a ready market and you won't have a bad back from carrying your goodies.

5. Diamonds and jewels are free from government hanky panky. Governments do not sell jewels and, therefore, they can't affect the market's stability.

6. The South African-based De Beers cartel sets the price of diamonds throughout the world. Even Russia, the largest source of diamonds outside of South Africa, sells its diamonds through the De Beers empire. So far, the cartel has generally supported prices by holding back diamonds if the price of the gem starts to fall. When De Beers holds back on selling diamonds, diamond prices go up. However, there are strong signs that De Beers cartel is breaking up, and when this happens, the price of diamonds will plummet.

When you sell jewels you sell at wholesale, and that is often only one-third to two-thirds of retail. Precious gem advocates suggest putting no more than 5 percent to 7 percent of your money in investment stones. So if you have $50,000 to invest you should, according to this formula, spend only about $2,500 on your gems. And we've seen that $2,500 won't go very far in the gems market! Tip—With high interest rates, investors flee sterile-asset investments and investment grade diamonds plunge.

THE YELLOW BRICK ROAD

The price of gold will peak on the day the world blows up! When news is bad, when a country is being invaded or a world leader is assassinated, gold prices rise because they are based as much on emotions as on economics. Fear and doom make the glitter of gold more intense!

If the lure of gold for the sake of its own beauty is a passion you can't resist, for you, it is best to hold it in the form of coins. The price you pay for the workmanship in fine gold jewelry is *not* recoverable. Gold coins, however, such as the South African Krugerrand and the Canadian Maple Leaf, are easy to buy and sell. If you can stand to hold sterile assets, gold coins are the most reasonable deal.

The next best way to hold gold is in certificates offered by large banks. The certificates state that you own a certain amount of bullion that is being held in storage for you. The minimum investment requirement is usually $1,000. A commission, as well as storage charges, must be paid. The certificates' appeal is that the banks buy them back at current market rates, so they are a fairly liquid asset.

Do not confuse ownership of gold with gold *stocks*, American and South African, which are sold on the stock market. These are shares in gold mines, and if you buy these shares you become a partner in the mine itself. These shares react sensitively to fluctuation in the price of the metal. (You can also invest in silver mines and the so-called strategic metals.) All these investments are very speculative and should be left to the experts. Most get-rich-quick-and-easy schemes are outright scams.

Survivalists like Howard Ruff and his band of doom-and-gloom-let's-head-for-the-hills-boys have been able to get very rich off of people's fear of apocalypse. These prophets of disaster tell us to turn our paper money into gold, store enough food for one hundred years, and build a supreme personal arsenal out in the country (preferably on high ground!). The next step is to circle the wagons. Were I to survive a catastrophe that called for these extreme measures, I would face these problems:

1. Do I feed my sons-in-law as well as my daughters?

2. Which friend do I feed and which do I shoot?

3. Where will I get my cigarets?

4. How will I keep my weight down on all those beans?

5. Will my beauty parlor still be able to stock my hair color and how many cans of beans will it cost me?

Survivalists are not into finance, economics, or politics. They are into survival at *any* cost, and I do not think they are playing with a full deck! The leaders of the survivalist movements are fakers, playing on the fears and phobias of people. Stay away from them. They promote bad news and they *are* bad news.

Remember, collecting can be a joy and everybody does it to some extent, whether it be string, salt-and-pepper shakers, or fur coats. It seems to be a part of human nature.

Collecting can be challenging, interesting, and educational, but it is rarely lucrative. If some salt-and-pepper shaker aficionado offers you a tempting piece of change for your collection, the decision to sell is all yours. However, I do not suggest collecting anything as a means of building financial security.

INVESTMENT ANALYSIS

1. Cash needed for investment. *Lots!* In order to collect for purposes of investment, you must buy the best, the one of a kind, the rarest, or the complete collection. This costs a bundle.

2. Risk. It is highly unlikely that when you come to sell you'll get your money back. If you have bought wisely, your heirs may see some profit. But then anything an heir receives is pure profit.

3. Return on investment. Pleasure, if you like what you bought.

4. Liquidity. Not liquid, except for gold coins and certificates. With jewels. You may take a beating, but there's always a market for them.

5. Active or passive. All collecting is active, and that's what makes it fun.

6. Age. Any age for pleasure, not profit.

III

Your Security

9

Love and Money,
or
Be Sure to Cover Your Assets

Karl Marx and Jane Austen both understood that marriage and the family were institutions of property. Women in many cultures *were* property until modern times—and still are in some parts of the world.

Marriage in America traditionally provided financial security for many women. Today, marriage and security are no longer synonymous. Soaring divorce rates, men's shorter life span, women's evolving independence, and the excessively high cost of living are a few of the obvious reasons that have radically altered the notion of marriage as security.

This is a chapter about how to provide your own security with knowledge and savvy. You are no longer property and may, in fact, be property owners. It's up to you to protect yourself and to realize that emotional security has very little to do with financial security.

SINGLE WOMEN

In New York you go to Bloomingdale's for cheese. In Cincinnati you go to Sevatti's for pastry; something special for the special Sunday brunch. In Rhode Island you go to Wright's Farm for delectable chicken and homestyle potatoes. In Boston, at Legal Seafood, it's fun and easy to blow $30 on a lobster. If you over-extend your budget you can always spend a few days eating tuna and eggs to put the exchequer back in balance. A vacation can be Club Med or two weeks in St. Croix, and the only consultation you need is with your checkbook and credit cards. Anything you earn is yours. Your take-home pay is for the basics and the treats you want. How you scrimp or splurge is your business.

Setting financial goals, however, is important for the single woman. You may decide to marry late or not at all. If you put all your excess money on your back or into your tummy, you'll miss many years of opportunities to invest. Your priorities may include clothes and travel, but should also include a pension plan, education, investments, and maybe even a home!

Most single young men are financially goal and career oriented. However you, as a young woman, may not have been brought up to set any other goal than marriage. If so, now is the time to reevaluate this position and make some solid financial plans for the future.

Don't buy into the pervasive myth that single women will be better off when they are married. In reality, two do not live as cheaply (or as free of financial conflict) as one. You may marry a man whose higher education *you* will finance. You may marry a man with ongoing past family obligations. You may marry a rising young executive who then loses his job in a bad employment market. Anything can happen when you are married, and there are two sets of expectations and two piles of bills to deal with.

Being single may not be what you want forever, but it is the easiest financial situation, even easier than being married to a rich man.

Living Together

If you have a roommate, you've probably worked out a fifty-fifty split of expenses. If your roommate turns out to be miserly or a deadbeat, you simply end the arrangement and find another roommate. The ending may not be pleasant, but it is uncomplicated. You both came with your own things, and one of you will pack up and go with your own things.

Why should a man and woman or lover of any gender present a different and more difficult situation? Well, human nature is one reason, and different expectations are another.

The romance might begin with staying the night at your place or his. Soon you're together weekends and most weeknights. When you want to wash your hair, your shampoo is often at the place that you are not! Each month both of you are paying rent and utilities for two places and living in only one. You don't have to be an Einstein to know that it would be less expensive, more convenient, and lots more fun to live together. However, there are potential pitfalls. Working out financial arrangements in advance can help avoid some of the many problems of living together.

One problem you'll face in any live-in love relationship is how to handle finances. A second problem is how to protect yourself if you break up. Remember, live-in relationships are *not* protected by law; finances, children, property rights—none of these are protected.

Therefore, the importance of having everything spelled out up front is twofold. First, it can help in defining expectations and thereby avoiding unnecessary friction. An example: If he makes twice what you do, do you expect him to contribute more than you? Does he expect to contribute more than you? Second, by knowing where you are financially, money problems cannot be used as a surrogate for more serious problems between you. Many disagreements and fights about money are in reality conflicts about deeper problems. Money is a convenient whipping boy when you want to fight without discussing the real issues. This is as true in marriage as in an affair, and can damage the relationship.

While You're Together

Many couples simply pool their resources and pay the bills. This can work well if you have almost the same salaries and many of the same values. This simple solution will not be available to lovers with other commitments, such as child support, alimony, or support of relatives. One-half of the couple may have less to contribute; this should be understood beforehand. It may seem that love can conquer all, and it can when love is at fever pitch. Day-to-day living together can temper love with deep friendship and respect or it can contaminate love with anger and contempt. No matter which way it turns out, don't let money matters be the catalyst for breaking up an otherwise good relationship.

Most people are too shy or too trusting or too afraid to ask that their lover put an agreement in writing. When you're in love you just naturally suspend critical judgment. If he says he'll take care of the food costs, you don't doubt him. After all, you're not in love with a man who'd go back on his word!

But things may change, and it's better for both parties to have a plan in writing. Having a written agreement doesn't mean you can't change things later, nor does it mean that everything will go exactly according to the written words. All a plan can do is help you confront the issue of money early on and give you a written memo to refer to later. Then if one person says, "But I never said that," or "that isn't what we decided," you can always look it up. There is less vagueness in the written word than in pillow talk.

When/If You Break Up

There are three ways for a live-in couple to go: continue on, get married, or break up. If you break up, it won't necessarily be friendly. A break-up is painful enough without feeling that you've been had financially.

Right from the start, whatever goods you bring into the household should be listed, and the list signed by both parties. Anything you buy for the house should be added to the list, and you should keep the sales receipt. I'm talking about big ticket items such as furniture or a stereo or something of emotional value to you. Items like a garlic crusher or an ashtray *should not* be included. That kind of nitpicking is counterproductive in a relationship.

Things that are bought jointly can present a problem. How do you split a waterbed, for instance? Generally, I advise against joint purchases. Certainly *never* buy on credit jointly because the cardholder is *solely responsible for payment*. Some unmarried couples do buy houses and cars together. When and if they break up, one is going to have to buy out the other's interest. Before making any major joint purchase, such as a car or an appliance, draw up an agreement spelling out what will happen to the item should you go your separate ways.

For the purchase of a house, have a lawyer draw up the agreement regarding ownership rights. This is *not* a casual transaction. A lot of money is at stake. Molly and Richard bought a house together, and lived in it for two years before the relationship broke up. It was an amicable parting because ownership terms had been hammered out and every *i* was dotted and every *t* was crossed. Molly lives in the house, and Richard contributes $100 per month and remains part owner. Meanwhile, the house has appreciated, so though Richard no longer lives there he has an excellent investment. This is only one example of how this problem can be handled.

Living together involves sharing. Each of us has a different tolerance for giving and taking. If you love to give and find a lover who loves to take, you'll both be fulfilled! There really is no formula or checklist that can tell you if your live-in can be saved. Whatever arrangement works for you, makes you comfortable and satisfied, is the one you will cherish. There are women who are the sole support of their lovers, and it works. There are men I know who not only support their lovers but pay for their education. Other lovers are strictly fifty-fifty on everything from money to housework.

The first rule in living together, as in financial investments, is to know thyself. The second rule is to beware of the financial pitfalls and protect yourself.

I'll give you two examples of what can happen in a live-in relationship. The first is a client of mine (Elaine) who did not protect herself. She gave up her rent controlled apartment and her job and moved into her lover's house. She stayed home and completely renovated his house. She stripped and refinished the floors, wallpapered the bathrooms, bricked the walks, and planted a garden—a year of domestic bliss! She looked like your typical young bride, only she wasn't. After one year, *he* abruptly ended the relationship. He was left with a vastly improved house and fresh salad from his garden. She had nothing except a little expertise in stripping and varnishing. She had to find a job *and* an apartment in a seriously inflated housing market. A written agreement between them as to how she would be compensated for her work would have left her better off financially and less bitter emotionally.

Jill is another story. She moved into her lover's co-op apartment and gave up her own place. She kept her job on a small trade magazine. She and her lover blended their possessions.

However, these lovers drew up a contract listing their belongings separately. The contract also provided for his paying her moving expenses and first and last month's rent should he terminate their agreement. If she wished to end the relationship, she got her own possessions back and the responsibility for the move was hers. Should the break-up be by mutual agreement, expenses would be split fifty-fifty.

Remember, when a relationship is over, the only thing left is to divide the property.

MARRIAGE

They met as classmates their sophmore year at Harvard, two beautiful young people so well-matched in every way. Five years later they married at her father's home in California, surrounded by friends and family from all over the country. They are each other's first love, and there are no ex-wives or ex-husbands or children from former marriages to consider.

He's in his last year of medical school, with an internship and then residency to complete. I figure he'll be making a living about when Halley's Comet reappears. They'll make it through those lean years, because the bride works in her own profession and the groom has student loans to pay for his education. All the blessings of the Chinese proverb—"Health, wealth, and the time to enjoy them"—are shining on the young couple. And I should know, I'm the mother of the bride.

The plot changed when I looked at the guest list. I know all the etiquette of a marriage when the parents of the bride are divorced, but I had two ex-husbands at the wedding. Also, my late husband's nieces and his son Louis were guests. All three families I've married into were there to show their love and pleasure at Susanna's wedding. Three of the nine step-children came with variations of the name Susan. Now the new unit is Karim–Susanna, with Karim's parents and three siblings added to this large and ever-changing family. Karim's parents have only been married to each other, so their side is simple.

I was once a bride in white, and then a mother with two children in a house with a fence of roses. Everyone in my neighborhood had a house, a husband, and a couple of kids. Today that typical American picture of the perfect family represents only 15 percent of the population!

MARRIAGE: AN ECONOMIC PARTNERSHIP

As recently as the mid-1970s, a woman who worked for wages in Louisiana had no rights over the disposition of her own paycheck. Louisiana is an extreme example. California is at the other end of the spectrum, where in the 1970s women became co-managers of any assets of their marriage. This demonstrates that the law recognizes marriage as an economic unit.

Marriage *is* an economic partnership, and as such is subject to the laws of the state in which you reside. There are tremendous variations in the law from state to state. Each state, has volumes of specific laws pertaining to marriage and property. There are community property states (California, Arizona, Nevada, Texas, Louisiana, Washington, Idaho, and New Mexico), and non-community property states as regards marriage. For divorce, there are community property states, equitable distribution states, and support states. (See p. 194.) Refer to the Appendix for a state-by-state breakdown of marriage, divorce, and property laws.

In community property states, anything acquired during a marriage is equally owned by husband and wife. In some of these community property states, the wife is also considered co-manager of assets with the same rights as her husband to pledge and mortgage the assets of the community to get a loan or pay a debt.

When Sid Luft married Judy Garland, he was too broke to maintain his alimony payments to his former wife. He was ordered by the court in California to pay his alimony out of his share of Judy Garland's current earnings, one-half of which were considered his!

This is an unusual example, since men are statistically the big earners. Community property states generally do give women the fairest break in recognition of their contribution to the economic unit of marriage.

Non-community property states do not confer property sharing rights until divorce or death. What he acquires is his, what she acquires is hers, and the twain only meet in divorce court or probate.

In community, as well as non-community property states, anything that belongs to you before the marriage or that you inherit during the marriage is considered your *sole* property. If you do not commingle your property with you and your husband's other assets, any income received from it is yours exclusively.

Also, in all states you have a right of inheritance. A man may not disinherit a wife or vice versa. Even if your spouse dies returning from the altar, you are entitled to some portion of his estate. That portion is decided by state law. Remember to change your will if you move to another state, to comply with your new state laws. (See Wills & Estate Planning.)

You can supersede any or all of these marital rights by prenuptial or postnuptial agreement.

Prenuptial Agreements

The day you marry, the possibility of divorce or widow-hood becomes a probability. One in every three marriages ends in divorce, and women outlive their husbands four times out of five. Thus, the odds are good that you will be alone or have a different partner for a substantial number of years.

You can't foresee the future, but you can take certain steps to avoid some of the most obvious elephant pits. In a first marriage for both people there are relatively few financial complications. However, as my life demonstrates, things get very complicated with second and third marriages. There are so many people involved and so many interests to protect.

If either person in a new marriage has susbstantial assets, I recommend a prenuptial agreement. This type of agreement, for instance, may state basically that the assets brought into the marriage shall remain the property of the owner and will not be shared in the marriage. This does not prevent either partner from using the *income* from his or her assets to make life easier. The idea behind a prenuptial agreement is to protect the ownership of property from an unforeseen future.

Prenuptial agreements are very common in second mar-riages, where the couple getting married may well have different heirs. You can write anything you want into a pre-nuptial agreement, so you may stipulate such things as what the future spouse will be entitled to if there is a death or divorce. Jackie Onassis, a woman wealthy in her own right, had a prenuptial agreement with Aristotle O. He was a man with vast wealth and two grown children. When they mar-ried, he was willing to settle a sum of money on her and her children. He did not wish her or her children to share in the empire that was his and his heirs'. He died when their marriage was already on the rocks but before a divorce. The prenuptial agreement, written with just such contingencies in mind, left his only living child as his heir.

The Onassis story is a modern fairytale full of unexpected twists, turns, and tragedies. However, it is played out on a

smaller stage in cities and towns across the country. A prenuptial agreement may not sound like the height of romance;
but remember, though you are married in the sight of God,
you are also married under the laws of the State of Wherever.
You are joined by God in love as well as by Caesar in law.

Prenuptial agreements are not in the category of do-it-
yourself legal agreements. Many states will consider such
agreements illegal unless both parties are represented by an
attorney. Be sure to check the requirements in your home
state!

What to Keep from Your Past

There are several things to keep for yourself when you
marry:

1. Your property. If you have some separate property from
your single days, keep it that way. Whether it's a house or a
bank account or stocks and bonds, hold the title in your name
only. However, if the income from your assets is needed for
the family cash flow, it should certainly be contributed.

2. Your name. In all fifty states, you can retain your maiden
name; and in many cases it's a very good idea. This is an
excellent way to keep separate property separate. If you are
licensed in a profession under your maiden name, have name
recognition in business under your maiden name, or hold
assets in your maiden name, why not retain that name for
business and professional reasons? You can use your husband's name socially, your own name in business.

When I was married to Jack, we had three checking accounts. His was John W. Dyckman, mine was Miriam A.
Brien, and ours was Miriam and John Dyckman. My Miriam
Dyckman was an AKA. AKA means also known as. I was
Miriam A. Brien, AKA Miriam A. Dyckman. A person may
use any name or combination of names as long as the name is
not used with the intention to defraud.

In case of divorce, it's vital to know who funded which
asset. In a divorce, you'll want to keep out of the settlement
that which was yours to begin with.

Holding assets in your own name will help identify your
own money, but it is by no means a foolproof method. As
I've discussed, there are different sets of laws in the United
States that affect marriage. It is necessary to check with an
attorney in your own state to insure that your separate assets

remain separate. Remember, in community property states, property laws cover only those assets acquired *during* the marriage.

3. Your credit. It is important to keep credit in your own name. Even if you had no credit before you married, you can still develop and maintain a separate credit history while married. Any joint account opened by you and your husband since 1977 must, by law, be maintained in both names. If your account predates 1977, you have the right to request that those accounts be listed in both names. This is vital. Remember, if you have no credit history, you will have a terrible time establishing credit should your marital status change.

If you do change your name, notify the credit card companies. Your new name is *not* Mrs. Robert Zek, it's Elvira Zek. This ensures that a separate credit history for you will be maintained. Perhaps one bank charge card can be held jointly for charging household goods. Cards held solely in your name should be used for your personal expenses. This may seem clumsy, but it's vital to keep your own credit alive and well in case of death, divorce, or desertion.

It's easier to get credit in a community property state, because anything your husband earns is half yours. It's also easier to blow your credit, because half his debts, incurred during the marriage, belong to you. In non-community states the laws regarding your responsibility for your spouse's debts vary from state to state and from situation to situation. Check with a lawyer *before* getting into debt, and be sure to read the Credit chapter in this book.

One Paycheck

If the paycheck is his, and you want to invest in a hot tub, you'd better build it yourself or consult with your husband to see if you can afford it. If you can afford it, you'll both need to agree you want to spend the money *that* way at *this* time. It's no longer a case of you and yourself deciding, rather it's you and your husband, together.

If you are working only in the home and not bringing in a salary, on the average you'll have less financial say-so than your working sister. The old saying "He who pays the piper calls the tune" states a simple reality.

If the only paycheck in the house is yours, reality goes out the window and in flies internal conflict. You pay the piper but the tune changes to sound something like this:

You: "I should decide *that*. I'm paying."

Yourself: "It's hard enough on his ego as is. I better let him decide. He'll feel badly enough about my supporting him."

You: "But I earned that money, he didn't!"

Yourself: "He has to deal with his macho image. I'm a woman and used to giving in. I love him and don't want to hurt him. He's so vulnerable now that he's not earning."

This story *can* be played out with compassion and understanding. If you do pay the piper, you should probably talk with your mate as to what tune to play.

Two Paychecks

When a family has two wage earners, it's important to decide how much each should contribute to the household. If husband and wife are earning approximately the same amount, then the fifty-fifty split may be the obvious solution. However, given the great inequity in pay for women, usually the husband earns considerably more than his wife. Marriages where the wife is the big earner are still few and far between.

Barring a financial crisis, both partners should also have some money of their own, after paying household expenses, to spend or invest as they personally wish. Even if the amount of money is small, it's important to have something of your own to show for your work. Whether you want the money for a theater ticket, clothes, an exercise class, or a financial investment, every month's income should provide some money just for you.

With this in mind, you must now find a way to equitably split the costs of your joint life. One way to do it is on a percentage basis. If your husband earns twice your salary he puts into the joint pot twice the money. Example: You earn $12,000, and he earns $24,000. You put in $10,000 a year, or about 83 percent of your income. He puts in $20,000 a year, or about 83 percent of his income.

This is only one idea. No suggestion I make or formula I devise will work unless it is followed with generosity of the heart. What if his mother needs money? What if your mother needs money? What happens if either of you loses your job or becomes ill? If you want your marriage to last, forget the formulas and look to the important matter of being good to each other when unexpected demands arise. Your goal should be to have a system that works *whenever possible*!

If your marriage ends in divorce, you might be sorry you were generous. But if you're not generous, I can guarantee your marriage will end in divorce!

There are many ways to figure each partner's financial contribution. With the infinite variations, demands, and complexities of family life, no one way will work for everyone all the time. My best advice on how to deal with money problems is to keep talking to each other as things come up. Deal frankly with new situations that change your money plans. Don't harbor silent grudges. Talk things out until you agree or agree to disagree. Don't be a martyr or a saint about money, because both postures are very out of date and also very unattractive.

"I've Grown Accustomed to His Face"

Is your husband a saver, a man with concern for the future, willing to put off gratification now for a long-range goal of security? Does he pay his bills the day they arrive and buy on credit only in a serious emergency? These traits can be wonderful, particularly when you operate the same way. Well, maybe not exactly the same way, but you do admire his thrift and you can adjust to his patterns and grow accustomed to his ways.

But what if that isn't the way you want to live? What if you want to enjoy things now? You have zest and enough optimism for the two of you, and you believe the future will take care of itself. You pay bills as soon as you see the words "second reminder." And what in God's name is credit for if not to buy now and pay later? Is he going to grow accustomed to your ways? This is only *one* possible script. Can a marriage contain such opposites in one frail institution? Sure it can. It always depends on the couple, their tolerance, understanding, and ability to compromise. A couple with two savers or two spenders can encounter serious problems, having nothing to do with money, that will flaw their marriage. We are faced again with the fact that when dealing with people there are no formulas. Haven't you said, "What in God's name does she see in him?" Or, "How could he ever stay married to her?" Louis Untermeyer ended a poem with these two lines in praise of variety:

> "And let us thank God in our songs
> There are as many tastes as tongues."

DIVORCE

Have you heard any of this before?

She: You never call when you're going to be late!

He: What's it to you? When I do come home, you're always going to some dumb class. You'd rather be at school than spend an evening with me anyway.

She: I like to learn new things. The least you can do is babysit the house and kids. God knows you never help around our home in any other way.

He: Some home! You sure do a rotten job of entertaining and you know that's important to my business.

She: Entertaining! You gotta be kidding. All you need to be entertained is the TV and a bottle of beer!

He: So I like a little beer occasionally. Obviously you like a little food.

And on and on and on. . . .

Family fights can cause an even gross of sins. You can be high scorer if you cover more points of dispute than your partner. But you can't have these multifaceted and creative fights when you're getting divorced. There are only two subjects left to argue about, money and the children.

I've seen hateful, painful break-ups, and others best described as more in sorrow than anger. The longer the marriage, the more difficult the divorce. It's only years after a divorce that some people can gain the perspective that permits them to appreciate the good things that were in the marriage. In a divorce, the focus is on the bad part of the marriage, the wasted time, the betrayed emotions. You may not be able to get back the time or the dreams, but you can make him pay! And so, money becomes the repository for all emotion.

Keep It out of Court

Courts in most states view a divorce as they would the dissolution of any business partnership. The men and women who generally get the worst divorce settlements are those that want their day in court. They will not settle, no matter how realistic the proposal worked out by the lawyers. They want to tell the judge, the court, the world, how bestial their mate has been. They believe that when they talk, the world, and God himself, will see once and for all the viper they have been married to. Everyone will know that they were saints to have lived with this monster. This ultimate denunciation, this total indictment, is of no interest to the judge whatsoever. He or she has heard it *all* before. In most states judges will not even listen to *J'accuse*. They want only to hear about the financial arrangements. Remember, if you do go to court for a financial settlement in a divorce, you can *always* lose. What seems so clear to you, what seems so obvious and just to you, may not be so to the judge. The law is interested in equitable distribution, not dirty pictures.

Don't misunderstand me. Sometimes you must go to court if you can't reach an agreement. However, if you do go, the only sure winners are the lawyers in this nasty business.

State Laws

The United States operates under several different types of law in the division of marital property. (See Appendix for state-by-state breakdown.)

1. Community Property States. In California, Arizona, Nevada, Texas, Louisiana, Washington, Idaho, and New Mexico, courts view all assets that a couple acquires during marriage as belonging equally to both partners. A couple has equal interest in their house and other assets. If the husband gets his pension, an asset of equal value is usually assigned to the wife.

Judges will rarely ask a woman with young children to move, so a wife is most likely to end up with the house. In a marriage of more than a few years, where the wife has not worked outside the home, spousal support (alimony) is likely to be awarded. This support continues for a stipulated number of years, during which time the wife is expected to acquire the necessary skills to enter the work force.

2. Marital Property States. Property acquired during the marriage is subject to equitable distribution. There are a number of different and changing interpretations of the word *equitable* in a divorce!

Equitable does *not* mean equal. Judges in these states have enormous powers to divide assets, and equitable means what the given judge decides it means.

Again, a wife with children is most likely to end up with the house. While this is an excellent asset, it produces no income for her day-to-day living.

3. Support States (mostly in the South). A nonworking wife is entitled to support, if she can prove she needs it, but has no legal share in property acquired during marriage. Her years of caring for home and children may or may not be counted as a contribution to family assets.

Support states are the least favorable to women, while community property states are the states where women usually get the fairest deal.

Divorce without Children

A divorce where there are no children is often comparatively simple. State laws set the guidelines, and the lawyers work out the particulars. If a woman is working or if a woman is quite young and able to work, the best settlement, in my opinion, is a lump sum settlement. You can invest it or you can go back to school to train yourself for a profession or qualify yourself for a higher paying job.

With a lump sum you can also avoid the wait by the mailbox for the alimony check, which is often less than expected, late, or not there at all. Statistically, only 15 percent of all men pay alimony or child support for more than five years. Just because there's a court order or an agreement saying he *must*, doesn't mean he *will*. Trying to find an ex-husband and hauling him into court for nonpayment is costly, time consuming, painful, and often impossible. If you can afford it, it's always better to cut clean and sever the financial ties with one blow. There is the added psychological benefit of putting it all behind you if you get a lump sum.

Many couples can't do a lump sum settlement because there isn't enough cash available. Monthly support until you are equipped to earn is the next best solution.

The case of an older woman who has had a long marriage is most tragic. She may not be able to go into the work force, and so must live on her lump settlement or depend on her ex-husband's paying as promised.

Divorce with Children

When dependent children are involved in a divorce, the parent receiving custody must do some serious financial planning. This has to be spelled out in an agreement. Items to work out are:

1. Monthly support payments.

2. Major additional costs, such as medical and dental bills, education, childcare, camp and summer vacations, life insurance, etc.

3. Length of time that payments will continue.

Have your ex-husband keep the children on his medical plan unless you have a better plan at your work. Have your ex-husband carry enough life insurance so that if he dies, your support and the children's is protected. Stipulate how long he will pay for, or contribute to, the children's education. College plus four years of graduate school will get your child through almost all professional education.

The best guarantee you and your children will have in a divorce is your ability to bring in money. Even if your ex-husband is the major contributor to the support of the children, you will always need extra money. I cannot stress strongly enough the need for preparing yourself for a job. If you can get support for a few years, use it to educate yourself for a career. If you were a college dropout or a French poetry major, you probably don't have marketable skills. Go to a reputable job counseling service or read your newspaper help wanted ads. Check what kind of skills the employment agencies and the ads are looking for and how much they pay. Take the first year or years after the divorce to train or retrain yourself. Try to arrange the time and the money through the divorce settlement to get yourself prepared to work at the highest level you can achieve.

There is a trend these days for courts to recognize the unpaid services performed by a woman in the home during the marriage. The estimate of the dollar cost of these services is anywhere from $12,000 a year on up. But let's look at a family of four with an income of $50,000 a year. By the time the children's support is decided on and support is given to the wife, if necessary, there isn't much left over for the husband to live on. After all, the $50,000 a year is before taxes. Obviously, it would be impossible to award the full amount to a woman for her past services in the home, but some settlement can and should be made.

Taxes and Divorce Settlements

There are a lot of tax consequences to a divorce, so you will need to consult with your attorney. The major thing to remember is that you do not pay taxes on child support, but you *do* pay taxes on alimony or spousal support. Get the most you can in child support, because tax-free dollars go a whole lot further.

Don't forget to spell out which spouse gets to claim the kids as a tax deduction. This must be worked out and agreed to by both parties. An example might be spouses claiming the kids every other year.

A good settlement should also include protection from prosecution for tax fraud or error committed by the other spouse during the marriage and protection from responsibility for unknown debts.

SECOND MARRIAGES, ETC.

If you get married for a second or third or fourth time, and statistics say you may, you'll be more self-protective. You'll also have more to protect, such as separate property or children from a previous marriage. And your new husband may have other obligations from a previous marriage. A prenuptial agreement in a second marriage is very important. It can spell out the extent of the financial responsibility that you will take for each other.

One of my clients, married to a very wealthy man, has a prenuptial agreement that reads that if there is a divorce, she will receive nothing. If she is widowed, she will be supported by her husband's estate in the style she has been accustomed to for a period of ten years. She receives nothing under his Will. My client is willing to sign this agreement because she has money of her own. Her two children from a former marriage will inherit money from *their* father. My client's husband has a Will leaving everything to his son from his first marriage.

If you make a prenuptial agreement, you should also make a will that conforms to the agreement. Your insurance beneficiary must also conform with your contract.

Keeping proper records of separate property is very important if you don't wish to commingle your monies. For example, keeping records of who put up how much for the down payment on the house is more vital in a second marriage. You and your husband may have separate heirs or separate and common heirs.

If you do not have a prenuptial agreement, keep *all* transactions separate. Second marriages can generate a lot of tension and unhappiness if financial matters are not discussed before the wedding. Your husband may have support payments that you should be aware of. He may be under an obligation that causes him to pay more money to his first family than he can contribute at home. This may also be true for an increasing number of women. This situation is never easy to deal with, but it's much harder if it comes as a surprise. In many second marriages, one spouse's children from a previous marriage may have financial advantages that the other children do not. If you know this before the second marriage, you can decide whether you can live with this problem or not.

Even if you've decided to wing it through a second marriage and then find that too much unpleasantness is connected with the family finances, you can always make a marital agreement (postnuptial agreement).

WIDOWS

Statistics tell us that four women out of five will be widowed. The time to prepare for widowhood is before it happens. (See chapters on Wills and Estate Planning and Retirement.)

Trying to cope with financial problems in the midst of grief is extremely difficult and can only add to your burdens. Be sure you have a current and completely filled out where-it's-at list (Chapter 1). Revise and update this periodically. The information on this form will be a great help to you and your attorney if you become a widow. Remember, one out of four widows do *not* collect their full benefits because they don't know about them. Don't let this happen to you!

During my husband Jacques's two-and-one-half-year terminal illness, we worked together to prepare me for life without him. Despite all this preparation, I still made the classic error of making a major decision in the midst of my grief. I sold my house. Even though real estate is my field and I *know* I would have told anyone else in my position to stay put, I still sold my home. Today, that home is worth a small fortune!

To all widows I say, make as few decisions as possible in the first year after your husband's death. If you can, stay in the home you've lived in and keep children in the same school district. If possible, make no important financial changes because you fear the future. You may feel that you are functioning well in those months immediately after your husband's death, but you are not really. You're in a period of mourning and your judgment is probably not the best.

The milestones during the first year are the hardest things to face: his birthday, your birthday, your anniversary, holidays. These are all difficult times, and bring back a flood of memories. Make a special effort to be with close friends and family on these days. Join a widows' group in your area. These are sponsored by mortuaries, Ys, churches, hospitals, community mental health groups, etc. They offer emotional support from other widows, as well as some professional counseling from psychologists, gerontologists, and financial experts.

If you are widowed or are helping a widowed relative, here is a brief checklist of things to remember:

1. In order to collect on your husband's insurance, Social Security, and anything else due you, you will need about a dozen copies of your husband's death certificate. These agencies will require this proof of death before you can collect. Social Security also requires proof of marriage and proof of the birth of any child who claims Social Security rights. You may be able to claim Social Security benefits of an ex-husband if you were married to him for at least ten years. You may also claim benefits for his children if they are minors. If they are legal adults, and have entitlement, they must claim for themselves. In addition, new Social Security laws now allow a widow over 60 years of age to remarry *without* losing her Social Security benefits. (See Retirement chapter.)

2. This may seem cold-hearted, but I suggest that you withdraw all the money in your joint bank accounts before your husband's death becomes public knowledge. Otherwise, the account might be frozen and you could have to go to court to get an order to distribute these funds.

3. The next step is to apply for all life insurance benefits that you are entitled to. You will generally be paid in four to six weeks. Check to see what burial benefits your husband is entitled to either from Social Security or the Veterans Administration.

4. Do not worry about hospital bills or outstanding debts, except for your mortgage, car payment, and utilities. All the rest can wait.

5. When the cash comes in from insurance policies and other sources, invest it in a high-yield, short-term lending

instrument such as money market funds or three-month Treasury Bills. Do not burden yourself with any long-range financial plans.

6. Widows are the natural target of a lot of well-meaning advice. Don't take any of it unless it's from someone who is reliable and is *not* personally involved.

10

Insurance

If you're blessed by the gods and believe nothing bad can happen to you, then don't buy insurance. If you're like me, however, you are going to buy and hope you won't have to collect!

When you buy insurance you are buying protection against financial loss due to loss of health, life, goods, or income. It is a contract between you and an insurance company whereby you contract to pay your insurance bill (premiums) and it contracts to cover the costs of certain losses. Depending on the contract, you could be covered for from 80 percent to 100 percent of a loss or for some stated flat amount.

Women are new to the insurance game. Until recent years, the buying and selling of insurance was reserved for men. But no matter which sex was purchasing it, insurance was and is a complicated business overrun with strange practices and even stranger jargon. Where else would you encounter the term "subrogate?" (It means, simply, to substitute one for another.)

Americans are great believers in insurance. We buy 80 percent of all the insurance policies sold in the world. Life insurance companies alone collect over $30 billion a year in premiums from more than 150 million consumers.

Insurance is a profit-making business, and the figures testify to its steady success. Insurance companies that report large insurance-related losses are not legally obliged to report their huge investment profits, which they made by investing *your* premiums. Unfortunately, the performance of the insurance companies falls far short of their promise to provide fair and adequate protection for their customers. Furthermore, many of the policies on the market today are so confusing that many buyers have given up trying to understand them. Some companies are beginning to sell policies with simplified language. Still, one of the great ironies of the insurance business is that medical policies rarely cover the cost of eyeglasses. To my way of thinking, this adds insult to injury, because you need the glasses to read the policy!

Women have been discriminated against by the insurance industry in a great variety of ways. Insurance companies divide human beings into two groups, men and high-risk factors!

Insurance sales handbooks are filled with sexist language and discriminatory advice for future insurance salespeople. For example, a brochure entitled *Selling to the Ladies* contains little tidbits of advice on how to respond to "feminine reactions to the subject of life insurance." This manual warns about women's "preference not to think about the future, their inability to reach a decision and their aversion to medical exams." Fortunately, many states are now taking action against unfair insurance practices against women. For more detailed information, you can write to the National Task Force to Investigate Discrimination Against Women in Insurance, 206 West State Street, Trenton, New Jersey 08608. Or you can contact your State Commission on the Status of Women.

Gone are the days when women's work in the home was protected by her extended family. Today, most women work outside the home and many are heads of households. Their deaths, illnesses, or disabilities would cause a substantial hardship in many a household. Even the tasks performed by women who work only in their homes have been assigned a minimum value of $12,000 annually! Insurance protection for women has become essential for their financial security and well-being.

Insurance companies are now beginning to recognize women as a vast, untapped market. They are hiring more women agents and are beginning to simplify their policy language. However, women need to educate themselves about insurance to avoid becoming a mark for unscrupulous insurance providers.

Basically, there are five insurance policies that a woman should look into: health, disability, life, automobile, and homeowners or renters insurance. Remember, these policies should be purchased with the same care and consideration used to buy a car or a refrigerator or a good dress. I can't stress enough the importance of *reading* your insurance policy—it's about as much fun as going to the dentist but just as necessary. In the insurance business, a key phrase is: Buyer beware. Remember, the large print giveth and the small print taketh away!

AGENTS VS. COMPANIES

You will buy insurance directly from a company or through an agent, unless you are adequately covered for your own needs by group insurance where you work. Premiums are less when you buy directly from a company, but you do sacrifice the services of an agent.

Good companies with fine reputations pride themselves on using good agents. There are a few ways to find a good company. Insurance companies are listed and rated in *Best's Insurance Reports*, which you can find in your local public library. Choose only those companies with ratings of "very substantial" or "most substantial." While at the library you should also check the findings of *Consumer Reports* on the various insurance companies. Ask for these from the reference librarian. Also, ask your friends how they like their insurance companies and agents. A good recommendation often goes a long way.

Once you have a feel for insurance companies, you'll be better equipped to choose a company or decide to use an agent. An agent can represent many companies or work for just one. He or she should try to find the policy that most closely fits your needs. If the agent is also an insurance broker, he or she can deal with any company doing business in the United States.

The added service provided by an insurance agent comes from his or her desire to keep you as a client. When you buy directly from the company, the salesperson gets a high percentage of your first year's premium. If you then renew, that salesperson only gets $5 or $10 each year for having brought you into the fold in the first place. An agent, on the other hand, gets a certain set percentage every time you renew, which provides him or her with a steady income. In order to keep you as a customer, the agent must provide fast, courteous service when you have a claim. If your agent doesn't come through for you, by all means get a new agent!

When I was married to my first husband, we owned an apartment building. We called our insurance agent every time we had a loss or a theft of equipment. No matter what we reported, we were told it wasn't covered. When we reported the lobby chairs missing and were again told that they weren't covered by insurance, we decided to change agents. Young and inexperienced as we were, we still felt that if we had an insurance policy it should cover something!

We went looking for an agent who knew his business and who would advise us on what kinds of insurance we should have. Through divorce, accidents, sickness, death, and re-marriage, we are both still with the same agent. We remain loyal because his service is fantastic.

Paying a bit extra for service is a policy I endorse. It often works out to be less expensive in the long run!

What Does a Good Agent Look Like?

First of all, if you go the agent route, you'll probably need two of them. One will handle casualty insurance, the other life, health, and disability. An agent rarely handles both. An insurance broker, on the other hand, can handle all of these. Remember, agents and brokers earn their living by receiving commissions on policies they sell to you, the consumer. They are salespeople first. Concern about your welfare comes second, if at all. When your agent's welfare and your welfare *both* are covered, then you'll probably have a good insurance policy and a happy agent!

Your agent or broker should be ready and willing to sit down with you to go over your personal financial portfolio. He or she will look at your income, expenses, career expectations, dependents, marital situation, and anything that would pertain to your insurance needs. Beware of oversell! If you're a middle-aged career woman with only yourself and a small dog to support, then a $100,000 life insurance policy is not necessary.

Like you, your insurance policies need annual checkups. In his or her service your agent should include regular updates on your policies. For instance, if you make more money this year than last in your work, your disability coverage should be greater.

As in the case of choosing and working with any professional, insist on good service from your insurance agent. Is he or she willing to explain everything to you cheerfully and patiently? After all, insurance *is* loaded with specialized language that must be understood. That's your agent's job! I can't repeat this enough: If you're not happy with the service provided by your agent, find another agent.

HEALTH INSURANCE

Health care costs have skyrocketed, and there is no end in sight. Even a fairly commonplace medical problem can seriously damage a person's financial health. Therefore, health insurance in the United States should be a primary concern for everyone, and especially for women with children.

Health and disability insurance are necessities, and statistics show that they are used more than any other kind of insurance. They are also the two areas of insurance where discriminatory practices against women are widespread. Women pay higher premiums than men for both these types of insurance. As we shall see later, the reasoning behind this practice is very shaky!

Health Plans

There are several ways to cover yourself against financial setbacks from health problems. The least expensive way to obtain health insurance is through a group plan, usually offered by employers. Some group policies are comprehensive; others are seriously limited. Your group policy may have to be supplemented by coverage through a private insurer.

If you are a student, are self-employed, or work for a small company without a health plan, then it is necessary for you to purchase a medical policy on your own. This can be an expensive proposition as private insurance providers often find themselves losing money on health plans. Naturally they pass these costs on to the consumer, which drives up the price of individual or family health insurance. Investigate private insurance plans carefully!

Blue Cross for hospital coverage and Blue Shield for surgery and other general medical expenses are called the Blues. Their notoriously slow payment schedules and frustrating mounds of paperwork can indeed give a person the blues! However, despite the aggravation, these non profit health care plans offer fairly broad coverage at a reasonable price. Blue Cross and Blue Shield, when worked together, can provide comprehensive coverage that is quite satisfactory. Other companies such as Washington National and Kemper should be looked into also before you decide.

Health Maintenance Organizations (HMOs) are membership groups composed of medical teams who own their facilities and offer medical care at a fairly reasonable cost. These costs are usually higher than those offered by the Blues, but benefits are more extensive. Routine physicals, not covered by the Blues, for example, are covered under most HMO plans. The focus of the HMOs is on preventive care, their aim being to reduce health care costs by *preventing* illness before it strikes rather than curing it after the fact.

While you should choose the plan that meets your own individual needs, there are several fundamental things to look at in any health plan. The first is to check to see what the limit of *basic* coverage is for treatment and care in a hospital. This includes drugs, surgery, nursing services, etc. There is a dollar amount schedule, which is usually fairly low. For example, some policies will only pay the surgeon $150 for an appendectomy. Such inexpensive surgeons no longer walk this earth!

Major medical coverage should pick up where basic coverage leaves off. This type of coverage protects you against the exorbitant costs of a prolonged or debilitating illness. It is crucial to be covered against a serious physical catastrophe that would wipe you out financially.

Research findings conclude that a minimum adequate package of medical benefits should cover at least 80 percent of the costs of fifteen days of hospitalization, all physicians' services, lab work and x rays, inpatient psychiatric care, and some outpatient services, prenatal care, and nursing home care. Also recommended is major medical coverage that offers a minimum lifetime total benefit of $250,000 with stop-loss protection of from $1,000 to $2,500 annually. This means that your share of costs will stop at $1,000 to $2,500 per year on any illness. These figures will need to be revised to keep pace with inflating medical costs.

Tips for Health Insurance Shoppers

1. Compare policies thoroughly page by page.
2. Unless you're covered by a group plan, a rule of thumb to remember is the higher the deductible, the lower your

premiums will be. Try to get a blanket deductible—for example, a flat $200 per year. If you have a $200 deductible *per* family member and per illness, you could end up paying more than you thought you would. Also, note the annual maximum payment. For instance, say you have an 80/20 policy with a $200 deductible, with your maximum payout being $2,500. You will pay your $200 deductible and 20 percent of expenses up to $2,500. After that, you are covered for 100 percent for that year. So your total liability in this example is $700. You may want to raise your deductible, if you can, and thereby lower your premiums.

3. Check what conditions *are* covered. Companies have differences in their lists of covered ailments and the allocations for each.

4. Check all exclusions—the list of what is *not* covered.

5. Check the length of the waiting period before coverage begins on illnesses or injuries that you had prior to applying for a health policy. These are known as pre-existing conditions. My ingrown toenails are an unpleasant but persistent pre-existing condition.

Ideally, the waiting period should be six months or less, and pre-existing conditions should refer only to recently diagnosed and treated problems. If you have to wait two years to be covered for an allergy that you've walked around with since first grade, shop for a better plan.

6. Study *all* restrictions and limitations noted in any health insurance policy. If the company does not cover short redheads, and you are five feet tall with gorgeous red hair—well, the solution is obvious: Find another policy. Of a more serious nature, be sure newborns are covered *from birth*, when most health problems arise, and not after a two-week waiting period! This is a fairly common health plan restriction, so watch out.

7. Make sure your plan is *guaranteed renewable* and *noncancellable* if you pay your premiums. In the event that you have a run of poor health, you will remain protected.

8. Private medical insurance only rarely covers normal pregnancy and delivery. Some will cover a high-risk pregnancy. However, each company defines high risk according to its own standards. Some require you to be confined to bed during your pregnancy before they'll pay your medical expenses!

Many insurers do not cover prenatal or obstetrical services, amniocentesis, postnatal, or well-baby care. The cost of having a baby is high and on the rise. Be sure to demand a complete breakdown from your health insurer of what is covered, if anything. A common situation is where employee coverage provides maternity benefits for the wives of male workers and not for women workers. If you find this to be true, your company is guilty of discrimination and is open to a lawsuit!

HMOs usually provide full maternity care, and should be investigated if you plan on having a child.

9. You and your children may be covered by the group medical plan through your spouse's employer. However, this will probably run out within thirty days of his death or if you were to divorce. If you are widowed, you should search for a medical plan immediately. A few companies are becoming less draconing and keeping the widow on medical insurance for a while. In the case of a divorce, there may be a conversion clause allowing you to transfer out of his plan and into a private plan with the same company. Generally, this can be expensive, and you'll probably have to apply for the policy as a new applicant. Also, if you're between jobs you may want to convert to a private plan until you can again receive group coverage.

When my husband and I divorced, I was dropped from his Blue Cross plan. I applied for an individual policy and discovered it cost quite a bit more. However, the extra cost became the least of my worries. I was turned down anyway—for my ingrown toenails!

10. Blue Cross offers an expensive High-Option Policy that will cover anyone-at-anytime-no-matter-what. If you keep receiving rejection slips from health care providers and have a host of ailments needing immediate attention, do check into this as a possibility for yourself.

In addition, Blue Cross and Blue Shield have open enrollment periods in certain states. Call your local office for exact dates. HMOs must, by law, have an open enrollment period each year. During these periods, anyone and everyone can join, no matter what the condition of their health.

11. Many private insurance companies offer comprehensive plans to supplement Medicare, often referred to as companion care plans. Check on these and by all means take advantage of them if you are eligible. And if you have any responsibility for an older family member, make *sure* that they are covered.

Medicare coverage is limited and has become even more restricted as Social Security benefits wither under Federal budget cuts.

Warning: These plans vary widely and should be shopped for with care. Some senior citizen organizations rate these plans annually and can be a valuable resource in helping you decide which plan is best for your situation.

DISABILITY INSURANCE

Disability insurance is protection against loss of income due to injury or illness. This is the most overlooked insurance by women and where discrimination has done the most damage. Working women were often denied access to disability insurance. If they *could* find a company to take them, their premiums were exorbitant! Today, with so many women working to support their households, income protection has become a must.

There are several types of disability coverage, including Social Security and Workman's Compensation for job-related injury or illness. Some states have adequate and reasonable disability programs for qualified workers. Your state insurance department can assist you with questions regarding coverage in your state. This agency also handles medical and disability insurance consumer complaints.

If you work for yourself, are not protected by a group plan at your workplace, or earn a good living—say over $16,000—then you should investigate private disability insurance plans. As with any insurance, you should shop very carefully for the plan that meets your needs.

Read the prospective policy to see what it will or will not do. Is the definition of disability acceptable or do you have to lose your leg to a great white whale in order to be considered disabled? Disability should be defined as an inability to perform the duties of your *particular* occupation. Otherwise you could be forced to consider accepting a different and lower paying job. You don't want to have to work as a file clerk if you are a personnel manager!

Two most important features in any disability policy are that it should be both *guaranteed renewable* and *noncancellable*. The waiting period should be reasonable and suit your particular circumstance. For example, you can afford a longer waiting period if you are covered by sick leave at work. There should also be a rehabilitation clause to give you a chance to really get back on your feet again.

The amount of protection you will need depends on your income and lifestyle. If you're a bank executive with two children in private school, then your needs are far greater than if you're a freewheeling young woman with no children! Figure your budget and what portion of it is covered solely by *your* income. What would happen to you and/or your family should you lose that income? When you've figured that, then you'll have an idea of the amount of income protection you will need. Remember that prices and benefits will vary from company to company. The rampant discrimination against women in disability insurance is only recently being turned around. It is essential to shop carefully *and* read that policy.

LIFE INSURANCE

Do you, as a woman, really need life insurance? Well, the answer is yes—and no. Yes, definitely, if you are the head of your household and have children to protect. Yes, too, if your contribution to family income would cause a hardship were it lost. On the other hand, if you are a single woman with no pressing responsibilities, or your kids are launched you probably don't need much, if any, life insurance.

We all lead different lives and have different needs for life insurance. Do you have a favorite niece that you'd like to see educated? Do you wish a giant funeral with a twenty-piece band, a horse-drawn carriage, and your name spelled out in exotic flowers? Do you need to leave a fund to care for your seventeen cats after you're gone? Do you adore your grandchildren and want to lend them a hand? All of these might be good reasons to carry some amount of life insurance.

Insurance companies would have you believe that if you don't need life insurance now then you will later, so better buy it now when it's cheaper and so that it won't be denied to you later. Does that seem logical? Sounds like a line from a used car salesman: "Better grab this deal TODAY because it won't be here tomorrow." A salesperson can use that *same* line every day for thirty years! Just as second-hand cars will be available as long as we use cars, so will life insurance be available. In fact, the Institute of Life Insurance reports that

97 percent of all life insurance applicants *are* accepted.

Remember, though, if you have no children or pet projects, or your children are grown and burgeoning entrepreneurs, then you should probably drop or cash in your life insurance policy. Don't be one of those women struggling to meet life insurance payments to insure the future of sons or daughters who have already become successful professionals, $30-an-hour plumbers, or wealthy gem smugglers! They can take care of themselves. (And if one of your male relatives has persuaded you to buy life insurance for investment purposes—read on.)

Only Five Variables

There are raging debates over the glories and the agonies of term vs. whole life insurance. Volumes are written on the proper amount to be insured for and how to figure this amount. But despite the debates and the confusing jargon, life insurance *only* varies in five ways. There are differences in the cost of a policy, its face value, time period, cash value accumulation, and its purpose.

Policy *costs* vary with insurance companies. For example, individual rates are higher than group rates.

What the insurance would pay in the event of death is known as the *face value* of a policy. You can be insured for as low a face value as $10,000 or as high as $1,000,000 or more.

Different kinds of life insurance have different *time periods* for being insured. For example, term life insurance often provides coverage for one year and must be renewed. Some whole life policies insure you for your lifetime so long as you meet your payment obligations.

Only whole life insurance has *cash value accumulation*. The variable with this is how much of your cash value can be borrowed out and when.

The *purpose* of a life insurance policy depends on what you want and need. For example, term provides straight protection on a year-by-year basis, and whole life offers a cash accumulation plan.

How Much Is Enough?

There is no easy answer to this question, as several factors must be considered, such as your age, marital status, income, status of dependents, earning power of your survivors, and so on.

Basically, though, life insurance should cover the income lost because of your death. It should also pay for your last expenses—funeral costs and back debts. So to figure what your coverage should be, add together an estimate of your final expenses and 60 percent to 70 percent of your income. This is what your family will need to get by on. Subtract from this amount any money that could be expected from Social Security, pension plans, savings, and investments. Multiply that figure times five and you'll have a ballpark idea of the amount of coverage necessary to give your family adequate protection for five years.

Remember, this figure is subject to change over the years as children are born, then grow and leave home, as your career blossoms, as your investments change, and so on. Your life insurance policy needs an annual review and revisions made whenever necessary.

Tip: For those who have kept life insurance policies to pay death taxes, a review is in order. Under the 1981 tax reform act, only very large estates will be taxed, so life insurance to cover taxes may no longer be necessary.

Term vs. Whole Life Insurance

Term insurance covers you for a specific period of time—a term. That term can be anywhere from one year to twenty years. Term provides pure protection and nothing else. It's the least expensive life insurance and offers the most bang for the buck.

There are several ways to purchase term insurance. Level term means that your premium remains the same for the life of the policy. At the end of the term of your policy if you decide to renew, your premium will go up because you are older. Renewable term means you can renew without a medical exam; convertible term means you can convert your term insurance to whole life, also without a medical exam. This gives you extra protection should you become terminally ill. All of these features add a small amount to the cost of your policy but are well worth it.

Whole, or *straight,* or *ordinary life insurance* are all names for a type of policy that offers life insurance protection combined with savings. The cost of this type of coverage is substantially higher than for term, and the premium remains the same for the life of the policy. When you buy a whole life insurance policy you are building up cash value that pays very low interest.

In my opinion, there are only two good reasons for purchasing straight life insurance:

1. If money runs through your fingers, then whole life insurance will force you to save. This form of savings should really be a last resort. It would be better to have a certain amount of money taken from your pay every month and put into a savings plan.

2. If you hit it big in an illegal poker game and want to hide your winnings from the tax man, you can buy a single premium life insurance policy and then borrow back the cash value.

There are a wide variety of policy names with specialized coverage here and variable coverage there. You can buy extended term, reduced paid up, split life, modified life, and so on. Remember, though, just as a rose by another name is still a rose, so life insurance, by another name, is still term *or* whole life.

There is a form of insurance that will cover any remaining payments on a car or a mortgage if the insured person dies. This kind of insurance is very expensive and suitable only for certain people. For example, mortgage insurance might be useful for a professional man with small children and a wife who does not work out of the home. Before purchasing this type of insurance, evaluate your own situation and requirements.

Cash Value

This is the portion of a whole life insurance policy that has actually been contributed by you. A low rate of interest is paid on it. It grows with every year that you hold the policy. Cash value can be borrowed out at a very low rate of interest. That sounds great until you remember that it's your money anyway. You are paying to borrow money from yourself!

Lest a whole life policy *still* look good to you, I'd like to remind you that those dollars of yours are eroding drastically over time. Refer to the inflation charts in Chapter 4. Even at a 5 percent inflation rate, your dollar looks pretty sad after twenty years. Furthermore, it takes almost that long—fifteen to twenty years—to build up a sizable cash value policy! Don't be fooled by the lure of a build-up of cash value. You'd do better in almost any other savings plan.

*   *   *

In any life insurance policy, you name a person or persons who will receive the benefits should you die. You can name your spouse, your lover, your friends or family, or a trustee to administer the money for your young children.

AUTOMOBILE INSURANCE

Automobile insurance protects your car and its occupants against financial loss resulting from an auto accident. If you own a car you should own car insurance, and some states require you to do so before you can register your car. Auto insurance, like any other kind of insurance, needs to be shopped for. But first, you have to know what to look for and make some decisions about what kind and how much coverage you need.

There are no standard price guidelines for car insurance, and there are vast cost fluctuations from one company to another. You will need to do some comparison shopping to get the best deal from the most honest and reliable company. *Consumer Reports* examines and rates auto insurance companies. I strongly recommend a trip to the library to read these. Ask the reference librarian.

Generally, there are five areas of coverage in any auto insurance policy: liability, collision, comprehensive, uninsured motorist, and medical payments. Some policies also offer a restitution clause for loss of wages and the cost of services, such as a housekeeper, due to injury in an auto accident.

Liability coverage is protection against total financial wipe-out when an accident occurs causing grave bodily injury or extensive property damage to others and you are at fault. Even if you have no other form of protection, liability is a must. And with today's exorbitant medical costs and auto prices, it is advisable to pay the extra money charged to carry *more* than just minimum liability coverage. Remember, however, that you can be insured to the limit with liability and it will not cover your own losses unless you live in a no-fault state. Rather, you will have to sue the other party in a two-or-more vehicle accident *and* prove the driver was at fault.

Collision insurance protects your property, no matter who caused an accident. Obviously, if you have a brand spanking new car, collision is essential. However, even if you dearly love your reliable, albeit beat-up, old clunker, this form of coverage is a waste of your money. An insurance company will only give you the cash value of your car, that is, its cost, less depreciation. They put no value on fuel-efficient, lifetime dependability. Alas, that old Chevy is *still* only worth $300 bucks.

Comprehensive covers loss due to theft, vandalism, fire, animals, or other such hazards. My friend Janet's car was broken into and her three-month-old tape deck was stolen and now offers solace to someone else driving home on the highway! Fortunately, her $50 deductible comprehensive insurance covered the cost of replacing the cassette player/radio combo. Unfortunately, Chrysler no longer stocks replacement dashboards for Janet's six-year-old car, and comprehensive does not cover irresponsible auto manufacturers!

Uninsured motorist covers damage to you, your passengers, or your property when involved in an accident where the person at fault has no insurance. That same little car with the sorry looking dashboard was hit, while parked, by a rude little reprobate with bloodshot eyes. Worse, he had no insurance. Thanks to Janet's excellent insurance policy, her car looks as good as new. (Her leaky trunk is a well-kept secret!)

Uninsured motorist coverage is very important as there are lots of people driving around without insurance. If they are as irresponsible on the highway as they are about insurance, then you can really see the need for this type of protection.

A medical payments clause covers medical expenses, up to a certain limit, for you or your passengers, no matter who was at fault in an accident. When a shiny new Buick became intimate with the passenger door of my friend's Chevy, the result was a painful whiplash in my neck! Fortunately, Sharon had a medical payments clause in her policy, and my ongoing medical expenses were all covered.

In car insurance, as in all forms of insurance, you can lower your premium by raising your deductible. You can also save by dropping collision and possibly comprehensive on an older car. Liability, uninsured motorist, and medical payments, however, are all essential for an adequate auto insurance policy.

HOMEOWNERS AND RENTERS INSURANCE

Homeowners insurance is essential to protect the equity in your property. It covers loss due to fire, theft, and certain other catastrophes. The minimum coverage that you should have is 80 percent of the current replacement value of your home and its contents, not including the land. Land doesn't burn! Remember, these figures should be updated periodically to keep pace with inflation. The home you bought for $40,000 many years ago is worth quite a bit more now.

On the other hand, beware of over-coverage. You can buy $150,000 worth of insurance on a $100,000 home. However, should the house burn to the ground, $100,000 is the maximum that you will be eligible to receive.

There are limits to the amount of cash that is covered in any policy. So clean out that mattress and put the green stuff into a safe investment! Also, many policies do *not* include coverage for fine arts, jewelry, collections, sporting or musical equipment, silver, crystal, antiques, and so on. To prevent the loss of one of your treasures, specific things should be listed in your policy for specific values. This is called scheduling and is crucial if you want to protect something special that is normally not included in a homeowners policy. It'll increase the cost of the policy, of course, but wouldn't it be terrible to lose that set of meticulously selected crystal and not be able to replace it?

There are essentially three different forms of homeowners insurance. Basic Form policy, or Homeowners A, is the least expensive and the most limited in its coverage. Broad Form, or Homeowners B, is the most popular. It's fairly comprehensive and offers extensive protection. Most of the mishaps that can occur to your home are covered by this type of insurance. Comprehensive Form, or Homeowners C, is the most expensive and covers virtually every possible risk except nuclear war, earthquakes, and floods.

A good homeowners policy covers many things:

Your house, of course.

Your garage, storage shed or outside unattached buildings.

Your personal property at home.

Your personal property away from home, such as your luggage on a trip.

Personal liability. For instance, should that dog of yours bite your best friend, who then sues you.

Medical payments. This will pay for your friend's medical expenses in caring for the dog bite.

Reimbursement for living expenses if your home becomes uninhabitable and you must live elsewhere temporarily.

Damage to somebody else's property while in your possession.

All of these areas will have certain deductible amounts. Remember, the greater the deductible, the lower the premium.

Renters insurance covers only the contents of your rented house or apartment. The contents must be listed and should be photographed with serial numbers noted. Costs for this kind of insurance are usually based on your area of residence. Your rates will be higher if you rent in the Soho district of New York than if you had a spiffy little place on the East Side. Renters insurance is fairly inexpensive but limits its coverage in the same ways that homeowners insurance does. Read the policy and attach a schedule for anything not covered.

If you have some fine pieces of art or jewelry, you should investigate separate policies to cover them. Be careful with these, though, because they are tricky. My brother insured a beautiful pre-Columbian bowl. A piece of it broke off and had to be repaired. Lo and behold, his insurance was cancelled! Now he's stuck with this beautiful, expensive piece of art and no way to protect it.

It Ain't Actuarially So

Webster defines an actuary as an expert who calculates risk and premiums. This person, usually dressed in a green plastic visor, figures out when and how we are likely to be injured, smash up our car, get sick, have our house cave in, and/or die. This strange person doesn't tell us—rather he or she passes on this information to our insurance companies. These bastions of American life digest this information and immediately raise (or *very* occasionally lower) our premiums.

Actuarial tables are the source for all insurance figures. They are updated every twenty years and, like all statistical data, are subject to interpretation.

For instance, women pay higher premiums for health and disability insurance. The reasoning behind this is because, actuarially speaking, women get sick more often than men and miss more work days than men. Well, current Labor Department statistics show women missing 5.3 days of work per year and men, 4.7 days. This is hardly a serious difference—six tenths of a day! Furthermore, Dee Dee Ahern, in *The Economics of Being a Woman*, points out that "both in frequency and duration of hospitalization, the overall cost of female claims is *less* than that of males."

Another complaint is that women go to the doctor more often. This is substantiated by the Census Bureau for women between the ages of seventeen and forty-four. Weighting these figures, however, is that visits to the obstetrician are included! Women between seventeen and forty-four are in their childbearing years, and each nine months of an uncomplicated pregnancy involves at least fifteen visits to the doctor.

Actuarial tables can be the source of continuing problems for women trying to purchase insurance. Even feminist insurance agents can be swayed. One favorite woman agent of mine, a staunch supporter of women's rights, said of insurance companies' health plans, "They don't discriminate against women, they just charge them more."

Insurance, for better or for worse, has become as much a part of the fabric of American life as apple pie and lawsuits. For women, this means having to learn a whole lot of new and sometimes confusing information. Remember, the insurance business is about as competitive and as ethical as the used car business. It has a history of unfair treatment of women. So you must be on your toes and equipped with some of the savvy necessary to purchase insurance wisely and realistically.

INSURANCE ANALYSIS

Casualty insurance (homeowners and automobile) is necessary if you own a home or car, regardless of what age or stage of life you are in.

Health, disability and life insurance needs if you are:

Young and Single

Medical
Disability, if you work

Young and Married

Medical
Disability, if you work

Married with Young Children

Medical

Disability

Term life, enough to see you through five years

Forty-Plus

Medical

Disability

Term life, reduced amount; necessary if your other assets are not sufficient to support a surviving spouse or dependent children

Fifty-Five-Plus

Medical

Disability

Term life, if other assets are insufficient to support a surviving spouse

Sixty-Five-Plus

Medical, supplementary policy to Medicare

Term life, if other assets are insufficient

11

Retirement Planning Now

Simone de Beauvoir wrote, "It is for women in particular that the last age is a liberation; all their lives they were subject to their husbands and given over to the care of their children. Now at last they can look after themselves." In order to really enjoy their last age, women, must prepare for it early on in their lives.

Remember, the only alternative to growing old is dying young. Retirement and estate planning may be of little interest to you now. It's difficult to think about the future when you are young, vigorous, and full of strength. However, it may be too late to adequately plan for your old age if you are already older.

One million aged Americans slip into poverty each year. Many of these people were middle class when they were younger. They were school teachers, managers, buyers, etc., and made substantial contributions to the welfare of their community. Many of them left the labor force before pension plans were widespread and, now, in the 1980s find themselves in serious financial trouble.

Nobody will have your best interests at heart as much as you. Nobody is out there waiting to take care of you—that's your job!

The fact is that retirement and the golden years bring loss of work, status, and collegial relationships, and a significant drop in income. It is also a time when most women are alone, their children grown, and their husbands dead. (Four women out of five survive their husbands.) If a woman retires at sixty-five, she can expect to live fifteen to twenty years in the golden years.

At the turn of the century, people didn't retire. They

worked until they died or until their strength was no longer adequate for the job and they were let go. When a woman grew old and dependent, she was often considered a valuable asset in her child's home, an extra pair of expert hands to help with the work. Today, without the extended family, married and single women must plan carefully for their retirement years.

Tony Lamb and Dave Duffy wrote in *The Retirement Threat*: "Retirement can be much more of a shock for the middle and upper-middle classes than for the very rich or poor. The very rich have resources to battle inflation, which usually robs the retired of buying power. And the poor have spent their whole lives managing on tight budgets. But people in the middle and upper-middle classes have limited resources to cope with the runaway cost of living. It is their standard of living that is apt to slip and this can be most upsetting."

What should women do now about retirement? First let's look at what makes a good retirement package, and then how to put one together.

An ideal retirement package consists of:

1. a paid-up residence (unless you are an apartment dweller)
2. adequate income-producing investments
3. realistic private and employee pension plans
4. Social Security as a *supplement* to all of these

When Should You Start Planning for Retirement?

A part of your retirement income starts building the moment you begin working. Social Security is taken out of your paycheck from day one. Another part of your check goes to a retirement plan if your company has one and you have joined it. An IRA or Keogh Plan (see below) is your responsibility; if you can possibly afford to do so, start one now. One thousand dollars a year (less than $100 a month) at 7.5 percent interest will give you $49,000 after twenty years. At 10 percent interest, that $1,000 a year in twenty years will have grown to $67,200. If you wait to start your plan until you're in your forties or fifties, you'll have to put in much more in order to play catch up!

The chart on p. 222 shows what inflation does to your pension dollars. This should be incentive to you to dig in and begin to amass your retirement package now.

Ever Shrinking Pension Dollars

Annual Pension Income	Annual Inflation Rate	*Purchasing Power After	
		5 yrs.	10 yrs.
	3%	8,600	7,400
$10,000 @	7%	7,000	4,800
	10%	5,900	3,500
	3%	21,500	14,700
$25,000 @	7%	17,400	12,100
	10%	5,900	3,500
	3%	30,050	25,800
$35,000 @	7%	25,350	16,900
	10%	20,700	12,200

* Figures rounded off

Before we discuss those elements of a retirement package that you must put together yourself, let's look at the involuntary plan of Social Security.

SOCIAL SECURITY

In 1940, a retired bookkeeper named Ida Fuller received the first Social Security payment, a grand and princely check of $22.54. Today she would get at least ten times that, a grand and princely check of $225.40 per month. I don't know how Ida made out then on her twenty-two bucks, but I know how she'd be living today if she had to depend only on her Social Security!

Social Security was originally conceived of as a *modest* retirement plan, and has since grown to become a broad-based insurance system. It is still, however, extremely modest, unpretentious, and oh, so humble.

Many older people confuse Social Security benefits with welfare. Social Security is a pay-as-you-go insurance plan. You pay for it out of your wages during your entire work life. It is a mystery to me how Social Security checks ever became a source of embarrassment! The rich people I know enjoy Social Security the most. They love the idea of getting a check from the government for a change, rather than sending one.

Social Security Know-How

Social Security benefits must be applied for at your local Social Security office. Contact the office three months before you are entitled to benefits as it takes a while to process your application.

There is a formula by which Social Security figures your benefits. It includes the length of time you've worked and the amount of money you've paid into Social Security. Naturally, you will receive the largest benefits if you've paid the maximum amount of money over a long period of time. If you are interested in seeing where you stand now, call your Social Security office and ask for the pamphlet entitled *Estimating your Social Security Retirement Benefits.*

You can take early retirement at age sixty-two. However, if you do you will be heavily penalized through reduced benefits. The Social Security Administration figures that if you retire early you'll receive checks for a longer period of time. Also, the present administration is against early retirement because it feels it will drain an already financially weakened system.

There is presently a ceiling on what you can earn after you have started collecting Social Security. If you earn more than allowed, Social Security will reduce or eliminate your payments. The age after which you may collect all the Social Security coming to you no matter how much you earn ranges from seventy to seventy-two. This keeps changing, so check.

Social Security has become a complex plan that includes burial and disability allowances, special supports for dependent children, and widow's benefits. I recommend a pamphlet entitled *Social Security, Government Benefits, Medicare,* put out by the editors of *Consumer Guide* as a helpful guide to this elaborate system. This is published by Fawcett/Columbine (New York) and can be ordered through your local bookseller.

The Future for Social Security

Social Security has expanded since Ida Fuller's day. It will change many more times during your life. A pamphlet can tell you how the system works and how to work the system but not where the system is going. Most changes in the system are front page news. You should follow these changes; it's *your* money they're dealing with.

Social Security is in trouble. There are too many older people due to collect and too few younger workers coming into the system to adequately support those who are retiring now. However, no administration will let Social Security go bankrupt. The benefits will change and shrink and eligibility rules will become more stringent, but the basic structure of this modest proposal will hold. It's the most sacred of the sacred cows—as well it should be.

For those retirees who saw Social Security as a supplementary income, the system has worked well. For the less fortunate, who could never save for retirement, the little income that Social Security does provide is better than nothing.

EMPLOYER PENSION PLANS

A decent pension plan could make an important difference to you when you are old, the difference between survival and sufficiency. You *must* take the time to understand the various employee pension plans. An article in the *Los Angeles Times* states, "As crucial as these extra benefits obviously are, only half of American workers are covered by pension plans—that is, retirement programs into which they or their employers have contributed and from which they later receive an income from the funds invested in the interim. Even fewer workers are assured of benefits once they retire because most plans require that a person have worked for an employer five or ten years before gaining pension rights—or as the jargon goes before being 'vested.'" Vested means that you get to keep whatever retirement you've accrued no matter how or why you leave a company. Your retirement fund must be given directly to you or transferred to your new place of employment.

ERISA

In 1974, the Employment Retirement Income Security Act (ERISA) was passed. This was designed to protect the interests of employees in their company pension plans. In many cases, ERISA has been worthwhile and important. However, the complexity and rigidity of its regulations have caused some smaller companies to drop out of pension plans entirely.

There are some aspects of this law that you should be aware of. For instance:

1. If you work for a company with a retirement plan, that

company must provide you with an annual financial statement about the plan. You must also receive a clearly worded pamphlet explaining the plan.

2. A company has the right to deny you access to its pension plan until it sees how you are going to work out. ERISA sanctions three eligibility standards for participating in a pension plan. A company can require that:

a. You be at least twenty-five and have worked for one year with the company.

b. You be at least twenty-five and have worked for three years with the company. (In this case, vesting takes place immediately upon enrolling.)

c. You be any age and have worked for three years with the company.

3. ERISA does permit a company to exclude you if you join the organization within five years of retirement age or if you are under twenty-five years old.

4. A retirement plan most probably will contain a vesting schedule either based upon years of service or a combination of age and years of service. The plan sponsor may choose the vesting schedule appropriate for its business. Some common schedules are 10 percent vesting per year, so that an employee is fully vested after ten years of service, or 20 percent vesting per year, so that an employee is fully vested after five years of service. Vesting really means the amount of your pension account that you may carry with you if you should leave the employ of the sponsoring company. As an example, if the vesting schedule is 10 percent per year and you leave the company after four years, you take with you 40 percent of your account balance. This is your accrued benefit. The remaining 60 percent is forfeited.

This rule looks good on paper, but statistics show the average man changes jobs every five years and the average woman every three years. Women are predominantly the ones stuck in low-paying jobs, and after a couple of years in the lingerie department at Macy's one might absolutely lust for a change of scene and go charging off to Gimbel's. You lose your Macy's retirement benefits as a result.

5. When you do leave a job, you may be entitled to partial pension at retirement or a lump sum payment immediately. Be sure to check on this should you change your job.

Pension Formulas

There are two types of pension formulas. One is a defined contribution plan. In this plan your company contributes a percentage of your salary up to 25 percent, which is invested for you. When you retire, the money credited to you will be used to buy an annuity or you can take it in lump sum or installment payments. If you buy an annuity, you'll receive monthly checks as your pension. How large your monthly check is will depend on the size of the annuity and how successfully your plan has been managed. This type of plan includes deferred profit-sharing and stock bonus programs.

The other plan is the defined benefit plan, which uses a formula to fix a definite dollar amount to your benefits. This formula is based on years of service and the amount of your salary, and actuarial tables are used to figure the actual amount. For example, you might receive 80 percent of your salary from the average of your top three earning years.

Remember, there are no provisions for cost of living increases in most plans. That nice check of $1,200 a month will, in times of inflation, buy less each year. Example: If you had received a pension in 1970, its purchasing power by 1980 would have been 70 percent less. Social Security, humble as it is, does have a built-in cost-of-living increase. A few pensions do have a wee annual raise of about 3 percent or so.

Prior to retirement, your company should inform you of the ways your retirement benefit may be paid to you. Most plans allow you to elect either an annuity (joint-and-survivor *unless* you positively opt for a sole annuity), periodic payments, or a lump sum distribution. As each choice carried different tax implications, as well as benefits to your spouse, it is important for you and your spouse to discuss this matter with your financial and tax advisors.

Besides retirement payout, most pension plans also provide for payout in the event of death or total disability.

PRIVATE PENSION PLANS

Individual Retirement Account (IRA)

This plan was established for people who worked for companies that didn't have a retirement plan. Under the Economic Recovery Tax Act of 1981, IRA plans can be set up even if you are already enrolled in a private or employee pension plan. You can start an IRA at a bank, savings institution, insurance company, or brokerage house. You and your working spouse can separately put in $2,000 or you can invest a total of $2,250 if you have a non-working spouse. You put in dollars earned from working before tax dollars and thereby lower your overall taxes—a great advantage. In many cases you are saving dollars that would, in large part, just go to the government in taxes. The interest you earn in an IRA isn't taxed until you take out your money. This is a wonderful investment and probably the only decent tax break for the middle class in our new tax reform package.

There is a wide range of choices among IRA accounts. This means you'll have to shop for the best investment package. The amount of interest that you will receive on your IRA account depends completely on what instrument you use to fund your account. The interest you earn is not taxed until it's withdrawn. Meanwhile, it compounds itself for your joy and profit!

Before 1982, the government permitted diamonds, gemstones, and other collectibles as IRA investments. Collectibles as instruments are no longer allowed.

When you open an IRA, invest in high-yield securities, such as stocks and Treasury Bills. If you have an unproductive, low-yield IRA, you are allowed a rollover. This means you can change your current account to a higher yielding one. A word of caution: Since IRA plans are retirement plans and not short-term investment vehicles, only one rollover is allowed per year without interest penalty.

IRA Payout

There are some rules governing how, when, and why you can take your money out of an IRA:

1. You can elect to take your money any time between the ages of fifty-nine-and-one-half and seventy-one-and-one-half.

2. You can take your money out earlier, but you'll have to pay a penalty of 10 percent of your accumulated interest and also pay income tax on the amount withdrawn.

3. You can take out your money any time without penalty if you're disabled. If you die, regardless of age, the money will be paid to the beneficiary you name.

4. You can elect to take your money back in a lump sum or on a periodic payment plan.

5. You can elect to rollover a lump sum into an annuity within sixty days after retirement. If you wait more than 60 days you will lose this option.

6. Each choice has very different tax repercussions, and you must decide, with your accountant, which is best for you.

The Keogh Plan

This plan is for self-employed people. If you fall into this group you may put 15 percent of your earned income, or $15,000, whichever is less, into a private plan. Again, you use before-tax dollars. A lot of the money you invest in your plan would otherwise go to Uncle Sam.

Even moonlighters have rights, so if you're self-employed on a part-time basis you can set up a Keogh. This is so, even if you work at a job that provides you with a pension plan.

When you are ready to take money out of your Keogh Plan, it falls under the same rules as the IRA plan. You must discuss your decision with an accountant, to understand the tax consequences of your decision.

It's not easy for anyone these days to come up with cash to put into an IRA or a Keogh Plan. Beg, borrow, or steal to do so. Remember, you'll have two advantages: You'll be saving for your future, and doing so with money you would otherwise pay to the government.

DIVORCEE'S AND WIDOW'S BENEFITS

Social Security and pension plans offer a range from full to no benefits to divorced women and widows:

Social Security

• Provides some benefits to divorced women and/or widows who were married for at least ten years.

• As a divorcee, you are entitled to ex-spouse's benefits if you are at least sixty-two and have not remarried.

• As a divorcee, you are also entitled to widow's benefits when your ex-husband dies, if you do not remarry before age sixty.

- If you are at least sixty-five and a widow, you can receive 100 percent of what your husband received when he died.

- You may collect widow's benefits at age sixty, but they will be reduced.

- As a widow of any age with dependent children, you and your children are eligible for benefits.

Company Pension Plans

- Do not recognize or pay out to a divorced spouse.

- Are considered as part of divorce settlement in many states, especially community property and equitable distribution states.

- In a divorce are often considered an asset of the husband's that should be offset by an equal asset going to the wife.

- Note: A person can work for a company for forty years but if he/she dies *before* retirement, the spouse receives nothing! Be careful of settling for interest in an ex-husband's pension plan—you could end up with one-half interest in nothing.

- A person can elect a joint and survivor pay-out plan, thereby guaranteeing income to a widow. These pay out less per month than sole benefits do.

- Pension benefits are considered the sole property of the employee. Check your spouse's plan to see what, if any, provisions are available to widows.

Private Pension Plans—IRA and Keogh

- As in company plans, IRAs and Keoghs should be negotiated for in divorce settlements.

- They are considered an asset of the husband's in divorce settlements (unless the wife has one established of her own) and should be offset by an asset of equal value to the wife.

- Beneficiaries are named. A widow who has been named beneficiary receives benefits at the appropriate age, in a lump sum, installments, or as an annuity.

ANNUITIES

An annuity is an investment that provides a fixed yearly income during one's lifetime or for a specific period of time. Annuities have had a bad name for a long time; and they deserved this reputation. They were what little old men and women lived on in genteel poverty. Annuities have taken a long time to develop into the sophisticated instrument they are today, but because of their bad reputation they are often overlooked in financial planning.

A very attractive and important aspect of qualified annuities is that the money they earn is tax-deferred until payout. It grows and compounds without a bite from the IRS.

Annuities can be bought through life insurance agents and through many stockbrokers. Annuity guidelines come from the *same* actuarial tables that life insurance companies use. Remember, annuity and insurance sellers are in the business of making money. Contrary to what they might have you believe, these are not charitable organizations. Therefore, purchase annuities, like anything else, carefully and wisely.

There are three ways to buy an annuity, depending on your particular financial situation:

1. You can buy in a one-shot lump sum purchase to start paying off now.
2. You can buy in a lump sum purchase to start paying off at some stipulated time in the future.
3. You can buy a future annuity by making payments into it over time.

Fixed vs. Variable Annuities

There are two kinds of annuities being sold today, fixed and variable. A fixed annuity guarantees you a fixed sum of money for life, paid out in monthly checks. An example of this type of annuity is a lump sum annuity bought for $24,000 that will pay $200 a month for life. A life could end tomorrow or go on for forty more years. (Women pay more than men because they live longer.)

What will the $200 a month mean in twenty years? Look at the inflation chart in Chapter 4 and you'll see. For example, if inflation is at 10 percent, your $200 will have the purchasing power of $29.80. One dollar at a 10 percent inflation rate has a purchasing power of .149 after twenty years. So, .149 x

200 = 29.80. Obviously this is a rotten investment and the reason annuities got their bad reputation.

A variable annuity, as its name suggests, will give you a varying sum of money each month. The sum you receive will depend on the value of a fixed number of investment units for as long as you live. The number of investment units you have depends on the amount you pay to buy into the annuity. Each month when your check is prepared, the company multiplies the number of units you own by that day's unit value. Since the value fluctuates, your check will, too.

Example: September check, forty investment units, each unit worth $7.40 x 7.00 = $280. October check, forty investment units, each unit worth $7.11. 40 x 7.11 = $284.40.

The variable annuity check is based on current economic realities rather than what looked good fifteen or twenty years ago. With this type of annuity, you have a fighting chance to maintain a good investment.

Why, then, does anyone ever choose a fixed over a variable annuity? Because with a fixed annuity the company guarantees the amount paid to you no matter what. It takes the risk. In the variable annuity, you don't get a guarantee. But while you take the risk, you also reap the rewards.

My gut instinct, not to mention the news headlines, tells me that the buying power of the dollar is eroding. Just as I won't buy long-term bonds, so will I not buy a fixed-income security. I believe it's far wiser to take your chances.

Wrap-around, or family fund variable annuities, are the latest vehicles for annuity investments and the type I recommend to my clients. They, too, can be bought from an insurance agent or stockbroker. They bring together a life insurance company and an investment management firm with a family of mutual funds. You decide which mutual fund you want, and then you're free to switch around in whatever manner and at whatever time you choose. If interest rates are high, you can move into a high-interest-yield fund. When you think stocks are good, you can move to a family fund member that is investing in growth stocks. After the annuities start paying out, you may still move from one family fund to another but only once a year.

Annuity Payout

The three major options for annuity payout are:
1. Guaranteed income for life.

2. Guaranteed income for husband and/or wife, for as long as either is alive.

3. Ten years certain—income guaranteed for at least ten years. If you die before ten years, a beneficiary of your choice receives the monthly check until the ten-year period is up.

You can take out any or all monies in the annuity, not to exceed what you put in originally, up until the day you get your first payout. The money you use to buy an annuity has been taxed already. When you are paid out, only the interest earned is taxed.

Rollovers into Annuities

When your IRA or Keogh is drawn out between the ages fifty-nine-and-one-half to seventy-one-and-one-half, it comes out with a bang! It's rather like the one-armed bandits in New Jersey and Las Vegas. That retirement money went in tax free, remember, and all you've made on it has also been tax free. When it comes out, you'll have to pay taxes on every cent. In some situations the government taxes IRAs and Keoghs differently, so check with an accountant. You might be better off rolling over your plan into a qualified annuity. *This must be done within sixty days of the end of the IRA or Keogh, or you lose the tax benefit of this option.* Some Keogh and IRA have specific payout plans; but if yours doesn't, an annuity may be just the thing for you. Check with your accountant on all options. This is very complex and always subject to change.

Some Other Reasons for Buying an Annuity

1. You have a child in need of protection. For instance, an annuity could be helpful for a handicapped child who will never be self-supporting, or for a spendthrift child who shows no sign of ever learning the value of money. The child could have a guaranteed income for life rather than a lump sum inheritance that he couldn't handle. However, parents need the dough to begin with to buy this type of investment.

2. You don't want to be an active investor. Annuities, with the exception of the wrap-around type, are passive.

3. You receive an inheritance and know you can't hold on to money. An annuity provides a good old-fashioned allowance. You get a certain amount every month with no opportunity to blow the whole thing on a new adult toy!

4. Your IRA or Keogh account doesn't have a payout plan, and you would benefit more from an annuity than you would from ten-year income averaging or other tax treatment.

REAL ESTATE AND RETIREMENT

Real estate appreciation has outpaced inflation, and a paid-up home is probably the single greatest asset you can have. You still have real estate taxes and maintenance, but you also have an asset you can live in. Most people have their peak earning power in their fifties. That is a time to think about paying more than required each month on your mortgage. See your banker and figure out how much more you need to pay each month so you can reduce the mortgage to zero by age sixty-five or seventy.

Some states permit older people to defer real estate taxes. The state will lien your home for the amount of the taxes you owe and get its money and interest back from the sale of your home if you sell or when you die. Check with the Department of Real Estate in your state.

Some lending institutions have reverse mortgages for older homeowners. They will pay you money each month and use your home as collateral. When you die or sell they will get paid back, with interest, from the proceeds of the sale. The Department of Real Estate in your home state can provide you with detailed information about where to get these mortgages if they are available.

These ideas are quite new in the mortgage business. I hope they'll spread, because they're sensible and humane.

If you own or inherit a second home and can afford to keep it for vacations now, it will be a great asset when you're old. You could use your second home as income property and rent it out when you have less income. Rents also have risen sharply and will probably continue to do so. Any asset that's not tied to a fixed income will obviously bring you more money in the future because it will become more valuable with inflation.

Some people, when they retire, want to sell their home and move to a smaller place in a better climate. The sale of your fully paid-up home will provide the necessary funds to reestablish yourself where you want. Any excess money can be invested to increase your retirement income.

There is another big plus should you decide to sell your

home. Under the new tax laws, $125,000 of the profit on the sale of your home is exempt from taxes! This is a one-time benefit. You must be at least fifty-five years old and have lived in your home for three years to take advantage of it.

WOMEN AND RETIREMENT

Women have an advantage over men at retirement. For most women, roles and role demands over the course of their lives change constantly. Women move in and out of a variety of roles: employee, wife, mother, housewife, divorcee, and widow. The impact of all these changes and repeated adjustments to change in life situations make women's adjustment to old age easier than men's.

However, moving from an active work life to a sedentary retirement is physically and mentally unhealthy. One should remain engaged with the world. There are part-time jobs suited to older women. While most of them are not very prestigious, they do provide extra money as well as continued interaction with the world.

A partial list of jobs that are in demand includes dog sitting, house sitting, plant sitting, baby sitting, part-time bookkeeping, part-time office work, or work through a temporary agency. Also, working at older adult centers, working for an organization like Meals on Wheels, driving for older people who don't drive, teaching or tutoring children and adults in a private practice or through an adult school.

Lobby for Your Future

Since we all expect to be older people some day, it is in our best interest to lobby now for some basic benefits for the aging. One such benefit would be a national health insurance program. The cost of medical care is highest for older people and the United States is the only major country in the western world without a national health insurance plan. It is a disgrace to this country that our middle-income and older people can be financially wiped out by a single major illness.

Tony Lamb, author of *The Retirement Threat*, in a recent interview told me horror story after horror story about the effects of medical bills on the aged. One typical story was about an eighty-year-old woman whose husband collapsed in front of their mobile home. She called the paramedics, and he was taken to the hospital and put into intensive care. He died ten days later. His wife now has a $10,000 hospital bill above and beyond what Medicare paid, and will have to sell her mobile home to pay it. As a widow her Social Security will be cut, and she'll have to go on welfare. She said to Tony, "Why did I call the paramedics, he was as good as dead when he arrived at the hospital? I should have let him die, it would only have taken a few minutes!" We cannot let our older Americans face these tragedies!

Another program that would be of great value to older people is a negative income tax. This means that any person whose income fell below a certain level would receive enough money from the state or federal government to have a subsistence income.

Once a child is born in this country that child must be fed and housed. The child must receive public education to equip him or her to work for a future with some dignity. And when people grow old, if they can no longer fully care for themselves, the community must care for them. I always believed that was what America was all about. Misfortune can be anyone's lot, and let me guarantee you that there is no safety net out there if you're old.

Other programs are desperately needed, such as affordable housing for the aged that caters to their special needs. Cheap public transportation should be provided for our country's aged. Utility rates should take into account the low income of the elderly. Some programs are in place already, but more are needed. Programs such as meals on wheels need to grow so that shut-ins get at least one well-balanced meal brought to them each day. We need a national program of visiting nurses and homemakers to help the bedridden. Many of these programs would open up new jobs and many would lower the cost of welfare.

We could use a tax law that would exempt people over sixty-five from paying taxes on the first $10,000 of income from investment; and this exempt amount should rise with the cost of living. This would provide a great incentive to saving and produce new money for investments.

Lobby for your future. Support candidates who are concerned with problems of an aging population. You'll be voting from self-interest, for you probably will be old some day too!

Reevaluating Your Investments

Anne, an older retired woman, came for a consultation. She wanted to see where she could cut down on expenses without too much pain. Besides Social Security, she had some investments that provided an income. However, each year her income's purchasing power was dwindling.

When looking at Anne's monthly expenses I saw some items that could indeed be cut. Each month she paid $25 for a life insurance policy for her son. The son is a very successful doctor in Chicago! Anne somehow still saw him as her child whose future she had to insure. Since the policy was a whole life policy and had cash value, we scooped out the cash and put it into a high-yield mutual fund paying over twice the interest.

I also saw another $25 item marked savings. Anne was saving for the future even in retirement! She had met the future and it was now, but she hadn't rethought her financial position. When I suggested that, because of her age, rather than saving she might consider going into capital and enjoying life more, you would have thought I had told a very unfunny dirty joke.

Anne's situation brought to mind this old story about two proper Bostonians:

First Bostonian: "I'm afraid I've got to use some of my capital to set up my son's medical practice."

Second Bostonian: "Living on interest is permitted, but capital! Invading capital! Why only a scoundrel would do that!"

Somehow, we, a nation of immigrants, have all developed into Boston Brahmins in two short generations! Not only do we wish to be financially independent in our retirement years, we also wish to leave our capital intact so our children can inherit money from us at our death.

As an older person, you must reevaluate all your past investment strategies. You are no longer interested in making your fortune. Growth, so important in your early years, is no longer a financial priority. Now is the time for comfort, a time to reap the rewards of a long working life.

I recommend that growth stocks be sold and put into reputable high-yield interest bearing investments. Today, these include such things as money market funds, T-Bills, certificates of deposit, and high-dividend stocks. Remember, retirement is the time to enjoy terrestrial rewards. Celestial rewards *may* come later, but these you can't save for. They are earned by other means.

Retirement can and should be a wonderful and relaxing period of your life. Your children are grown and your confinement to a strict work routine is over. With proper planning and a bit of watchfulness, you can indeed look forward to that last age as a liberation.

12

Wills and Estate Planning

WILLS

Free Will vs. Predestination

If your permanent address is the Sunshine Mission downtown, you probably don't need a Will. However, every other person needs one, RIGHT NOW! Most people say, "If I were to die—," "Were I to die—," etc. Make no mistake, you're going to die! (Remember, you read it here first.) And if you want *your* desires rather than those of the states carried out, a Will is essential.

There are two reasons to write a Will. The first and most important reason is to leave money to whom you want and in the manner you desire. The second reason is to minimize taxes on estates left to someone other than a spouse if your estate is over the current taxable limit, which will rise from a 1982 ceiling of $225,000 to $600,000 by 1987. Sometimes these two ideas do not jibe. When they don't, *remember it is more important to leave the money to those you choose in the manner you choose,* than to save on estate taxes.

You might think you have nothing to leave but a stack of bills. But remember, you may have a house, furniture, silver, jewelry, a future inheritance, ten little acres in Texas left you by Grandpa, three thousand cash you lent a friend, and a couple of kids to boot. All your assets are appreciating with inflation—except the kids. The disposition of these things must be taken care of by a Will.

If you don't have a Will (seven out of ten people die without leaving one), the state decides what happens to your things and your kids. Depending on your home state, your surviving spouse will get one-third to one-half of your estate and your children will get the rest. Do them a favor and make a Will. It will lessen the burdens of that first year after a death, which is an emotional ferris wheel.

Many formerly close sisters and brothers aren't speaking to each other today because of their parents' Wills. If a Will is not explicit about who gets what, there can be a lifetime falling out among the heirs. The disposition of a scratched table or an ugly coral ashtray can cause an emotional firestorm. Money can be easily divided but personal effects are loaded pistols. So do list who should get what in your Will. Then if some of your heirs feel slighted they can be angry with you; wherever you are, I don't think you'll care!

If you do not write a Will, and if you have no spouse and no children, generally your money goes first to your parents, then to surviving siblings, then to cousins, etc. If you have no living relatives, your heir will be the state in which you live.

A Legal Bargain

A Will is the only loss leader—the cheap special used to lure you in—in the legal supermarket. A simple Will can run from $35 at a legal clinic to a couple of hundred dollars at your attorney's—or you can write your Will in your own handwriting.

Pay a lawyer, and get it done correctly. A famous case study for law students offers a wonderful example of "The Mystery of the Misplaced Comma," or "What Did Daddy *REALLY* MEAN?" A man wrote, "I leave my estate in equal shares to Jeremy and Stephen Smith, and to John Smith." Because of the comma, the court ruled that Jeremy and Stephen should each receive 25 percent and John received 50 percent.

Things to Decide Before You See a Lawyer

Before you go to an attorney to have your Will drawn up, there are several decisions you must make. They are:

1. Whom do you want to leave your money to: spouse, children, relatives, friends, educational institutions, charities?

2. How much do you want to leave to any one person or institution?

3. In what form do you want to leave it, outright or in a trust?

4. Whom do you want to leave your personal property to—jewelry, art, furniture, memorabilia?

5. Whom do you want to be guardians of your minor children?

6. Whom do you want to act as trustee of your minor children's money?

7. Whom do you want as executor of your Will?

Joint Wills, Oral Wills, and Handwritten Wills

Joint Wills should not be drawn up under any circumstances. Two separate Wills are the best way to go. A joint Will has absolutely nothing to recommend it. It can lead to an inability to change your Will without the consent of your spouse and possible legal complications should there be simultaneous death.

Oral Wills are recognized in only a few states. They *are* valid in military combat—but only if you die in action!

Handwritten Wills hold more danger than just a misplaced comma. The requirements of each state for the validity of a handwritten Will are stringent, and each state has its own set of rules. The only valid use for this type of Will is as an emergency measure. Once the emergency is over, get thee to a lawyer!

Where to Keep Your Will

The original Will should be at your attorney's office, with a copy at home. Your Will should not be in a safe deposit box because in some states these are sealed until the contents are inventoried for the estate. This could unnecessarily delay the administration of your estate.

Revising Your Will

Your Will should be changed as your life changes. When Aliza, my first daughter, was born, my parents came out from New York City to see their first grandchild. My mother, an attorney, took one fast look through the nursery window and came to my room. Her first words were approving and practical, and I quote, "Cute baby! Have you changed your Will?" I did, within a week, and so did my mother, because when my life changed and I became a mother, my mother became a grandmother. My mother assigned a certain portion of her estate to any children born or to be born to her children. Another portion went to her three favorite charities and to an old dear friend.

The birth or adoption of a child is only one reason for writing a new Will and changing or adding beneficiaries. Some other events that may trigger you to write a new Will are: separation, divorce, remarriage, death of an heir, a change of heart, a change in the law, a change of guardians or executors, or a move to another state. I recommend that you dust off and reread your Will periodically to be certain that it still meets the needs of your family.

With the extraordinary changes due to the passage of the Economic Recovery Tax Act of 1981, it is vital that you take your Will out and dust it off *right now*. Read it and have your attorney make the necessary changes, to take full advantage of the new laws.

For example, if your Will (or your husband's) reads "I leave my spouse the maximum marital deduction. . . ," you will get the old *limited* deduction. This can cost you a bundle. Amend your Will to get rid of this clause!

Guardians

A most important decision when making a Will is who will raise your children if you die. The person chosen is called "guardian of the person."

If one parent dies the other parent will usually be the one to raise the child. You cannot by Will take this right away without good cause. If both parents die, someone must be designated for the job. Consult with this most important person to see if he or she wants the job. Pick someone whose lifestyle and child rearing philosophy you find most appealing. There is nothing wrong with stipulating a friend and ignoring family. If you don't consider members of your family suitable, bypass them! If your relatives fight for guardianship of your child after your death, a court hearing will be held. The judge will decide what is in the best interest of the child. And nowadays, the ruling usually honors the parents' wishes.

Trustees

A trustee is needed to administer the money left in trust for a child. The same person you would choose to raise your child might not be the type who could best serve as trustee.

To handle your child's money you'll want someone whose thinking is akin to your own financially.

Trusts can be set up for children in many different ways, depending on the philosophy of the parents. Basically, the trust should provide the guardian with money for the child's support.

When Jacques died, I became trustee under the Will for my stepson, Louis. I have the widest powers under the trust and am allowed to use Louis's money for anything that would enrich his life. I can use the money to send Louis to Europe or for psychotherapy, for summer camp or scuba diving lessons, if that's what Louis wants and I think it's reasonable. According to the trust, Louis will receive half the money in the trust at age twenty-four and the other half at age twenty-eight.

Each state has laws that govern trustees and hold them accountable. Some types of investments are not considered prudent enough to protect the rights of the beneficiaries, and are thus not used. Some states demand an annual accounting to the courts of the investments of the trustees. A trustee can be sued by his or her charge if blatantly unwise investments have seriously depleted the trust.

A trustee may handle a small estate for nothing, but a large estate should provide fees to pay for the trustee's time and effort.

Banks are often named as trustee, but I would do so only as a last resort. You should choose a bank *only* if you can't find someone who is honest and competent. Why? In my opinion, most banks are unimaginative, ultra conservative, impersonal, rigid, prejudiced, sexist, and slow. If somebody in your family is good at handling money, pick him or her or a savvy friend or your family lawyer to serve.

A trustee is often required to furnish a bond (money to insure an honest performance), but you can do away with this requirement in your Will. Trustees age and die, so when you do a periodic review of your Will, change your trustee to a younger and more vigorous person if necessary.

Executors

Find an obsessive compulsive who is good at business to be executor for your Will. The executor sees that a Will is probated, (see below) insures that all debts are paid, keeps account of the assets, and distributes the assets according to the Will. Before the assets are distributed to the heirs, the executor should keep the monies of the estate invested at the highest possible rate of return so the estate will grow while in probate.

The usual choice for an executor is an adult child or a spouse. Anyone who stands to inherit has the extra motivation to get the job done fast and well.

Your executor will almost always work with a lawyer, who in reality does most of the gritty work. The lawyer works for the executor and is chosen by the executor. If you serve as an executor, pick a lawyer you can work with comfortably—you may be in each other's pocket for a year or more.

The attorney is in charge of filing the estate tax return, but the executor will sign it. You know death and taxes are the two constants of life, but there are also taxes after death. The estate must file an income tax return for the deceased showing everything he or she earned till the date of death. The estate must also file a return showing everything made by the estate since death, and pay the taxes on that sum annually.

The executor may be required to be bonded, but the Will can stipulate that the executor serve without bond. Bonding can be costly and a hardship, so if you don't think your executor will abscond with the money stipulate that he or she may serve without bond.

An executor can be held personally responsible for errors or misspent money, and the job of an executor is time-consuming. Before you name someone in the Will to this job, be sure this person is willing to serve.

Fees are paid to executors. The maximum is usually set by state law. A lawyer or attorney will want to receive that fee for the time they've spent. Heirs and family members will usually waive the fee.

You may have more than one executor. My mother's Will named her three children. Do not slight your daughters by naming only your sons. My women clients have made good, conscientious executors—usually even better than the men!

It is possible for an executor to handle a simple estate without a lawyer, but I think it is ill-advised. The time and the paperwork, the bureaucracies and the technicalities, the forms and the figures are endless. If you are appointed an executor, get a lawyer.

Estate Lawyers

A lawyer usually charges a percentage of the estate for work done; the fee is tax deductible. From sea to shining sea, this country is blessed with an overabundance of lawyers, some of them competent. Get a referral to two or three good attorneys and shop price. No smart shopper pays the maximum fee.

Probate

To probate a Will is to have it filed in court and declared valid. Assets are inventoried and appraised. This preliminary step is usually handled by a lawyer. A few states have simplified their laws, making it possible for executors to settle small uncomplicated estates.

The negative aspects of probate all revolve around time and money. Probate can easily take a year or two. Complicated estates can drag on much longer. Unless your lawyer is on top of things, probates can drag on and on—and on.

As probate proceeds, fees are running like a taxi meter—lawyers' fees, accountants' fees, appraisal fees, executor fees. The estate may not have to bear all these expenses, which will be minimized if the deceased's affairs are in good order. However, an estate is bound to have some of these expenses, so shop for a lawyer who is knowledgeable, fast, and willing to negotiate the fee.

Some people have estates that largely pass outside the Will and thus avoid probate. This type of estate consists of assets that pass outside the Will, (see below), plus any trusts set up during the deceased's lifetime, and all business interests that so stipulate by contract. In this case, there are no fees and no probate. Everything is fast and easy; and all assets can be distributed right away, except what's owed in taxes to the government. Personal (solely-owned) property must still be left by Will, but unless there is a lot of personal property it should be a simple matter to settle.

Assets that are not passed by Will and do not go through probate are:

1. Life insurance. This goes to the named beneficiary.
2. Certain U.S. Savings Bonds. These go directly to the person listed on the front of the bond.

3. All property held in joint tenancy. This may be real estate, cars, checking, or savings accounts. Owning in joint tenancy carries with it the automatic right of survivorship. You may hold assets in joint tenancy with anyone.

(Thank you very much, but I'd rather have my Will probated! Holding my assets in joint tenancy doesn't fit in with my need for independence. Real estate and stocks can be impossible to sell unless the joint tenants agree to sell. I also want the tax advantages of real estate all to myself and freedom to take my losses or gains in the market without consultation—even with my darling daughters.)

4. One-half of the community property in community property states (California, Arizona, New Mexico, Nevada, Louisiana, Texas, Washington, and Idaho). On death, either spouse can will only half of the community property. The other half already belongs to the surviving spouse!

Remember that some of these items that pass without Will are still part of your taxable estate.

ESTATE PLANNING

The Economic Recovery Tax Act of 1981 has revolutionized the area of estate taxation. It is now possible for the rich to pass their money on to their spouses and children, paying little or no taxes and providing little or no revenue to the federal government. Because of this, the United States will now have an institutionalized upper class. The revenue that the government used to receive in the form of estate taxes from the wealthy is largely lost and will be made up by cuts in social programming.

By the simple use of a Will, it is possible for a person to leave an unlimited amount of money to a spouse without paying taxes. In 1987 a couple can leave one million, two hundred thousand dollars to their heirs without any federal tax. Through the use of gifts, it is possible for a couple to transfer out of an estate multiples of $20,000 per year (instead of the old rate of $6,000) to any child, relative, or friend. A family with three married children and four grandchildren can give away as much as $200,000 per year without paying gift tax. And the recipients receive the money tax free!

For most people, this provision is of zero importance. Only a very few have that kind of money to give away. However, every time you are asked to tighten your belt, remember that a select group of wealthy people are being allowed to loosen theirs!

Trusts

Trusts are a major tool for estate planning. They are legally binding contracts for the management of assets by one person for the benefit of another. There are two types of trusts. One is a testamentary trust, set up by you in your Will, which becomes operative when you die. This can be used for the protection of beneficiaries. The other is a living trust, set up for use while you're alive.

Testamentary Trusts—for Children

A good example of a protective testamentary trust is one held for a child until that child develops some mature judgment about handling money. You have the widest lattitude when making this kind of trust. It is your Will and must be followed. You can tailor-make a trust to your own philosophy and lifestyle. For example, you could dictate that all monies in the trust be used to enrich your children's early years in hopes they will grow to be self-supporting and responsible adults.

You can stipulate that:

1. The money be given to the child in a lump sum at a certain age.

2, The money be given in installments at different ages.

3. The interest go to the child at a certain age and the capital at a later age.

4. Your trustee decide when the child is mature enough to handle the money.

5. Any combination of the above or any way you decide as long as the method is legal. A lawyer should be able to tailor-make a trust that fits your needs.

Do not, however, continue a trust beyond a reasonable time, unless a child is mentally or psychologically disabled. If your adult child is going to blow the money or make a dumb investment, so be it. You can't control from the grave, really you can't! I have heard of too many young adults who lack incentive to find meaningful work, knowing they have a trust coming. Other adults have suffered from the humiliation of having their money handled by others when they are in their forties and fifties. A reasonable trust condition might read, "until the completion of college or age twenty-five, whichever comes first" or "trust income until age thirty, distribution of all assets at age thirty."

Leave a trustee the widest powers to invade the capital in the trust so she can distribute monies in case of emergencies. Provide in your Will for a substitute trustee in case the trustee turns out to be an unfit person, is unable or unwilling to serve, or dies.

If a woman has children from a previous marriage, she can't expect her present spouse to provide for them should she die. In order to protect her own children, she should leave money in trust. The trust could provide some income for the surviving spouse during his lifetime, but the children would be the major beneficiaries.

Testamentary Trusts—for Widows

Be sure that your husband does not leave money to you in trust. Trusts for widows can be punitive to the extreme. A man shouldn't leave his wife dependent on the whim or judgment of others. Neither should he leave her with a fixed allowance. You and your husband should sit down with a lawyer when drawing Wills and openly discuss your objectives. A few women may choose to leave the management of their money to a male member of the family or a bank. This decision should be made by you, when and if you become a widow, after your husband's death, rather than be written in concrete into the Will. Many women in widowhood find a new independence and should not be stuck in the infantile position of having financial decisions made for them.

My client Heidi was widowed fifteen years ago. She was left a trust that provided $2,300 per month for herself and her three sons. She was considered well-off at the time, and her future and the children's education seemed assured. Today, however, she faces exorbitant college tuitions and an ever-increasing cost of living. Her husband, while very well-intentioned, could not foresee the tremendous surge in living and education costs. Nobody can. Heidi should have been left with a great deal more discretion over the estate.

Living Trusts

There are two types of living trusts that take effect during your life. One is an irrevocable trust, which cannot be undone since a completed gift is made. The other type of living trust is a revocable trust. This trust remains under your control, and you can change or cancel it at any time. Both types of living trusts have complicated tax advantages, especially in large estates, and should be discussed with your lawyer. If you set up your AB marital trust (explained later) as a living trust, it does not go through probate. As a lawyer friend said, "It is a help for the secretive." Those things that go through probate become a matter of public record and anybody can find out how much money you left. Many people find this idea distasteful. There may well be practical reasons for keeping the size of an estate a secret from the public. A troublesome child or relative could hound a rich widow for loans or gifts. Many people in the public eye use the living AB marital trust so that the amount of their estates won't be splashed across the newspapers at death, thus enticing every rip-off artist and thief to befriend or rob the surviving spouse.

A Clifford Trust

This is a living trust with unique features. It is considered a short-term trust, with the minimum time being ten years. During the ten-year period you cannot cancel the trust. The trust's purpose is to provide money or support to someone for a limited time while you reap tax advantages. When the trust is terminated, the assets that funded the trust come back to you.

An example of this would be a trust set up to support elderly parents who are in a very low tax bracket or not paying taxes at all. The income from the trust would go to support the parents, and any taxes on that income would be taxed to the trust itself or the parents. Since they are in a lower tax bracket than you, you save tax dollars while meeting obligations you would assume in any case. This way you get benefits just by being a dutiful child. You have moved some of your income into a lower tax bracket without giving away assets.

This type of trust is also popular for paying a child's way through college and graduate school. Again, the child is probably not paying any taxes so the income from the trust would pass to the child without tax or only minimal taxes. You cannot use this trust for support of a minor child, because support of a minor child is a legal obligation.

Tip: There is a hitch—if you *add* money to this trust, your ten-year minimum is extended from the date of the addition. Watch out!

AB Marital Trusts

An AB Marital Trust is a good estate planning tool for many couples. It is not a complicated trust and can save many dollars from taxation when the second generation inherits. While the trust is simple, the explanation should come from an estate planning attorney. When you make your will or review it, ask your lawyer whether this trust would be good for you and your husband.

Laws Against Perpetuity

There are laws that prevent the dead hand from controlling endless generations through trusts. According to law, you can set up a trust only for lives in being plus twenty-one years after death. "Lives in being" is a legal phrase meaning anyone now alive, and includes a child in the womb. It is the social policy of the law that the money vest (completely pass to, without strings) in the hand of a living heir. This is interpreted differently from state to state and needs to be checked out with an attorney.

DEATH AND TAXES

Under the Economic Recovery Tax Act of 1981, only extremely large estates will be subject to federal inheritance taxes as of 1987. Many states also impose a death tax, which is unaffected by the change in federal law. An adjusted gross estate (estate of the deceased less funeral expenses, administrative expenses, and debts) of $600,000 or less will be exempt from taxes in estates passing to heirs other than your spouse. Also deductible from your adjusted gross estate is money donated to charity and some exotic deductions that are allowed by the government. Check with your lawyer.

Until 1982, estates of $175,625 or under were not subject to taxes. Now, money passed to a spouse upon death is totally tax-exempt. Money or assets passed to children or other heirs have new limits set for tax exemption. Under the latest tax laws, the new limits being phased in are:

1982	$225,000	sheltered
1983	$275,000	sheltered
1984	$325,000	sheltered
1985	$400,000	sheltered
1986	$500,000	sheltered
1987	$600,000	sheltered

If you pay a state death tax you get a credit from the federal government. However, when you pay a federal estate tax, the state gives you no credit. You are taxed in the state in which you reside. This can cause bitter fights between states vying for the loot. At least two states proudly claim Howard Hughes as a resident in the hope of being able to tax his estate. If you live in New York State and have a place in Maine, you'll pay estate taxes in New York *and* death taxes on your home in Maine.

Flower Bonds

If you have an extremely large estate, there will be taxes no matter how well you plan. The proceeds from life insurance is one way of paying estate taxes. Another less well-known method is the purchase of Flower bonds. Flower bonds are U.S. government bonds paying a meager interest of around 3.5 percent. They were issued by the government for one purpose, to help pay Federal estate taxes. Flower bonds are purchased by a person in contemplation of death. Because of their low interest they are bought at a discount.

When my mother was dying she estimated the size of her estate and the tax that would be due on it. She then sold off stock and bought Flower bonds with a redemption value that would cover federal estate taxes. The bonds were discounted by 30 percent at that time. For each $1,000 she paid $700. When Mom died, the executors for the estate were allowed to redeem the Flower bonds at full value, 100 percent on the dollar. We paid the federal estate taxes with bonds that cost seventy cents on the dollar.

Here are a few cautions to remember:

1. The Flower bonds must be bought by a living person in sound mind or by someone with power of attorney that permits them to act.

2. The bonds must be bought in that person's lifetime, not after death.

3. The Flower bonds can only be used to pay federal estate taxes.

4. Flower bonds are bought from a stockbroker, who will give you an exact price.

5. The government is not issuing new Flower bonds; it is phasing them out. Since they are becoming scarce (supply and demand), they are not being discounted so heavily. Today you would probably have to pay $800 to $900 for a $1,000 bond.

6. When estimating how many Flower bonds are needed, consult with an accountant to find out the federal estate tax rates you'll be paying. By doing this you can make an educated purchase of flower bonds.

7. Try to sell stocks that are in a loss position, so there will be no capital gains tax.

Gifts—Another Estate Planning Tool

As I've mentioned, under the Economic Recovery Tax Act of 1981, the limit for gifts has been raised from $3,000 annually to $10,000. This means that you can give a gift of $10,000 annually to each of your heirs. This serves to reduce your taxable estate before you die, and your heirs will not have to pay taxes on it. You and your husband can give a combined gift of $20,000 annually.

Before my mother died, she gave each of her three children, their spouses, and her five grandchildren the former legal limit of $3,000, thereby removing $33,000 from her taxable estate. Had she died in 1982 she would have been able to reduce her taxable estate by $110,000 by giving her eleven heirs $10,000 each.

Attitudes—Thy Will Be Done

People are really wonderfully funny. On the question of estate planning, they fall into one of three groups. Group one believes that somehow if you don't plan your estate and make your Will you won't die. Group two loves to make plans and write Wills; it gives a great sense of power and order. This group firmly believes that if your affairs are in order you won't die. Group three keeps its affairs in order with the same emotional involvement you use to brush your teeth. It's just another task. Of course, this group knows that if you don't do so you'll be struck dead on the spot. I am firmly stuck in Group three.

THINGS TO REMEMBER

1. You must plan your estate or the state will divide what you leave according to law.

2. You may have very little now, but with inflation your estate may grow to be much larger than it is today.

3. Protecting your minor children with life insurance isn't enough. They must have a trustee *and* a guardian named in your Will.

4. Protecting special children who may never be able to care for themselves is something you must discuss with a lawyer. Each state has complicated and different laws that can reduce your best intentions to dust.

5. Don't make unnecessary trusts. Stick to those that protect minors. A Will should be as simple and forthright as possible, not a maze to enrich an attorney!

6. Remember the old joke about the two men who met in the street.

First man, "I heard Joe died yesterday. Did he leave anything?"

Second man, "Yes, he left everything."

Afterword

A delightful sense of virtue will descend on you when your finances and investments are in order. Changing one aspect of your life has a wonderful and strange effect. Remember the kaleidoscope you played with as a child? One small twist and all the pieces fell into a whole new magic pattern. So it will be when you are in charge of your financial future. You will find the entire pattern of your life has subtly changed, and I hope the effort is as rewarding for you as it has been for me.

Appendix

Glossary

abstract—The summary of the history of the legal title for a particular piece of property.

accrued interest—The amount of interest earned but not paid since the last payment date.

accumulation plan—A plan whereby mutual fund shares are purchased on a regular basis in regular amounts.

adjuster—The insurance person who decides what damage has been sustained in an accident or catastrophe and also the liability of the insurance company.

administrator—Person or institution appointed by the court to handle the estate of a person who dies without leaving a Will or who fails to name an executor in the Will.

amortize—Practice of paying off a debt, including loan costs, such as interest or deferred charges, in a series of regular installments.

analyst—Not your psychiatrist. Person who makes detailed studies of a business or industry within the context of the current political and economic atmosphere, in order to determine investment value.

annual report—A formal financial statement issued by a corporation every year. This report lists assets, liabilities, and earnings, and highlights a company's financial progress during the previous year.

annuity—A vehicle used primarily to save for retirement. It is usually sold through insurance companies, with money paid regularly into an interest-earning account. It can be either a deferred payment or lump sum payment annuity. Both guarantee income to the holder for life.

appraisal—1. An impartial determination of property value. 2. Estimate of the amount of loss sustained by a car in an auto accident.

appreciation—1. A feeling we have for the finer things in life! 2. An increase in the dollar value of an asset over a period of time.

assets—All types of real and personal property owned by an individual or a company that have value.

assigned risk auto insurance—Insurance that offers basic and minimal protection to drivers with poor driving records.

automatic payroll service—Service offered by some banking institutions to companies. On payday you receive a deposit slip from the bank indicating your salary and deductions.

automatic teller machine (ATM)—A bank device that eats plastic cards while promising to give you your money, deposit it, or pay your bills.

averages—A method of measuring the trend of stock prices. The Dow Jones Industrial Average totals the price of the thirty stocks on its list and divides by a number that theoretically compensates for stock splits and dividends. The Standard and Poor's index uses 500 stocks to figure its average.

basic coverage—A type of homeowners insurance that protects against loss caused by certain catastrophes, such as fire, explosion, storm, smoke, vandalism, and theft.

bear market—A declining market with prices generally dropping.

bearer bonds—A bond that is payable to the holder; it does not have the owner's name registered with the company of issue. Whoever has possession of the bond certificate is assumed to be its rightful owner.

beneficiary—Person named to receive benefits in the form of funds or property from an estate, trust, or insurance policy.

bequest—Gift of personal property through a Will.

bid and asked—A stock price quote. The bid is the highest price anyone will pay for a given security at a given time; the asked is the lowest price anyone will take at that same time.

Big Board—Nickname for the New York Stock Exchange, Inc.

binder—Tentative agreement in real estate between the buyer and the seller of a piece of property, usually involving a dollar amount deposit.

blood bath—This refers to a serious loss suffered by many investors because of a sharp market decline.

blue chips—Stocks from companies with a very high rating in terms of consistent earnings and dividend payments in good as well as bad times; established leaders in established industries and solid prospects for continuing to earn, grow, and pay dividends.

blue sky laws—A popular name for laws of various states designed to protect the public against securities fraud. The term originated when a judge ruled that a certain stock had the same value as a patch of blue sky.

bond—An IOU issued by a corporation or the federal, state, or municipal government. A bond is proof of a debt on which the issuer (borrower) usually promises to pay the bondholder (lender) a specified amount of interest for a specified period of time and to repay the loan in full on a designated date. A bondholder is a creditor of the corporation or government.

book value—This value is arrived at by figuring a company's total assets less its liabilities and the liquidating value of its preferred stock. This sum is then divided by the number of common shares outstanding. The result is book value per common share. Book value may bear little or no relation to market value.

broker—An agent, working on a commission basis, who handles orders by the public to buy and sell commodities, securities, or other property.

bull market—An advancing market with prices generally on the rise.

call—An option contract that permits the holder to buy a number of shares of a security at a specific price on or before a fixed date.

capital assets—Stocks, bonds, real estate, autos, jewelry, and household furnishings, paintings, etc.

capital gain or loss—Profit or loss from the sale of an asset. Under federal tax law, a capital gain or loss can be short-term (twelve months or less) or long-term (over twelve months). Long-term capital gains are taxed at a lower rate than short-term.

capitalization—The value of all securities issued by a corporation; can include bonds, debentures, preferred and common stock, and surplus.

cash flow—1. Net income of a corporation plus depreciation. 2. Cash surplus from an investment regardless of the amount of taxable profit.

certificate of deposit—A time-deposit savings account with a specific minimum amount to be deposited for a specific period of time; it pays a higher rate of interest than regular passbook accounts.

certificate of title—Legal statement to establish property ownership as a matter of public record.

charitable trust—A trust that names a qualified charity as beneficiary of all or a portion of the trust funds.

churning—An excessive and highly suspicious amount of trading in a customer's account by a broker without proper justification. Usually gives the broker large commissions without substantial gains to the investor. Brokers guilty of churning are subject to disciplinary action by regulatory agencies.

claim—Demand by policyholders for benefits promised by their insurance contract or by another person's contract.

closing—When buyer and seller of a piece of property—or their representatives—exchange payment and subsequent ownership of the property.

closing costs—Costs of transactions necessary to close a real estate deal. These can include lawyers' fees, taxes, title insurance, and other miscellaneous fees.

codicil—Postscript to a Will that is drawn up separately as an addition to a Will.

collateral—Property or assets pledged by a borrower to a lender to insure repayment of a loan.

collision insurance—Covers loss from damage to the policyholder's car if a collision or single-car accident occurs.

commission—A fee, usually a percentage of the transaction amount, paid to an agent or employee for transacting business or performing a service. Stockbrokers, insurance agents, and real estate people work on commission.

Commissioner of Insurance (Superintendent or Director of Insurance)—Key state official whose responsibility is to oversee and enforce compliance with state insurance laws.

common stock—Securities that represent an ownership interest in a corporation or industry. Common stockholders assume the greater risk, but also exercise greater control and stand to reap the greater rewards in the form of capital growth and dividend payments.

community property—Personal and real property acquired and held jointly and equally by a husband and wife.

compound interest—Interest paid on accumulated interest as well as on the principal.

comprehensive insurance—Insurance that pays for damage to your car from mishaps other than collision, including such perils as fire, theft, explosion, storm, and so on.

condominium—A form of home ownership in which a person owns a dwelling unit with one or more walls in common with another unit and also an undivided interest in joint facilities such as the foyer, pool, and hallways.

convertible—A bond, debenture, or preferred stock that provides a fixed rate of return and can be converted into shares of the same company's common stock in accordance with the terms of the issue.

convertible debenture—Bond issued on the general credit of a corporation that can be converted into common and sometimes preferred stock of the same corporation at a specified price under specified conditions.

convertible term policy—A life insurance term policy that can be converted into a whole life policy or other cash value plans without a medical checkup.

cooperative apartment—A type of real estate ownership in which each person owns a portion of a building containing dwelling units. Ownership of a percentage of the property gives the owner a right to live in one of the units.

cosigner—A person who signs another person's loan agreement and who becomes equally responsible for the loan.

covering a short—Buying shares of stock to pay back previously borrowed stock used in a short sale.

credit—Ability to buy goods or borrow funds on trust; loans made on the promise of ability and willingness to repay.

credit bureau or credit reporting agency—An agency that collects consumer credit information on people and provides this information to its members for use in evaluating a credit application.

credit history—The record of a person's borrowing and repayment history. This is usually available from a credit bureau or credit reporting agency.

creditor—A person, bank, or business to whom money is owed.

credit union—Non-profit savings and lending cooperatives comprised of persons with a common bond, such as place of employment, union membership, area of residence, and so on. Their purpose is to extend credit to its members at lower rates than commercial banking institutions.

current ratio—A ratio of current assets to current liabilities that is used to determine the financial soundness of a company.

current yield (return)—The income from an investment for twelve months is divided by the current value of the investment; the resulting figure is that investment's current yield.

cyclical stocks—Stocks that go up or down with the trend of business. When business is in a period of improvement and growth, cyclical stocks climb; when business is bad, cyclical stocks decline.

dealer—A person in the securities business who acts as a principal rather than an agent. A dealer buys for his own account and then sells directly to a customer from her own inventory.

debenture—A promissory note or type of corporate bond backed only by the general credit of a company and usually not secured by a mortgage or lien or specific property.

deductible clause—A provision in any insurance policy that directs the insured to pay up to a certain specific limit; the insurance company will pay the balance.

deductions—Tax-deductible expenses that can be subtracted from income when computing income taxes.

deed—Proof of ownership of a piece of property; describes property in detail.

default—In real estate, failure of a buyer to meet the mortgage payments or other requirements that could result in foreclosure.

deferred annuity—An annuity that pays out at some stipulated future date.

depreciation/cost recovery system—Decline in the dollar value of property over time, the amount of which is figured and deducted on an income tax return.

disability insurance—Coverage against loss of earnings due to injury or illness.

discount—Reduction of the original price on any item for sale, including stocks or bonds.

discount rate—The rate of interest that the Federal Reserve System charges Federal Reserve member banks when they borrow money.

discount the news—When the price of a stock or the level of a market indicator changes dramatically in *anticipation* of a news event and then barely changes when the event actually occurs, the stock or the indicator is referred to as having discounted the news.

discretionary account—An account where a broker or agent is given full or partial authority to buy or sell securities or commodities for you.

diversification—The practice of reducing risk by spreading investments among different instruments and different companies in different fields.

dividend—A share of the profits of a company paid to the shareholders.

dollar cost averaging—A system of investing at regular intervals with a *fixed* amount, regardless of the condition of the market.

Dow Jones Average—See averages.

Dow theory—A market analysis theory based upon the performance of the Dow Jones industrial and transportation stock price averages. The Dow theory does not predict or forecast; rather, it defines the market as in a basic upward trend if the Dow reaches and surpasses a specific previous high and in a downward trend if it passes a previous low.

down payment—Money put as a deposit toward the purchase of real property.

endowment insurance—A kind of cash value life insurance where savings accumulate more rapidly than other types of cash value plans; used to accumulate money for a specific purpose, such as a child's college education or for retirement.

equity—Value built up in a property over the years; total current value of the property minus debts against the property.

ERISA—Employee Retirement Income Security Act passed in 1974 that drew up comprehensive guidelines regarding employee pension rights.

escrow—The process where property and/or money is held by a third party for safekeeping until transactions between buyer and seller of the property are completed.

estate—Personal assets and liabilities left by a person at death.

exchange privilege—The right to exchange the shares of one mutual fund for shares of another under the same sponsorship for little or no cost.

executor—The person or institution named in a Will to administer the disposition of an estate according to the directions in the Will.

exemption—The amount that a taxpayer is allowed to deduct from gross income for self and any dependents, to determine taxable income.

face value—The dollar value that appears on the front of an insurance policy or a bond; it is ordinarily the amount promised at maturity.

fall out of bed—Jargon meaning the stock market declined very sharply.

FDIC—Federal Deposit Insurance Corporation, which insures deposits of up to $100,000 in commercial banks.

Federal Reserve System—Established under the 1913 Federal Reserve Act; regulates the banking system of the United States and sets monetary policy.

FICA—Federal Insurance Contributions Act; the Social Security payroll deduction.

fiduciary—A trustee.

fiduciary account—An account opened by a trustee, executor, or guardian to hold funds held in trust.

financial responsibility laws—State laws requiring automobile owners to prove that they are financially responsible, usually met by carrying adequate car insurance.

fiscal year—The accounting year for a business or company; it does not necessarily run from January 1 to December 31. Typically, a fiscal year may run from July 1 to June 30.

fixed income securities—Securities, such as bonds or preferred stocks, that return a fixed income over a specified period of time.

fixed rate—A set amount of interest that one pays for a mortgage.

float—Time between when one writes a check or uses a debit card and when it actually reaches the bank and is cleared.

floor—The actual trading area of any of the world's stock exchanges.

floor broker—A stock exchange member licensed to buy and sell securities on the floor but not affiliated with a specific brokerage house.

flower bonds—Nickname for certain U.S. Treasury bonds that can be redeemed at face value for payment of federal estate taxes if the bonds are owned by the decedent at the time of death.

foreclosure—The legal process whereby a borrower's real property is sold by a lender to cover defaults on payments.

foreign exchange—Securities exchanges operating in other countries. Also, international currency transactions.

FSLIC—Federal Savings and Loan Insurance Corporation, which insures deposits of up to $100,000 in savings and loan institutions.

going public—The process whereby a private company offers its stock for sale to the public for the first time.

good-till-cancelled order—An order to a broker to buy or sell a specific security; it remains in effect until either executed or cancelled.

gross income—Total income *before* deductions.

group insurance—Any kind of insurance written for a specific group of people; usually less expensive than individual coverage.

growth stock—Stock in a company with a history of rapid increase and a forecast of continued increase in earnings.

guaranteed renewable—Clause in an insurance policy that guarantees renewal up to a certain age or for a certain number of years.

Health Maintenance Organizations (HMOs)—An organized health care system for a specific enrolled population with emphasis on preventive medicine.

hedge—To try to minimize or eliminate risk by taking steps to offset the risk.

holographic will—Handwritten Will; only legal in certain states under specific conditions.

inflation—A rapid rise in prices over a relatively short period of time resulting in erosion of a currency's buying power.

insider—The directors, officers, and principal security holders of a corporation with access to detailed inside information as to how a company is faring financially.

interest—Money paid for the use of money.

interest rate—The percentage rate charged for borrowing money or received for lending money.

intestate—Dying without leaving a Will.

investment company—A company that invests its money in other companies.

investment portfolio—See portfolio.

IRA—Individual Retirement Accounts for employed people.

issue—Children and direct descendants.

joint tenancy—Ownership of a piece of property by two or more people, the title to which passes completely to the last survivor.

Keogh—Private retirement plan available to self-employed individuals.

leverage—To use someone else's capital to increase an individual's equity in personal property.

liabilities—Obligations and debts, either current or long-term.

liability insurance—Coverage against claims due to accidents or injuries caused by you.

lien—Claim against a piece of property as security for the repayment of a debt.

limit order—An order to buy or sell a specific security at a stated price.

line of credit—The maximum amount that a lender will extend to a borrower at a given time.

liquidity—The ability of any asset to be quickly converted to cash.

listed stock—Stock that is listed and traded on a national securities exchange.

living trust—A trust that goes into effect during one's lifetime.

load—Sales charge that a mutual funds investor must pay to cover the costs of administrative and sales work.

major medical—Insurance against loss from the huge expenses of a catastrophic injury or lengthy illness.

management company—Company that manages a mutual fund.

margin—Proportion of the purchase price you must pay when you use your broker's credit to buy a security.

margin call—A demand by your broker to you to put up money or securities in order to bring the equity in your account up to the maintenance requirements stipulated by the exchange.

market order—Order to buy or sell a specific security at the best price obtainable.

market price—The last reported transaction price of a security.

maturity—The date on which a loan or a bond or debenture comes due.

monetary policy—Policy set by the Federal Reserve Board to influence the supply of bank credit and other monetary conditions that in turn affect interest rates and the entire U.S. economy.

money market funds—Funds that invest in short-term money market instruments.

money markets—Markets where short term securities of various borrowers are traded.

mortgage—Legal claim on property given as security by the borrower to the lender to insure repayment of the loan.

municipal bonds—Offered by cities, towns, villages, states, etc. and exempt from federal tax.

mutual funds—An investment company that sells its shares to the public and invests the proceeds in various securities for the benefit of its shareholders.

NASD—National Association of Securities Dealers, Inc. An association of brokers in the over-the-counter securities business.

NASDAQ—National Association of Securities Dealers Automated Quotation; an automated information network providing brokers with price quotes on over-the-counter securities.

new issue—A stock or bond sold by a corporation for the first time in order to raise money.

no-fault—Type of automobile insurance in which an accident victim is reimbursed for certain accident expenses regardless of who caused the accident.

notary public—A person licensed to verify a signature.

NOW (Negotiable Order of Withdrawal)—A check written on an interest-paying checking account.

odd lot—An amount of stock shares that is less than the round lot figure of one hundred shares for frequently traded active stocks or ten shares for seldom traded inactive stocks.

option—A right to buy or sell a fixed amount of a security at a specified price within a specified time period.

over-the-counter—Biggest securities market in the world, where the stocks and bonds not listed on any exchange are traded. (See NASD and NASDAQ.)

par value—For common stock, its nominal dollar amount. For preferred stock or bonds, par value often signifies the dollar value upon which dividends or interest are figured.

payroll deduction plan—An arrangement where employees may accumulate shares in a mutual fund by authorizing the employer to deduct a specified amount from their salary at certain times for investing in the fund.

penny stocks—Extremely speculative stocks that usually sell for one dollar or less.

p/e ratio—Price/earnings ratio. The relationship between the current price of a stock and the company's earnings per share, calculated by dividing the current market price of a stock by the earnings per share of the previous twelve months.

points—For stock prices, a point is one dollar; so a one-point rise or fall in the price of a stock is a rise or fall of one dollar. For bond prices, a point is $10; so a rise or fall in the price of a bond of one point is a rise or fall of $10. In real estate, points are part of settlement costs, with one point being one percent of the amount of the mortgage, and are charged to the buyer and paid to the mortgage lender.

portfolio—The collection of investments held by an investor.

preferred stock—A category of stock with a claim on company earnings ahead of common stockholders should a company liquidate; dividends usually paid at a fixed rate.

premium—The amount by which a preferred stock, bond, or option may sell above its par value. Insurance companies call their bills premiums.

prepayment penalty—A clause in the note for a loan that provides for a penalty in the event of an early loan payoff.

probate—The legal procedure that establishes the validity of a Will and sees that the Will's provisions are carried out.

prospectus—An official statement describing a security or mutual fund and offering shares for sale.

proxy statement—A written power of attorney given by a stockholder to another person if he or she is unable to attend a stockholders' meeting.

puts—Options to sell a specified amount of a particular stock at a specific price within a specific period of time.

quote/quotation—The highest bid to buy and the lowest offer to sell a security at a specific time.

real rate of return—Annual yield from fixed-income securities reduced by yearly cost-of-living increases.

redemption price—The price at which a bond or a preferred stock may be redeemed before maturity.

refinancing—New securities are issued by a company to pay off other securities and debts.

registered bond—A bond whose owner's name is registered with the issuer and appears on the face of the certificate. (See bearer bonds, serial bonds.)

retained earnings—That portion of a company's profit that is not paid out to stockholders.

return—Also called yield; the rate of income from an investment.

rollover—Moving funds from one retirement account into another.

round lot—A unit of trading securities, usually one hundred shares for active stocks, ten shares for inactive stocks.

seat—An expression meaning membership in a stock exchange; entitles the owner to trade securities on that exchange.

SEC—Securities and Exchange Commission; federal agency established to protect investors by enforcing regulations regarding securities trading.

second trust deed/second mortgage—A loan secured by interest in real property that is subordinate to the first or principal mortgage.

security—A stock, bond, or note.

serial bond—A bond that matures in small amounts in sequential order over periodic stated intervals.

settlement day—The deadline by which the seller must deliver sold securities certificates and the buyer must pay for the securities purchased.

short—A term to describe debt to your broker, either cash or securities.

short position—Stocks sold short and not covered as of a particular date.

short selling—Strategy used when it is believed a stock will decline. Seller sells stock which is borrowed to cover the sale and then buys for delivery at a later time and hopefully at a lower price.

simple interest—Interest that is computed and paid only on the principal. (See compound interest.)

specialist—A stock exchange member with two functions: 1. Maintains an orderly market by buying and selling from his or her own account when necessary; 2. Acts as a broker's broker.

speculator—A person who buys and sells securities in an attempt to multiply capital very quickly.

split—Dividing a company's outstanding shares of stock into a greater number of shares of proportionately less value.

spread—The difference between bid and asked price or between purchase and sale price.

stock dividend—A dividend of additional stock shares instead of cash.

stop order—Standing instructions to a broker to sell a particular security if its price falls to a specified level.

street—The New York financial community of Wall Street.

street name—Securities held in the name of a broker instead of the owner's name.

taken to the cleaners—Stock market jargon meaning to be hit with tremendous losses; also called taking a bath and bloodbath.

tax liability—The amount of tax that a person is responsible for paying.

tax shelter—An investment that offers certain income tax advantages; a place to shelter money from the tax man.

tenancy in common—Two or more owners of a piece of real property.

tenants by entirety—Husband and wife who are joint owners of a piece of real property.

term bond—A bond with a single maturity date.

term insurance—Life insurance without a cash value accumulation; offers protection for a specified period of time.

testamentary trust—Trust established by a Will to take effect when that person dies.

thin market—A market where there are few bids to buy or offers to sell or both; or where small numbers of shares of a company are available to trade.

ticker—The instrument that prints prices and the volume of security transactions worldwide within minutes after each trade is completed.

tight money—Financial conditions that result when the Federal Reserve adopts a monetary policy that restrains the supply of credit, thereby increasing interest rates.

time order—An order to your broker that becomes a market order or a limited price order at a specified time.

tips—Supposedly, tips are inside information on corporate financial affairs from someone in the corporation.

title—Legal document proving ownership of a piece of real property.

title search—Checking title records to be sure that a piece of real property is being bought from the legal owners and that there are no liens or encumbrances in the title.

trader—One who buys and sells for his own account for short-term profit.

trading post—One of the twenty-three locations on the floor of the New York Stock Exchange at which stocks assigned to that location are traded.

trust—Assets held for a certain person and managed to his or her best advantage by a trustee.

trustee—Person or institution designated to manage a trust.

two-dollar broker—Members on the floor of the New York Stock Exchange who execute orders for brokers who are too busy to do so themselves or for firms who do not have their exchange members on the floor. The name is from the days when these brokers were paid $2 per hundred shares for executing such orders.

underwriter—Middleman between a company issuing new securities and the investing public and between sellers of large blocks of stock and investors.

United States Securities Market—The vast over-the-counter market in which U.S. Treasury Bills, notes, and bonds are bought and sold.

variable rate—Refers to interest rates that vary with overall interest rates.

vested—Having claim to accrued retirement benefits that cannot be taken away for any reason.

volume—The number of shares traded of a particular security or an entire market during a given period of time.

warrant—A certificate granting the holder the right to purchase securities at a specified price within a specified period of time or perpetually.

W-4 form—A form filled out by employees that indicates how many deductions are claimed.

W-2 form—Annual record showing the amount of income a person has earned and the amount withheld from earnings for tax purposes.

yield—Dividends or interest paid by a company expressed as a percentage of the current price. (See return.)

yield to maturity—True total rate of return, determined by figuring the purchase price of a bond, the interest to be received, and the price the bond will be paid off at on its maturity date.

State-by-State Guide to Marriage and Property Laws

Alabama

Separate property state.
1. Prenuptial/live-in agreements:

   (a) Valid for married couples.

   (b) Valid for live-ins if used to protect property interests.

   All agreements must be made with full disclosure of assets and other pertinent information, and without duress.

2. Property: Each controls and manages his or her property.

3. Division of property in contested divorces: Separate property is retained by its owner; the court may divide joint property. Property division must be fair but does not have to be equal. Division of property is not required; alimony can be given in lieu of property division.

Alaska

Separate property state.
1. Prenuptial/live-in agreements:

   (a) Valid for married couples.

   (b) Valid for live-ins if used to protect property interests.

   All agreements must be made with full disclosure of assets and other pertinent information, and without duress.

2. Property: Each controls and manages his or her property.

3. Court division of property in contested divorces: The court divides all separate property, including property owned jointly, as it deems fair.

Arizona

Community property state.

1. Prenuptial/live-in agreements:

   (a) Valid for married couples.

   (b) Probably valid for live-ins if used to protect property interests.

   All agreements must be made with full disclosure of assets and other pertinent information, and without duress.

2. Property:

   (a) All property owned by a spouse prior to marriage or acquired by gift or inheritance during marriage is considered separate property.

   (b) All property acquired during marriage, including wages, (except as provided in (a) above) is community property.

   Each spouse controls his or her separate property. Both spouses must sign for the sale or lease of real community property. Either spouse can buy or sell property, other than real property.

3. Division of property in contested divorces: The court divides all community property equally; separate property is retained by the owner. Marital misconduct is only considered if there is an economic impact as a result.

Arkansas

Separate property state.

1. Prenuptial/live-in agreements:

   (a) Valid for married couples if acknowledged before a court in state where it was drawn up.

   (b) Valid for live-ins if used to protect property interests.

   All agreements must be made with full disclosure of assets and other pertinent information, and without duress.

2. Property: Each controls and manages his or her property. The wife may *not* claim her separate property if she allows her husband to use it as his own.

3. Division of property in contested divorces: Each spouse keeps his or her separate property acquired before the marriage; property acquired during the marriage is divided equally *or* as the court deems fair. Marital misconduct may be considered in all cases.

California

Community property state.

1. Prenuptial/live-in agreements:

   (a) Recognized for married couples.

   (b) Valid for live-ins if used to protect property interests.

   All agreements must be made with full disclosure of assets and other pertinent information, and without duress.

2. Property:

   (a) All property owned by a spouse prior to marriage or acquired by gift or inheritance during marriage is considered separate property.

   (b) All real and personal property acquired during marriage (except as provided in (a) above) is considered community property with spouses having equal ownership. Property acquired out of California is treated as community property in the event of a divorce or death of a spouse; this is referred to as quasi-community property.

   Each spouse controls his or her separate property. Each has management and control of community property, but both must give written consent to dispose of community property other than real estate. Both must sign to sell or lease real estate.

3. Court division of property in contested divorces:
   (a) The court divides all community property equally. (Equally has been defined to mean "substantially equally" so that the court may balance one piece of property against another, i.e., the husband receives his pension in total and wife receives something of "substantially equal" value.

   (b) Family home held in joint tenancy is community property. Other joint tenancy properties are not divided since each spouse already owns a half share.

Colorado

Separate property state.

1. Prenuptial/live-in agreements:

    (a) Valid for married couples, but will not necessarily be followed by the court when dividing property in a divorce.

    (b) Valid for live-ins if used to protect property interests.

    Agreements must be made with full disclosure of assets and other pertinent information, and without duress.

2. Property: Each spouse controls and manages his or her own property.

3. Division of property in contested divorces: The court may order division of marital property (includes joint property and the amount of increase in value of separate property during marriage) acquired during marriage, except by gift or inheritance, without regard to marital misconduct. Court may divide separate property acquired prior to the marriage.

Connecticut

Separate property state.

1. Prenuptial/live-in agreements:

    (a) Valid for married couples.

    (b) Probably valid for live-ins if used to protect property interests.

    All agreements must be made with full disclosure of assets and other pertinent information, and without duress.

2. Property: Each controls his or her property.

3. Division of property in contested divorces: The court may divide joint property and assign it to either spouse or may assign all or part of either spouse's separate property to the other spouse as it deems fair.

Delaware

Separate property state.

1. Prenuptial/live-in agreements:

   (a) Valid for married couples.

   (b) Probably valid for live-ins if used to protect property interests.

   All agreements must be made with full disclosure of assets and other pertinent information, and without duress.

2. Property: Each controls his or her own property.

3. Division of property in contested divorces: The court divides marital property, including joint property, as it deems fair. Marital property includes all property acquired during the marriage. Separate property acquired prior to the marriage is retained by its owner.

District of Columbia

Separate property state.

1. Prenuptial/live-in agreements:

   (a) Valid for married couples.

   (b) Valid for live-ins if used to protect property interests.

   All agreements must be made with full disclosure of assets and other pertinent information, and without duress.

2. Property: Each controls his or her property.

3. Division of property in contested divorces: Marital separate property is divided by the court whether it is held individually or jointly. Each spouse retains his or her separate property whether acquired prior to the marriage or acquired by gift or inheritance during the marriage.

Florida

Separate property state.

1. Prenuptial/live-in agreements:

   (a) Valid for married couples.

   (b) Probably valid for live-ins if used to protect property interests.

All agreements must be made with full disclosure of assets and other pertinent information, and without duress.

2. Property: Each controls his or her property. Both spouses must sign to sell or encumber the family home.

3. Division of property in contested divorces: Jointly-owned real estate can be ordered sold by the court and the proceeds divided if both spouses so request. Otherwise, jointly-owned real estate or personal property becomes tenancy in common. The court has no power to distribute separate property.

Georgia

Separate property state.

1. Prenuptial/live-in agreements:

   (a) Valid for married couples.

   (b) Probably not valid for live-ins and *only* if used to protect property interests.

   All agreements must be made with full disclosure of assets and other pertinent information, and without duress.

2. Property: Each controls his or her own property.

3. Division of property in contested divorces: Each spouse's separate property is retained by its owner; the court has the power to divide all jointly-owned property as it deems fair.

Hawaii

Separate property state, with a modified form of the community property system in effect.

1. Prenuptial/live-in agreements:

   (a) Usually valid for married couples.

   (b) Probably valid for live-ins if used to protect property interests.

   All agreements must be made with full disclosure of assets and other pertinent information, and without duress.

2. Property: Property acquired during the marriage between

July 1, 1945 and June 30, 1949 is community property because that is the period during which the community property system was in effect. All property acquired before or during a marriage outside of that period is considered the separate property of the acquiring spouse. Each controls his or her own separate property. Each has individual control over community property acquired when the community property system was in effect.

3. Division of property in contested divorces: The court divides community property, as well as separate and joint property, as it deems fair. The court determines each spouse's responsibility for any debts.

Idaho

Community property state.

1. Prenuptial/live-in agreements:

   (a) Valid for married couples. May modify community property by prenuptial contract.

   (b) Probably not valid for live-ins, and if valid only if used to protect property interests.

   All agreements must be made with full disclosure of assets and other pertinent information, and without duress.

2. Property:

   (a) All property owned by a spouse prior to marriage or acquired by gift or inheritance during marriage is considered separate property.

   (b) All property acquired during marriage (except as provided in (a) above), including income from separate property, is considered community property.

   Each spouse controls his or her separate property. Either spouse may control and manage community property. Neither spouse may sell or lease real estate unless both sign to do so.

3. Division of property in contested divorces:

   (a) The court divides community and joint property as it deems fair.

(b) Each spouse retains his or her separate property regardless of when it was acquired.

(c) The family home is retained by the innocent spouse.

(d) Retirement and pension benefits are considered community property and are divisible at the time of divorce.

Illinois

Separate property state.

1. Prenuptial/live-in agreements:

    (a) Valid for married couples.

    (b) May be valid for live-ins if agreements are in writing.

    All agreements must be made with full disclosure of assets and other pertinent information, and without duress.

2. Property: Each controls and manages his or her property. Both spouses must sign to sell the family home.

3. Division of property in contested divorces: Each spouse retains his or her separate property. The court divides marital property as it deems fair and without regard to marital misconduct. The court disposes of family home as it deems fair.

Indiana

Separate property state.

1. Prenuptial/live-in agreements:

    (a) Valid for married couples.

    (b) Possibly valid for live-ins if used to protect property interests.

    All agreements must be made with full disclosure of assets and other pertinent information, and without duress.

2. Property: Each controls and manages his or her own property.

3. Division of property in contested divorces: The court distributes all separate and joint property as it deems fair.

Iowa

Separate property state.

1. Prenuptial/live-in agreements:

   (a) Valid for married couples if not contracted for the performance of traditional marital obligations or to change the interest that one spouse has in the other's property.

   (b) Probably valid for live-ins if used to protect property interests.

   All agreements must be made with full disclosure of assets and other pertinent information, and without duress.

2. Property: Each controls and manages his or her property. Both spouses must sign to sell the family home.

3. Division of property in contested divorces: The court divides all separate and joint property as it deems fair and without regard to marital misconduct.

Kansas

Separate property state.

1. Prenuptial/live-in agreements:

   (a) Valid for married couples.

   (b) Probably valid for live-ins if used to protect property interests.

   All agreements must be made with full disclosure of assets and other pertinent information, and without duress.

2. Property: Property acquired before the marriage or by gift or inheritance during the marriage is considered separate property. All property acquired during the marriage is considered marital property. Each spouse controls and manages his or her property. Both must sign to sell the family home in which he or she has dower rights.

3. Division of property in contested divorces: The court divides all real and personal property, separate or joint, as it deems fair and without regard to when or how property was acquired.

Kentucky

Separate property state.

1. Prenuptial/live-in agreements:

   (a) Valid for married couples.

   (b) Probably valid for live-ins if used to protect property interests.

   All agreements must be made with full disclosure of assets and other pertinent information, and without duress.

2. Property: Each controls and manages his or her property. Both spouses must sign to sell property affected by dower rights.

3. Division of property in contested divorces: Each spouse retains his or her separate property. Marital property (all property acquired during the marriage except by gift or inheritance) is divided by the court as it deems fair.

Louisiana

Community property state.

1. Prenuptial/live-in agreements:

   (a) Valid for married couples.

   (b) Probably valid for live-ins if used to protect property interests.

   All agreements must be made with full disclosure of assets and other pertinent information, and without duress.

2. Property:

   (a) All property owned prior to marriage or acquired with separate funds or by gift or inheritance during marriage is considered separate property.

   (b) All property acquired during marriage (except as provided in (a) above), including profit from separate property and earnings of both spouses, is considered community property.

   Each spouse controls his or her separate property. Each spouse may manage and control the community property. Both spouses must consent to sell any real or personal property. Both must sign to sell or lease the family home.

3. Division of property in contested divorces: The court divides community property as it deems fair; each spouse retains his or her separate property.

Maine

Separate property state.

1. Prenuptial/live-in agreements:

   (a) Valid for married couples.

   (b) Probably valid for live-ins if used to protect property interests.

   All agreements must be made with full disclosure of assets and other pertinent information, and without duress.

2. Property: Each controls and manages his or her property.

3. Division of property in contested divorces: The court divides marital property (any property acquired during the marriage), including joint property, as it deems fair. Each spouse retains his or her separate property.

Maryland

Separate property state.

1. Prenuptial/live-in agreements:

   (a) Valid for married couples.

   (b) Probably valid for live-ins if used to protect property interests.

   All agreements must be made with full disclosure of assets and other pertinent information, and without duress.

2. Property: Each controls and manages his or her property.

3. Division of property in contested divorces: The court can order division and sale of joint property as it deems fair. The court can determine value of marital property (all property acquired during marriage except by gift or inheritance) and

order money to non-owning spouse as it deems fair. Each spouse retains his or her separate property. Court may award family home to either spouse.

Massachusetts

Separate property state.

1. Prenuptial/live-in agreements:

   (a) Valid for married couples, but contract must be recorded within ninety days following marriage or it will be null and void.

   (b) Valid for live-ins if used to protect property interests.

   All agreements must be made with full disclosure of assets and other pertinent information, and without duress.

2. Property: Each controls and manages his or her property.

3. Division of property in contested divorces: The court divides separate and joint property as it deems fair. Property may be awarded in lieu of alimony.

Michigan

Separate property state.

1. Prenuptial/live-in agreements:

   (a) Valid for married couples.

   (b) Probably valid for live-ins if used to protect property interests.

   All agreements must be made with full disclosure of assets and other pertinent information, and without duress.

2. Property: Each controls and manages his or her property. Both spouses must sign to sell joint property or the family home.

3. Division of property in contested divorces: The court divides all property, separate and joint, as it deems fair. Tenancy by entirety or joint tenancy becomes tenancy in common. Wife must receive an award equal to her dower right. Husband

may be entitled to a portion of wife's separate property if he helped acquire or improve it for her.

Minnesota

Separate property state.

1. Prenuptial/live-in agreements:

   (a) Valid for married couples.

   (b) Valid for live-ins if contract is in writing.

   All agreements must be made with full disclosure of assets and other pertinent information, and without duress.

2. Property: Each controls and manages his or her property.

3. Division of property in contested divorces: The court divides marital property (all property acquired during marriage) as it deems fair. Separate property usually retained by its owner. Property may be awarded in lieu of alimony. The court may divide separate property if necessary.

Mississippi

Separate property state.

1. Prenuptial/live-in agreements:

   (a) Valid for married couples.

   (b) Probably not valid for live-ins, and then only if used to protect property interests.

   All agreements must be made with full disclosure of assets and other pertinent information, and without duress.

2. Property: Each controls and manages his or her property. Homestead law is in effect; both spouses must sign to sell the family home.

3. Division of property in contested divorces: The court cannot divide separate property; each spouse retains his or her property. Joint property is not affected by divorce, but it may be partitioned or sold and the proceeds divided.

Missouri

Separate property state.

1. Prenuptial/live-in agreements:

   (a) Valid for married couples if in writing and acknowledged by each spouse or witnessed by a third party.

   (b) Probably valid for live-ins if used to protect property interests.

   All agreements must be made with full disclosure of assets and other pertinent information, and without duress.

2. Property: Separate property is all property acquired prior to marriage, acquired by gift or inheritance or purchased with income from other separate property. All other property acquired during the marriage is marital property and subject to division by the court. Each spouse controls and manages his or her separate property. Each spouse must sign to sell or encumber the real estate of the other or the family home.

3. Division of property in contested divorces: The court divides all marital property (all property acquired during marriage except by gift or inheritance). Each spouse retains his or her separate property.

Montana

Separate property state.

1. Prenuptial/live-in agreements:

   (a) Valid for married couples.

   (b) Probably valid for live-ins if used to protect property interests.

   All agreements must be made with full disclosure of assets and other pertinent information, and without duress.

2. Property: Each controls and manages his or her property. Both spouses must sign to sell the family home.

3. Division of property in contested divorces: The court can divide all separate and joint property as it deems fair, regardless of when or how property was acquired.

Nebraska

Separate property state.

1. Prenuptial/live-in agreements:

   (a) Valid for married couples.

   (b) Probably valid for live-ins if used to protect property interests.

   All agreements must be made with full disclosure of assets and other pertinent information, and without duress.

2. Property: Each controls and manages his or her property. Both spouses must sign to sell any real estate and household goods.

3. Division of property in contested divorces: The court can divide all separate and joint property as it deems fair, except property that was acquired prior to the marriage or by gift or inheritance.

Nevada

Community property state.

1. Prenuptial/live-in agreements:

   (a) Valid for married couples. However, they may not alter marriage laws by agreement.

   (b) Probably valid for live-ins if used to protect property interests.

   All agreements must be made with full disclosure of assets and other pertinent information, and without duress.

2. Property:

   (a) All property acquired prior to marriage or acquired by gift or inheritance or awards for personal injuries and profits from separate property is considered separate property.

   (b) All property acquired during the marriage (except as provided in (a) above) is considered community property.

   Each spouse controls and manages his or her separate property. Either spouse may control community property but may not will away more than his or her one-half share. Neither may give away, sell, or encumber real or personal community property without consent of the other.

3. Division of property in contested divorces: The court divides all community property and joint property as it deems fair. Each spouse retains his or her separate property. However, the court may set aside separate property for the support of either non-owning spouse or children in need.

New Hampshire

Separate property state.

1. Prenuptial/live-in agreements:

   (a) Valid for married couples.

   (b) Probably valid for live-ins if used to protect property interests.

   All agreements must be made with full disclosure of assets and other pertinent information, and without duress.

2. Property: Each controls and manages his or her property. Both spouses must sign to sell or encumber the family home.

3. Division of property in contested divorces: The court can divide all separate and joint property as it deems fair.

New Jersey

Separate property state.

1. Prenuptial/live-in agreements:

   (a) Valid for married couples.

   (b) Probably valid for live-ins if used to protect property interests.

   All agreements must be made with full disclosure of assets and other pertinent information, and without duress.

2. Property: Each controls and manages his or her property.

3. Division of property in contested divorces: The court divides all separate and joint property acquired during the marriage

as it deems fair. Separate property acquired prior to the marriage is retained by its owner.

New Mexico

Community property state.

1. Prenuptial/live-in agreements:

   (a) Valid for married couples if in writing.

   (b) Valid for live-ins if used to protect property interests.

   All agreements must be made with full disclosure of assets and other pertinent information, and without duress.

2. Property:

   (a) All property acquired before marriage or by gift or inheritance or designated by written agreement or held in joint tenancy or tenancy in common, including profits of such, is considered separate property.

   (b) All property acquired during marriage (except as provided in (a) above) is considered community property.

   Each spouse controls and manages his or her separate property. Either spouse may mortgage or control community property. Both must sign to sell community real estate.

3. Division of property in contested divorces: The court divides community property equally. Each spouse receives his or her share of any joint property. Court may award either spouse a portion of the other's separate property.

New York

Separate property state.

1. Prenuptial/live-in agreements:

   (a) Valid for married couples.

   (b) Probably valid for live-ins if used to protect property interests.

   All agreements must be made with full disclosure of assets and other pertinent information, and without duress.

2. Property: Each controls and manages his or her property.

3. Division of property in contested divorces: The court provides for the equitable distribution of all separate and joint property.

North Carolina

Separate property state.

1. Prenuptial/live-in agreements:

   (a) Valid for married couples.

   (b) Probably valid for live-ins if used to protect property interests.

   All agreements must be made with full disclosure of assets and other pertinent information, and without duress.

2. Property: Each controls and manages his or her property. Both spouses must sign to sell the family home.

3. Division of property in contested divorces: The court has no power to divide property beyond awarding it for alimony. Each spouse retains his or her separate property and his or her share of any joint property.

North Dakota

Separate property state.

1. Prenuptial/live-in agreements:

   (a) Probably valid for married couples.

   (b) Probably valid for live-ins if used to protect property interests.

   All agreements must be made with full disclosure of assets and other pertinent information, and without duress.

2. Property: Each controls and manages his or her property. Both spouses must sign to sell or encumber the family home.

3. Division of property in contested divorces: The court divides separate and joint property as it deems fair, regardless of when or how it was acquired. Family home is usually retained by the innocent spouse.

Ohio

Separate property state.

1. Prenuptial/live-in agreements:

    (a) Valid for married couples.

    (b) Probably valid for live-ins if used to protect property interests.

    All agreements must be made with full disclosure of assets and other pertinent information, and without duress.

2. Property: Each controls and manages his or her property. Both spouses must agree to remove real estate dower rights.

3. Division of property in contested divorces: The court divides separate property as alimony.

Oklahoma

Separate property state.

1. Prenuptial/live-in agreements:

    (a) Probably valid for married couples.

    (b) Probably valid for live-ins if used to protect property interests.

    All agreements must be made with full disclosure of assets and other pertinent information, and without duress.

2. Property: Each controls and manages his or her property. Both spouses must sign to sell or encumber the family home.

3. Division of property in contested divorces: The court divides joint property as it deems fair. Each spouse retains his or her separate property.

Oregon

Separate property state.

1. Prenuptial/live-in agreements:

    (a) Valid for married couples.

(b) Probably valid for live-ins if used to protect property interests.

All agreements must be made with full disclosure of assets and other pertinent information, and without duress.

2. Property: Each controls and manages his or her property.

3. Division of property in contested divorces: The court divides all separate and joint property as it deems fair. The court considers homemaking as a marital asset and presumes equal contributions by both spouses to marital assets unless there is evidence to the contrary.

Pennsylvania

Separate property state.

1. Prenuptial/live-in agreements:

   (a) Valid for married couples.

   (b) Probably valid for live-ins if used to protect property interests.

   All agreements must be made with full disclosure of assets and other pertinent information, and without duress.

2. Property: Each controls and manages his or her property.

3. Division of property in contested divorces: The court provides for the equitable distribution of all separate and joint property except separate property acquired prior to the marriage or acquired by gift or inheritance.

Rhode Island

Separate property state.

1. Prenuptial/live-in agreements:

   (a) Valid for married couples.

   (b) Probably valid for live-ins if used to protect property interests.

   All agreements must be made with full disclosure of assets and other pertinent information, and without duress.

2. Property: Each controls and manages his or her property.

3. Division of property in contested divorces: The court divides joint property as it deems fair. The court may divide separate property acquired during the marriage as it deems fair. Income from separate property acquired prior to the marriage may be divided by the court. Court may award property as well as or in lieu of alimony.

South Carolina

Separate property state.

1. Prenuptial/live-in agreements:

   (a) Valid for married couples.

   (b) Probably valid for live-ins if used to protect property interests.

   All agreements must be made with full disclosure of assets and other pertinent information, and without duress.

2. Property: Each controls and manages his or her property. Both spouses must sign to sell or encumber the family home.

3. Division of property in contested divorces: The court may divide any property acquired during the marriage as it deems fair and recognizes a special equity of one spouse in the separate property of the other because of homemaking contributions. Separate property acquired prior to the marriage is retained by its owner.

South Dakota

Separate property state.

1. Prenuptial/live-in agreements:

   (a) Valid for married couples.

   (b) Probably valid for live-ins if used to protect property interests.

   All agreements must be made with full disclosure of assets and other pertinent information, and without duress.

2. Property: Each controls and manages his or her property.

Both spouses must sign to sell or encumber the family home.

3. Division of property in contested divorces: The court divides separate property as it deems fair. Joint property can be divided by the court or ordered sold, with proceeds evenly divided.

Tennessee

Separate property state.

1. Prenuptial/live-in agreements:

   (a) Valid for married couples if in writing.

   (b) Probably valid for live-ins if used to protect property interests.

   All agreements must be made with full disclosure of assets and other pertinent information, and without duress.

2. Property: Each controls and manages his or her property. Both spouses must sign to sell or encumber the family home.

3. Division of property in contested divorces: Each spouse usually retains his or her separate property. The court may divide separate property as it deems fair, and distributes joint property as it deems fair.

Texas

Community property state.

1. Prenuptial/live-in agreements:

   (a) Valid for married couples.

   (b) Probably valid for live-ins if used to protect property interests.

   All agreements must be made with full disclosure of assets and other pertinent information, and without duress.

2. Property:

   (a) All property acquired prior to marriage or by gift, inheritance, or as a personal injury award is considered separate property.

(b) All property acquired during the marriage (except as provided in (a) above), including profits from separate property, is considered community property.

Each spouse controls and manages his or her separate property. Community property is controlled and managed by the spouse who acquired the property or by the spouse whose name is on the title. Both spouses must sign to sell or encumber the family home.

3. Division of property in contested divorces: The court divides community and joint property as it deems fair, with marital misconduct a consideration for division. Separate property may also be divided by the court, although separate real property may not be awarded to the non-owning spouse.

Utah

Separate property state.

1. Prenuptial/live-in agreements:

   (a) Valid for married couples.

   (b) Probably valid for live-ins if used to protect property interests.

   All agreements must be made with full disclosure of assets and other pertinent information, and without duress.

2. Property: Each controls and manages his or her property. Both spouses must sign to sell or encumber the family home.

3. Division of property in contested divorces: The court divides all separate and joint property as it deems fair.

Vermont

Separate property state.

1. Prenuptial/live-in agreements:

   (a) Valid for married couples.

   (b) Probably valid for live-ins if used to protect property interests.

   All agreements must be made with full disclosure of assets and other pertinent information, and without duress.

2. Property: Each controls and manages his or her property. Both spouses must sign to sell or encumber the family home.

3. Division of property in contested divorces: The court divides all separate and joint property as it deems fair.

Virginia

Separate property state.

1. Prenuptial/live-in agreements:

   (a) Valid for married couples.

   (b) Probably valid for live-ins if used to protect property interests.

   All agreements must be made with full disclosure of assets and other pertinent information, and without duress.

2. Property: Each controls and manages his or her property.

3. Division of property in contested divorces: Tenancy with right of survivorship becomes tenancy in common, with each spouse receiving his or her share. Each spouse retains his or her separate property.

Washington

Community property state.

1. Prenuptial/live-in agreements:

   (a) Valid for married couples.

   (b) Probably valid for live-ins if used to protect property interests.

   All agreements must be made with full disclosure of assets and other pertinent information, and without duress.

2. Property:

   (a) All property acquired prior to marriage or by gift or inheritance is considered separate property.

   (b) All property acquired after the marriage (except as provided in (a) above) is considered community property.

Each spouse controls and manages his or her separate property. Either spouse may control and manage community property, but may not will away more than one-half or sell or encumber community property without the other's consent. Both must sign to sell the family home.

3. Division of property in contested divorces: The court divides all community and separate property as it deems fair.

West Virginia

Separate property state.

1. Prenuptial/live-in agreements:

   (a) Probably valid for married couples if in writing and signed.

   (b) Probably not valid for live-ins, and then only if used to protect property interests.

   All agreements must be made with full disclosure of assets and other pertinent information, and without duress.

2. Property: Each controls and manages his or her own property.

3. Division of property in contested divorces: Each spouse retains his or her separate property. The court divides joint property.

Wisconsin

Separate property state.

1. Prenuptial/live-in agreements:

   (a) Valid for married couples as they pertain to property rights during marriage.

   (b) Probably valid for live-ins if used to protect property interests.

   All agreements must be made with full disclosure of assets and other pertinent information, and without duress.

2. Property: Each controls and manages his or her property. Both spouses must sign to sell or encumber the family home or any other property owned by both.

3. Division of property in contested divorces: The court divides all separate and joint property, except that which was inherited.

Wyoming

Separate property state.

1. Prenuptial/live-in agreements:

    (a) Valid for married couples.

    (b) Probably valid for live-ins if used to protect property interests.

    All agreements must be made with full disclosure of assets and other pertinent information, and without duress.

2. Property: Each controls and manages his or her property. Both spouses must sign to sell or encumber the family home.

3. Division of property in contested divorces: The court divides all separate and joint property as it deems fair.

Credit Regulatory Agencies

National banks
> Comptroller of the Currency
> Consumer Affairs Division
> Washington, DC 20219

State member banks
> Federal Reserve Bank serving the area in which the state
> member bank is located

Nonmember insured banks
> Federal Deposit Insurance Corporation,
> Regional Director, for the region in which the nonmember
> insured bank is located

**Savings institutions insured by the FSLIC and members of the
FHLB system (except for savings banks insured by FDIC)**
> The Federal Home Loan Bank Supervisory
> Agent in the district where the institution is located

Federal credit unions
> Regional office of the National Credit
> Union Administration serving the area in which the federal
> credit union is located

Creditors subject to Civil Aeronautics Board
> Director, Bureau of Enforcement
> Civil Aeronautics Board
> 1825 Connecticut Avenue, N.W.
> Washington, DC 20428

Creditors subject to Interstate Commerce Commission
    Office of Proceedings
    Interstate Commerce Commission
    Washington, DC 20523

Creditors subject to Packers and Stockyard Act
    Nearest Packers and Stockyards
    Administration area supervisor

Small Business Investment Companies
    U.S. Small Business Administration
    1441 L Street, N.W.
    Washington, DC 20416

Brokers and dealers
    Securities and Exchange Commision
    Washington, DC 20549

Federal Land Banks
Federal Land Bank Associations
Federal Intermediate Credit Banks
Production Credit Associations
    Farm Credit Administration
    490 L'Enfant Plaza, S.W.
    Washington, DC 20578

Retail department stores
Consumer finance companies
All other creditors
All nonbank credit card issuers
    Federal Trade Commission
    Equal Credit Opportunity
    Washington, DC 20580
(Lenders operating on a local or regional basis should use the
address of the FTC Regional Office in which they operate.)

Bank cards issued by national banks
(the word "National" appears in the bank's name)
    Comptroller of the Currency
    Consumer Affairs Division
    Washington, DC 20219

Bank cards issued by state banks
    Contact the Federal Reserve Bank serving the area in which
    the state member bank is located

Federal Trade Commission
Regional Offices

Federal Trade Commission
1718 Peachtree Street, N.W.
Atlanta, GA 30308
> For Alabama, Florida, Georgia, Mississippi, North Carolina, South Carolina, Tennessee, Virginia

Federal Trade Commission
150 Causeway Street
Boston, MA 02114
> For Connecticut, Maine, Massachusetts, New Hampshire, Rhode Island, Vermont.

Federal Trade Commission
55 E. Monroe Street
Chicago, IL 60603
> For Illinois, Indiana, Iowa, Kentucky, Minnesota, Missouri, Wisconsin

Federal Trade Commission
1240 E. Ninth Street
Cleveland, OH 44199
> For Delaware, Maryland, Michigan, Ohio, Pennsylvania, West Virginia, Western New York

Federal Trade Commission
2001 Bryan Street
Dallas, TX 75201
> For Arkansas, Louisiana, New Mexico, Oklahoma, Texas

Federal Trade Commission
1405 Curtis Street
Denver, CO 80202
> For Colorado, Kansas, Montana, Nebraska, North Dakota, South Dakota, Utah, Wyoming

Federal Trade Commission
1100 Wilshire Boulevard
Los Angeles, CA 90024
> For Arizona, Southern California

Federal Trade Commission
26 Federal Plaza
New York, NY 10007
> For Eastern New York, New Jersey

Federal Trade Commission
450 Golden Gate Avenue
San Francisco, CA 94102
> For Northern California, Hawaii, Nevada

Federal Trade Commission
915 Second Avenue
Seattle, WA 98174
> For Alaska, Idaho, Oregon, Washington

Current addresses can be found in: *Federal Regulatory Directory*, Congressional Quarterly, Inc., Washington, DC, available in most libraries.

Consumer Credit Counseling Services

Look in your phone directory under credit or counseling services or write to:

National Foundation for Consumer Credit
1819 H Street, N.W.
Washington, DC 20006

Family Service Association
44 E. Twenty-third Street
New York, New York 10010
> (Family Service Associations are located nationwide, and offer credit counseling as one of their services.)

State Insurance Commissioners

Superintendent of Insurance
Alabama Insurance Department
Room 453
Administrative Building
Montgomery, AL 36104

Director of Insurance
Alaska Insurance Department
Room 410 Gooldstein Building
Pouch "D"
Juneau, AK 99801

Director of Insurance
Arizona Department of Insurance
1601 West Jefferson
Phoenix, AZ 85007

Commissioner of Insurance
Arkansas Insurance Department
400 University Tower Building
Little Rock, AR 72204

Commissioner of Insurance
California Insurance Department
600 S. Commonwealth Avenue
Los Angeles, CA 90005

Commissioner of Insurance
Colorado Insurance Department
106 State Office Building
Denver, CO 80203

Commissioner of Insurance
Connecticut Insurance Department
State Office Building
165 Capitol Avenue
Hartford, CT 06115

Commissioner of Insurance
Delaware Insurance Department
Dover, DE 19901

Superintendent of Insurance
District of Columbia
Insurance Department
614 H Street, N.W.
Washington, DC 20001

Commissioner of Insurance
Florida Insurance Department
The Capitol
Tallahassee, FL 32304

Commissioner of Insurance
Georgia Insurance Department
State Capitol
Atlanta, GA 30334

Commissioner of Insurance
Hawaii Insurance Department
P.O. Box 3614
Honolulu, HI 96811

Commissioner of Insurance
Idaho Insurance Department
206 State House
Boise, ID 83707

Director of Insurance
Illinois Insurance Department
525 W. Jefferson Street
Springfield, IL 62707

Commissioner of Insurance
Indiana Insurance Department
509 State Office Building
Indianapolis, IN 46204

Commissioner of Insurance
Iowa Insurance Department
Lucas State Office Building
Des Moines, IA 50319

Commissioner of Insurance
Kansas Insurance Department
State Office Building
Topeka, KS 66612

Commissioner of Insurance
Kentucky Insurance Department
Old Capitol Annex
Frankfort, KY 40601

Commissioner of Insurance
Louisiana Insurance Department
Box 44214, Capitol Station
Baton Rouge, LA 70804

Superintendent of Insurance
Maine Insurance Bureau
State House Annex
Capitol Shopping Center
Augusta, ME 04330

Commissioner of Insurance
Maryland Insurance Division
1 S. Calvert Street
Baltimore, MD 21202

Commissioner of Insurance
Massachusetts Division of Insurance
100 Cambridge Street
Boston, MA 02202

Commissioner of Insurance
Michigan Insurance Bureau
111 N. Hosner Street
Lansing, MI 48913

Commissioner of Insurance
Minnesota Insurance Department
210 State Office Building
St. Paul, MN 55101

Commissioner of Insurance
Mississippi Insurance Department
910 Woolfolk Building
P.O. Box 79
Jackson, MS 39205

Superintendent of Insurance
Missouri Division of Insurance
Department of Business and
    Administration
P.O. Box 690
Jefferson City, MO 65101

Commissioner of Insurance
Montana Insurance Department
Capitol Building
Helena, MT 59601

Director of Insurance
Nebraska Insurance Department
1335 L St.
Lincoln, NB 68509

Commissioner of Insurance
Nevada Insurance Division
Department of Commerce
Nye Building
Carson City, NV 89701

Commissioner of Insurance
New Hampshire Insurance Department
78 N. Main Street
Concord, NH 03301

Commissioner of Insurance
Department of Banking and Insurance
201 E. State Street
Trenton, NJ 08625

Superintendent of Insurance
New Mexico Insurance Department
P.O. Drawer 1269
Santa Fe, NM 87501

Superintendent of Insurance
New York Insurance Department
123 William Street
New York, NY 10038

Commissioner of Insurance
North Carolina Insurance Department
P.O. Box 26387
Raleigh, NC 27611

Commissioner of Insurance
North Dakota Insurance Department
State Capitol
Bismarck, ND 58501

Director of Insurance
Ohio Insurance Department
447 E. Broad Street
Columbus, OH 43215

Commissioner of Insurance
Oklahoma Insurance Department
Room 408
Will Rogers Memorial Office Building
Oklahoma City, OK 73105

Commissioner of Insurance
Insurance Department
Department of Commerce
158 Twelfth St. N.E.
Salem OR 97310

Commissioner of Insurance
Pennsylvania Insurance Department
108 Finance Building
State Capitol
Harrisburg, PA 17120

Commissioner of Insurance
Rhode Island Insurance Division
169 Weybosset Street
Providence, RI 02903

Commissioner of Insurance
South Carolina Insurance Department
Federal Land Bank Building
1401 Hampton Street
Columbia, SC 29201

Commissioner of Insurance
South Dakota Department of Insurance
Capitol Building
Pierre, SD 57501

Commissioner of Insurance
Tennessee Department of Insurance
114 State Office Building
Nashville, TN 37219

Commissioner of Insurance
Texas Insurance Department
1110 San Jacinto Street
Austin, TX 78701

Commissioner of Insurance
Utah Insurance Department
115 State Capitol
Salt Lake City, UT 84114

Commissioner of Insurance
Vermont Insurance and Banking
    Department
State Office Building
Montpelier, VT 05602

Commissioner of Insurance
Virginia Insurance Department
700 Blanton Building
P.O. Box 1157
Richmond, VA 23209

Commissioner of Insurance
Washington Insurance Department
Insurance Building
Olympia, WA 98501

Commissioner of Insurance
West Virginia Insurance Department
1800 E. Washington Street
Charleston, WV 25305

Commissioner of Insurance
Wisconsin Insurance Department
212 N. Bassett Street
Madison, WI 53703

Commissioner of Insurance
Department of Insurance
State of Wyoming
500 Randall Avenue
Cheyenne, WY 82002

Be sure to check the telephone directory or with telephone information for current street addresses; some of these may have changed.

Money Market Funds

Alliance Capital Reserves
140 Broadway   (none/none)*
New York, NY 10005
212/344-9200
800/221-5672†

American General Reserve Fund
2777 Allen Parkway   ($1,000/100)
P.O. Box 3121
Houston, TX 77001
713/522-1111
800/421-5666

American Liquid Trust
Keystone Building   (none/none)
99 High Street
P.O. Box 2121
Boston, MA 02104
617/338-3300
800/225-2618

CG Money Market Fund, Inc.
Hartford, CT 06152   ($300/50)
203/726/6000

CMA Money Trust
165 Broadway   ($20,000/none)
New York, NY 10080
212/766-6310
800/221-4146

Capital Preservation Fund, Inc.
Capital Preservation Fund II, Inc.
755 Page Mill Road   ($1,000/none)

Palo Alto, CA 94304
415/858-2400
800/982-6150 (California only)
800/227-8380

Cardinal Government Securities Trust
155 E. Broad Street   ($2,500/500)
Columbus, OH 43215
614/464-6985
800/282-9446 (Ohio only)
800/848-7734

Carnegie Government Securities Fund
831 National City Bank Building
Cleveland, OH 44114   ($1,000/500)
216/781-4440
800/232-2321

Cash Equivalent Fund, Inc.
120 S. LaSalle Street   ($1,000/100)
Chicago, IL 60603
312/236-3223
800/621-1048

Cash Management Trust of America
333 S. Hope Street   ($5,000/50)
Los Angeles, CA 90071
213/486-9200
800/421-8791

Centennial Capital Cash Management
    Trust
One New York Plaza   ($1,000/none)
New York, NY 10004
212/825-4000
800/221-5833

---

*minimum initial investment/minimum subsequent investment
†All 800 numbers are toll free.

Colonial Money Market Trust
75 Federal Street   ($3,000/100)
Boston, MA 02110
617/426-3750
800/225-2365

Columbia Daily Income Company
621 S.W. Morrison Street   ($1,000/500)
Portland, OR 97205
503/222-3601
800/547-1037

Composite Cash Management Company
Fourth Floor   ($1,000/500)
Spokane & Eastern Building
Spokane, WA 99201
509/624-4101

Current Interest, Inc.
711 Polk Street   ($1,000/100)
Suite 500
Houston, TX 77002
713/751-2400

Daily Cash Accumulation Fund, Inc.
3600 S. Yosemite Street   ($2,500/100)
P.O. Box 300
Denver, CO 80327
303/770-2345
800/525-9310

Daily Income Fund, Inc.
230 Park Avenue   ($5,000/100)
Suite 3300
New York, NY 10017
212/697-8088

Delaware Cash Reserve, Inc.
Seven Penn Center Plaza
Philadelphia, PA 19103
215/988-0133
800/523-4640

Dreyfus Liquid Assets, Inc.
600 Madison Avenue   ($2,500/100)
New York, NY 10022
212/223-0303
800/223-5525

Eaton & Howard Cash Management Fund
24 Federal Street   ($1,000/none)
Boston, MA 02110
617/484-8260
800/225-6265

Fidelity Cash Reserves   ($1,000/250)
Fidelity Daily Income Trust
                         ($10,000/500)
82 Devonshire Street
Boston, MA 02109
617/726-0200
800/225-6190

First Investors Cash Management, Inc.
120 Wall Street   ($1,000/100)
New York, NY 10005
212/825-7900

First Variable Rate Fund for
Government Incone, Inc.   ($1,000/250)
1700 Pennsylvania Avenue, N.W.
Washington, DC 20006
202/328-4000
800/424-2444

Florida Mutual U.S. Government
Securities Fund, Inc.
Landmark Bank Building   ($1,000/100)
Suite 1507
Ft. Lauderdale, FL 33394
305/522-0200
800/432-1592 (Florida Only)

Franklin Money Fund
Franklin Money Fund II
155 Bovet Road   ($500/100)
San Mateo, CA 94402
415/574-8800
800/227-6781

Government Investors Trust
1800 N. Kent Street   ($2,000/none)
Arlington, VA 22209
703/528-6500
800/336-3063

Gradison Cash Reserves
580 Building   ($1,000/50)
Cincinnati, OH 45202
513/579-5700
800/582-7062 (Ohio only)
800/543-1818

IDS Cash Management Fund, Inc.
1000 Roanoke Building   ($2,500/100)
Minneapolis, MN 55402
612/372-3131
800/328-8300

INA Cash Fund, Inc.
3531 Silverside Road   ($2,500/500)
Bedford Building
Wilmington, DE 19811
215/241-2723
800/441-7786

Intercapital Liquid Assets Fund, Inc.
5 World Trade Center   ($5,000/100)
New York, NY 10048
212/938-4500
800/221-2685

John Hancock Cash Management Trust
P.O. Box 111   ($1,000/25)
Boston, MA 02117
617/421-6320
800/343-7180

Johnston Cash Management Fund, Inc.
One Boston Place   ($2,500/100)
Boston, MA 02106
617/722-7250 (collect, Massachusetts only)
800/343-6324

E.D. Jones & Co., Daily Passport
   Cash Trust
421 Seventh Avenue   ($5,000/1,000)
Pittsburgh, PA 15219
412/288-1900
800/245-2423

Kemper Money Market Fund, Inc.
120 S. LaSalle Street   ($1,000/100)
Chicago, IL 60603
312/346-3223
800/621-1048

Legg Mason Cash Reserve Trust
421 Seventh Avenue   ($5,000/500)
Pittsburgh, PA 15219
412/288-1900
800/245-2423

Lehman Cash Management Fund, Inc.
55 Water Street   ($10,000/250)
New York, NY 10041
212/588-2020
800/221-5350

Lexington Money Market Fund
476 Hudson Terrace   ($1,000/100)
P.O. Box 1515
Englewood Cliffs, NJ 07362
201/567-2000
800/526-4791

Liquid Capital Income
831 National City Bank Building
Cleveland, OH 44114   ($1,000/500)
216/781-4440
800/321-2321

Liquid Green Trust
207 Guaranty Building   ($1,000/500)
Indianapolis, IN 46204
317/634-3301
800/622-4921 (Indiana only)
800/428-4492

Lord Abbett Cash Reserve Fund
63 Wall Street   ($1,000/none)
New York, NY 10005
212/425-8720
800/221-9995

Lutheran Brotherhood Money Market
   Fund, Inc.
701 Second Avenue South   ($2,500/100)
Minneapolis, MN 55402
612/339-8091
800/328-4552

Massachusetts Cash Management Trust
200 Berkeley Street   ($1,000/none)
Boston, MA 02116
617/423-3500

Merrill Lynch Institutional Fund
125 High Street   ($25,000/1,000)
Boston, MA 02110
617/357-1460
800/225-1576

Merrill Lynch Ready Assets Trust
165 Broadway   ($5,000/1,000)
One Liberty Plaza
New York, NY 10080
212/637-6310
800/221-7210

Midwest Income Investment Company
508 Dixie Terminal Building   ($500/50)
Cincinnati, OH 45202
513/579-0414
800/543-0407

Moneymart Assets, Inc.
100 Gold Street   ($1,000/500)
New York, NY 10038
212/791-7123
800/221-7984

Money Market Management, Inc.
421 Seventh Avenue   ($1,000/100)
Pittsburgh, PA 15219
412/288-1900
800/245-2423

Money Shares, Inc.
One Wall Street   ($1,000/100)
New York, NY 10005
212/269-8800
800/221-5757

Mutual of Omaha Money Market
Account, Inc.
3102 Farnam Street   ($2,500/100)
Omaha, NE 68131
402/342-3328
800/228-09011

NEL Cash Management Account
501 Boylston Street   ($1,000/none)
Boston, MA 02117
617/266-3700
800/225-7670

National Liquid Reserves, Inc.
605 Third Avenue   ($2,500/100)
New York, NY 10016
212/661-3000
800/223-7757

Nationwide Money Market Fund
One Nationwide Plaza   ($2,500/100)
Columbus, OH 43216
614/227-4901

Oppenheimer Money Market Fund
Two Broadway   ($2,500/100)
New York, NY 10004
212/825-4000
800/221-5833

Paine Webber Cashfund, Inc.
c/o Paine, Webber, Jackson & Curtis, Inc.
140 Broadway   ($5,000/500)
New York, NY 10005
212/437-2121

Phoenix/Chase Money Market Fund
535 Boylston Street   ($1,000/100)
Boston, MA 02116
617/262-3600
800/343-2798

Plimoney Fund, Inc.
111 N. Broad Street   ($2,500/50)
Philadelphia, PA 19107
215/569-9300

Putnam Daily Dividend Trust
265 Franklin Street   ($2,000/500)
Boston, MA 02110
617/423-4960
800/225-2465

Rowe Price Prime Reserve Fund, Inc.
100 E. Pratt Street   ($1,000/100)
Baltimore, MD 21202
301/547-2000
800/638-1527

Scudder Cash Investment Trust
175 Federal Street   ($1,000/none)
Boston, MA 02110
617/482-3990
800/225-2470

Security Cash Fund, Inc.
700 Harrison Street   ($1,000/100)
Topeka, KS 66636
913/295-3127
800/432-3536 (Kansas only)
800/255-3509

Selected Money Market Fund, Inc.
Sixth Floor   ($1,000/100)
111 W. Washington Boulevard
Chicago, IL 60602
312/630-2762
800/621-7321

Shearson Daily Dividend
Shearson Government & Agencies
14 Wall Street   ($5,000/1000)
New York, NY 10005
212/522-7405
800/221-7136 (ME, VT, NH, MA, RI,
  CT, PA, NJ, DE)
800/221-2990 (other states)

Sigma Money Market Fund, Inc.
Sigma Government Securities Funds, Inc.
Greenville Center, C-200   ($500/100)
3801 Kennett Pike
Wilmington, DE 19807
302/652-3091
800/441-9490

Steinroe Cash Reserves, Inc.
150 S. Wacker Drive   ($2,500/100)
Chicago, Il 60606
312/368-7800
800/621-0320

Supervised Cash Account, Inc.
120 S. LaSalle Street   ($1,000/100)
Chicago, IL 60603
312/346-3223
800/621-1048

Union Cash Management Fund, Inc.
One Bankers Trust Plaza   ($1,000/none)
New York, NY 10006
212/432-4000
800/221-2450

United Cash Management Fund, Inc.
One Crown Center   ($1,000/100)
P.O. Box 1343
Kansas City, MO 64141
816/283-4000
800/821-5664

Value Line Cash Fund
711 Third Avenue   ($1,000/100)
New York, NY 10017
212/687-3965
800/223-0818

Vanguard Money Market Trust
P.O. Box 876   ($3,000/100)
Valley Forge, PA 19482
215/964-2600
800/523-7910

This is a partial list. For more information write to:
Investment Company Institute
1775 K Street, N.W.
Washington DC 20006

Index

Index

accountants
  for real estate investments,
    124, 126, 127
  reconstruction of assets by, 8
  records on, 4
  selection and treatment of,
    17–19
age and financial goals, 14–17,
  135–137
alimony, 195
All Savers Certificates, 70, 77,
  84–85,
annual reports, 157
annuities, 226, 228, 229,
  230–233
art, 173
associations
  credit counseling, 52
  for credit rights violations, 58
  diamond and gem, 174
  for insurance discrimination, 202
  to insure municipal bonds, 91
  for investment clubs, 21–22
  for networking, 20
  real estate, 107
  for widows, 199
attorneys
  estates and, 243–245
  for investment clubs, 22
  for real estate transactions,
    113–114, 123–124
  records on, 4
  selection and treatment of,
    17–19
  wills and, 5, 239–240

balloon payments on
  mortgates, 108
banks and banking, 23–40
  abandoned accounts in, 5
  account records, 4, 5, 7
  bank cards, 42–43, 49
  bank paper, 84
  changes in, 23–24, 29–30
  checking accounts, 28,
    30–32, 49
  competitors of, 24–26
  credit discrimination in,
    44–45, 57
  debit cards, 43
  Federal Reserve System,
    74–75, 87
  insider information and,
    158–159
  insurance for, 39–40, 83, 86
  loans, 34–38, 43–44 ·
  selection of, 26–29
  services of, 27–28, 29,
    30–35
  as trustees, 33, 242
  widowhood and, 199
Blue Cross/Blue Shield, 205,
  208
bonds, 88–92
  flower, 250–251
  municipal, 90–91
  ratings of, 88–90, 140, 147
  zero-interest, 91–92
brokers and brokerages
  insurance, 204
  real estate, 22, 101–104, 127

313

ABOUT THE AUTHOR

MIMI TARCHER BRIEN, born and raised in New York City, graduated from NYU with a B.S. in economics. She came to Los Angeles for graduate studies where she met and married her first husband. Mimi worked with him in all aspects of real estate for the next ten years. After her divorce, she worked for the Office of Economic Opportunity on a research and development project.

Mimi was remarried to Jacques Brien, a French-Canadian psychoanalyst. Five years later, she was tragically widowed. It was during that time that she realized the special needs women have for financial planning and so began to organize a system to meet those needs. While continuing to work as a licensed real estate broker, Mimi founded "Moneywise," a financial planning firm geared to provide necessary financial services to women.

Mimi has been a regular contributor to the Los Angeles "Widow-to-Widow" program. She has appeared nationally on the "Mike Douglas Show." She frequently lectures on television and at many special financial planning seminars offered by large department stores, temples, churches and businesses in the Los Angeles area.

Mimi has two married daughters, one a speech pathologist and one a lawyer.

WOMEN:
YESTERDAY
AND TODAY

☐	01428	**ALWAYS A WOMAN** K. Pickford & J. F. Smith (A large format book)	$9.95
☐	20202	**THE GIRL I LEFT BEHIND** Jane O'Reilly	$3.50
☐	22672	**GETTING RICH: A SMART WOMAN'S GUIDE TO SUCCESSFUL MANAGEMENT** Diane Ackerman	$3.95
☐	22872	**WOMEN & THE CRISIS IN SEX HORMONES** Barbara Seamans	$4.50
☐	14711	**WOMAN'S MONEY BOOK** Gene MacKevich	$2.95
☐	14999	**EVERYTHING-A-WOMAN NEEDS TO KNOW TO GET PAID WHAT SHE'S WORTH** Caroline Bird	$3.50
☐	20762	**A HISTORY OF WOMEN IN AMERICA** Carol Hymowitz and Michaele Weissman	$3.95
☐	20857	**AN UNFINISHED WOMAN** Lillian Hellman	$3.50
☐	20131	**THE DIALECTIC OF SEX** Shulamith Firestone	$2.75
☐	14912	**KISS SLEEPING BEAUTY GOODBYE** Madonna Kolbenschlag	$3.95
☐	20078	**OF WOMAN BORN: Motherhood as Experience and Institution** Adrienne Rich	$3.95
☐	20443	**THE FEMALE EUNUCH** Germaine Greer	$3.95
☐	22908	**THE BELL JAR** Sylvia Plath	$3.50
☐	20603	**THE FEMINIST PAPERS, From Adams to de Beauvoir** Dr. Alice S. Rossi, editor	$4.95
☐	20338	**AGAINST OUR WILL** Susan Brownmiller	$4.95

Buy them at your local bookstore or use this handy coupon for ordering:

MONEY TALKS!
How to get it and How to keep it!